Unwifeable

One of the "Best Books of 2018."

—*Refinery29*

"There's honest, and then there's *honest*. This book is so honest it will blow you away. With *Unwifeable*, Stadtmiller establishes herself as the Erica Jong of her generation—with storytelling as addictive as Jay McInerney's."

—Colin Quinn, creator and star of *The New York Story*

"The filthiest—and most moving—fairy tale you'll ever read."

—*SHESAID*

"A blisteringly candid depiction of party-girl carnage and the struggle to stop pointing the gun directly at your own foot. Mandy Stadtmiller is funny, messy, and real. I couldn't put this book down."

—Sarah Hepola, *New York Times* bestselling author of *Blackout*

"Candid, messy, and outrageously funny."

—*PureWow*

"Many of us hide our warts and scars, but Mandy celebrates them with such humor. *Unwifeable* is dark, honest, and always entertaining."

—Jim Gaffigan, *New York Times* bestselling author of *Dad Is Fat*

"In her hilarious yet earnest memoir, dating columnist Mandy Stadtmiller chronicles high-profile hookups—only to realize it's not who you're with, but who you are that truly matters."

—*US Weekly*

"I loved reading *Unwifeable*. A fascinating kind of chaos with the realization of addiction, and then recovery. What stood out to me most was Mandy Stadtmiller's optimism all the way through."

—Fred Armisen, creator and star of *Portlandia*

One of the "most rewarding experiences of 2018."

—*Shondaland*

"Wonderful, funny, heartbreaking, and redemptive."

—Kimberly Rae Miller, *New York Times* bestselling author of *Coming Clean*

"*Unwifeable* is at once an inspiring coming-of-age story, a visceral addiction memoir, and an extended gossip column full of boldface names—like its brash-yet-sensitive, goofy-yet-glamorous author, this book amounts to much more than the sum of its fascinating parts."

—Sarah Knight, *New York Times* bestselling author of *The Life-Changing Magic of Not Giving a F*ck*

"Unforgettable and unputdownable. I loved it."

—Pamela Redmond Satran, *New York Times* bestselling author of *Younger*

"A hit book . . . She spills secrets."

—*Bravo*

"A savagely personal memoir that pulls no punches when it comes to exposing its author's humanity. It's as deeply intimate as it is extremely relatable. Mandy Stadtmiller is a stunning writer, equally comedic and sobering."

—Ira Madison III, columnist for *The Daily Beast*

"If all people were as entertaining and vigilant about excavating their self-deceptions, desires, and fears, clowns like me would have no one to write books for."

—Greg Behrendt, *New York Times* bestselling author of *He's Just Not That Into You*

"Brilliant."

—Jon Ronson, *New York Times* bestselling author of
So You've Been Publicly Shamed

"Mandy Stadtmiller speaks the unspeakable in *Unwifeable*: All those things you think, but never tell anyone. And all those things you do, and hope no one finds out. Mandy lays it all out, and in the process, gets to the real issues of healing and self-discovery."

—Neil Strauss, nine-time *New York Times* bestselling author

"Smart, funny, warm, brave, generous, totally raw, sometimes shocking, *Unwifeable* is filled with wisdom, insight, and profundity about a lot of things—authenticity, self-discovery, stand-up, connection, stigma shattering, and, yes, even parenting. It's also a wonderful love story. Mandy Stadtmiller is a true voice and a real talent."

—Amy Chua, *New York Times* bestselling author of
Battle Hymn of the Tiger Mother

"Genius."

—Artie Lange, #1 *New York Times* bestselling author of
Too Fat to Fish

"*Unwifeable* is a hilarious, unfiltered plunge; its laugh-out-loud candor will have you rolling on the floor, then getting up and cheering for Mandy every step of the way."

—Jill Kargman, creator and star of *Odd Mom Out*

"Equal parts hilarious and heartbreaking. It's one of those books that you read when you just want to feel like someone else GETS IT."

—Abigail Breslin, Academy Award–nominated actress

"Mandy Stadtmiller has written a rollicking and wildly honest tale that includes lots of sex, vodka, Andy Dick, comedy, and self-doubt. The big disappointment was that it ended and I had to go back to my life, which is a lot less interesting than Mandy's."

—A. J. Jacobs, *New York Times* bestselling author of
The Year of Living Biblically

"She's brash, she's sexy, and she's scary real. Mandy's optimism throughout her gritty growth is insightful and enlightening. She makes you feel alive."

—Sonja Morgan, entrepreneur and star of
The Real Housewives of New York City

"So rewarding."

—Charlaine Harris, #1 *New York Times* bestselling author of
the Sookie Stackhouse series

Unwifeable

a memoir

Mandy Stadtmiller

GALLERY BOOKS

New York   London   Toronto   Sydney   New Delhi

G

Gallery Books
An Imprint of Simon & Schuster, Inc.
1230 Avenue of the Americas
New York, NY 10020

First Gallery Books paperback edition January 2019

GALLERY BOOKS and colophon are registered trademarks of Simon & Schuster, Inc.

For information about special discounts for bulk purchases, please contact Simon & Schuster Special Sales at 1-866-506-1949 or business@simonandschuster.com.

The Simon & Schuster Speakers Bureau can bring authors to your live event. For more information or to book an event, contact the Simon & Schuster Speakers Bureau at 1-866-248-3049 or visit our website at www.simonspeakers.com.

Interior design by Bryden Spevak

Manufactured in the United States of America

10 9 8 7 6 5 4 3 2 1

The Library of Congress has cataloged the hardcover edition as follows:

Names: Stadtmiller, Mandy, author.
Title: Unwifeable : a memoir / Mandy Stadtmiller.
Description: First Gallery Books hardcover edition. | New York : Gallery Books, [2018] |
Identifiers: LCCN 2017048816 (print) | LCCN 2018000414 (ebook) | ISBN 9781501174056 (ebook) | ISBN 9781501174032 (hardback)
Subjects: LCSH: Stadtmiller, Mandy. | Advice columnists—United States—Biography. | Women journalists—United States—Biography. | Interpersonal relations—United States. | Wit and humor. | BISAC: BIOGRAPHY & AUTOBIOGRAPHY / Personal Memoirs. | BIOGRAPHY & AUTOBIOGRAPHY / Women.
Classification: LCC PN4874.S623 (ebook) | LCC PN4874.S623 A3 2017 (print) | DDC 070.4/44092 [B] —dc23
LC record available at https://lccn.loc.gov/2017048816

ISBN 978-1-5011-7403-2
ISBN 978-1-5011-7404-9 (pbk)
ISBN 978-1-5011-7405-6 (ebook)

For every person who was told they couldn't

If you cannot—in the long run—tell everyone what you have been doing, your doing has been worthless.

—Erwin Schrödinger

Contents

Contents

Unwifeable

chapter one

The Black Box

I f you look deep inside every woman, you will find a black box that records the wreckage of her past relationships. Internal recordings that can withstand the g-force impact of total obliteration that comes with a coupling's end. *"We've got bonding failure. Tell the world I'm sorry. We're going down."*

It starts when we are babies.

Our black box records the looped attachment issues that play in our subconscious. A therapist tries to determine if it's pilot error, unfavorable conditions, or faulty wiring. And we try to present as heroic a defense strategy as we can, explaining how we did all we could in light of the circumstances given.

My black box is horrific—even by black-box standards.

I've behaved terribly, predictably, and embarrassingly—and most shameless of all, I wrote about the journey in the *New York Post* and on *xoJane* with such an excruciating lack of self-awareness I finally had to reconcile the fact that there might be no one out there left for me at all.

I considered myself unwifeable. And I liked it.

Well, the vague empowerment narrative of it, anyway.

I wasn't *just* a self-destructive exhibitionist whose crippling neuroses manifested in navel-gazing narcissism and random acts of implosion. Instead, I told myself I was a feminist. My warp-speed career in personal memoir I claimed to be the ultimate act: making myself as terrifying to men as possible.

I was a living don't, and I was okay with that.

Instigating sexual chaos provided me with the perfect excuse for my inability to save myself or learn from past mistakes. I had plausible deniability that way. Massive backlog. An unrelenting influx of more pressing cases. All to avoid confronting the most devastating moments of original impact or having to assume personal responsibility for my failures along the way to correct course.

That's the problem with any emotional investigation: You need an unwavering focus in the face of overwhelming shame and regret and distraction. No matter what unsettling evidence emerges as all the ugly secrets start inevitably spilling out, you must resolve to never give up.

It's a tricky endeavor—even for the bravest among us.

Because do you know what humans will do to avoid the pain of personal discovery? Nearly any-fucking-thing.

. . . .

IT IS EARLY 2015, and my favorite escape-the-moment drug of choice is sex.

I am lying perfectly still on a hand-me-down bed in Manhattan, desiring nothing more than to please a mysterious forty-five-year-old man I barely know. He's tall, dark-humored, and handsome, and I first begin seeing him after receiving $20,000 from an online dating site to meet as many men as possible—all while driving up website traffic.

Summoning my favorite seduction trick from my well-worn repertoire, I make my voice as breathy and helpless as possible, asking, "Do you want me to touch myself?"

We have been on a few dates before, but I can tell already, he isn't like all the others. This guy stares daggers through my bull-shit.

"I want you to cut it out," he says. "What's this thing you do, where it's like you're doing a show?"

"It's just easier," I say in my actual voice, not having intended to open up until I realize I am doing so. "Sometimes just pretending to be someone else feels safer."

"The only thing that turns me on is seeing who you actually are," the man says, moving his hand up my body.

"Tell me," he asks. "Do you need me?"

"Yes," I say, answering what I know to be true. "I do."

"Why, baby?"

"Because I love you," I say without thinking, then quickly try to reel it back in. "I didn't mean it like, you know . . . It was just . . ."

"It's okay," he stops me. "I love you, too."

Panic creeps in goose-bump inches up my body. This guy *is* different. I don't know how yet, but he is very, very different.

"See how easy it is," he says, "to just tell me what you're thinking?"

Effortlessly, this man is breaking everything down to its most elemental form. Somehow, I have just let slip something I swore never to say to a man in the heat of the moment—especially without running it past an emergency preliminary hearing before a hand-picked Council of My Girlfriends and Peers.

I am terrified. My throat feels dry and the sheets beneath me are drenched in sweat and excitement. Against all logic and precaution, I feel like I can tell this man exactly where I've been in my past and how far down my sex and lies have taken me. I feel freedom from the cover-up, release from the conspiracy.

"I know you, Mandy," he says. "You were bad, weren't you?"

I nod, eyes squeezed shut tight.

"Nothing is wrong," he says, "unless it's untrue."

My God, how I ache to open that little black box inside of me.

"Did you fuck a lot of guys?" the man asks. "You *love* sex, don't you?"

"I have," I say. "I do," I say.

I can feel it now. Something changing inside me. And I make a promise to myself. *I refuse to give up—until I can uncover the cause of the crash.*

"Tell me everything," the man whispers to me.

My eyes flutter open.

"Okay."

chapter two

....

The Big Break

2005

I'm standing outside the giant News Corp structure at 9:45 a.m., afraid the sky-high behemoth of an architectural phallus at 1211 Avenue of the Americas might just disappear. It is December 12, my first day as a general assignment reporter for the *New York Post*. My size 4 dark-blue fur-lined Balenciaga coat fits like a glove on my 143-pound six-foot-two body (all thanks to the magic of the Divorce Diet), my hair is dyed bimbo-with-a-heart-of-gold blond, and my carefully applied makeup is done to appear as if I'm not wearing any. But even with my best fashion armor on, trying to summon something like confidence, I'm having trouble mustering the courage to go inside.

The whirlwind of changes in my life, the singularly reliable constancy of chaos, is the *only* certainty that I can count on at the moment.

All in the last few months:

- I quit my safe job in public relations.
- I turned thirty.
- I got divorced after five years married to my college
  sweetheart.
- I watched my parents remarry one another (with their
  divorce lasting the same length of time as my doomed
  marriage).
- And only a few days ago, I picked up an entire lifetime of
  belongings, stuffed them into the trunk of a beaten-down
  sedan, and moved in the dead of night from Chicago to
  New York to return to the newspaper industry for the first
  time in half a decade.

It was like I had won the Most Stressful Life Events All at
Once lottery. But after ten years with my college sweetheart
James, I couldn't take it any longer. I left him one day after yet
another of his indiscretions was revealed. It was somewhere before the bombshell about the group bukkake he partook in with
some chick off Craigslist but sometime after his confession about
soliciting sexual favors from prostitutes. Somewhere before I woke
up to James coming downstairs after getting oral sex from a "girlfriend" whom I'd recommended for a job and sometime after I
found out he was fucking a married coworker while we were in
marriage counseling.

On the bright side, I stumbled onto this great new diet.

The Divorce Diet is easy, really. You cry. You complain. And
you just don't eat.

I drink in everything around me now, trying to ignore the demons of a raging impostor complex lodged deep in my gut telling
me that I don't belong here. That I will fail. That I can't do this.

Standing next to the giant snow-covered potted plants strategically placed in between the sidewalk and the entrance after 9/11,
my eyes drift heavenward toward the enormous slab of concrete
and steel towering above, which is home to not just the *Post* but
also Rupert Murdoch's expansive Fox News empire. Bringing my
gaze back down to the ground again, I catch the shadow of Fox TV
host Shepard Smith smoking a cigarette, glued to his BlackBerry
while pacing furiously in front of a giant sign that says, WE REPORT.
YOU DECIDE.

There is no getting around it. This is *really* happening.

I force my legs to move, one after the other. Through the revolv-
ing doors I go, clutching my knockoff Gucci bag, which I make a
mental note to replace ASAP. I check in at the front desk.

"Mandy Stadtmiller," I relay to the stone-faced black-suited re-
ceptionist. "I'm here for Stephen Lynch."

I wait and fidget with my conspicuously naked left ring finger.
That's another thing. I need to get new rings. It feels too weird not
having the gold band there, and I don't want people to think I am
weird, always fidgeting and uneasy.

As if it's part of a pregame Welcome to News Corp show, I watch
a nearly nonstop pageant of bleach and hairspray and red stilettos
parading in and out of the lobby past the giant abstract mural at the
front desk. I pull out my flip phone and try to look busy as I stare
at the 773 number.

Yeah, this area code needs to go, too.

Steve walks down to greet me—looking only slightly older than
he had when he was my editor years ago at the *Daily Northwestern*
in the mid-'90s. Short reddish-brown hair, an intelligent smile, and
the slightly worn-down look that comes from having a love for all
things newspaper.

STEVE HAD FIRST reached out to me nine months ago when our journalism school email-alumni group put our names directly in each other's in-boxes. I would occasionally sound out idiotic updates about, I don't know, Big Ten awareness or something while I was working my very safe nine-to-five writing job for Northwestern University Medical School's alumni magazine. The press release-y environment was a far cry from what Steve might've expected from the college student who'd graduated years earlier with a plum internship in the style section of the *Washington Post* and whom he'd championed for entertainment editor at our college daily.

"Hi, Mandy," Steve's email began to me back in March. "I'm on the alums list and got your recent missive, and just wanted to say hello. Also, don't know if you still write features, but I edit the Sunday features section of the *New York Post*. So if you're looking for freelance outlets, would love to hear from you."

As I read over his message in my tiny windowless cubicle in Chicago, I let out a little yelp of excitement. Every letter in his email seemed to vibrate off the computer like a living thing— overpowering the sad little tropical desert island screen saver that formed the background on my ancient monitor.

I felt like a prisoner receiving a stay of career execution. I wrote back immediately: "Hey, Steve, I would love to write for you."

Of course, I had nothing in the way of recent clips (my last newspaper job after the *Washington Post* had been a short stint at the *Des Moines Register* from 1998 to 1999 covering cops and courts and drunkenly hooking up with fellow reporter Jeff Zeleny before he came out as gay and rose to fame in TV news). But I did have Steve's curiosity on my side. Like any good Internet user in 2004,

Steve had googled me and found something that showed where I was *really* at in my writing life beyond my oh-so-professional email signature that read "Assistant Director of Publications and Public Relations, Northwestern University Medical School."

In 2004, I had secretly started a blog.

My relationship with my husband, James, was on the rocks, my career was going nowhere, and so for the first time in years, I tried writing for myself again—this time for fun. During this uncertain period, I somehow stumbled into chronicling the dissolution of my own marriage.

"I learned something disheartening recently," I wrote in one extremely coded, euphemistic blog post about finding out a woman who'd lobbied hard to be my best friend ("Hey, Mandy, love your blog, let me take pictures of you!") was actually taking it in the ass from James all the while. "It disheartened me. I guess we covered that."

The minute I got the email from Steve, I obsessively checked my blog's StatCounter and there I saw it: again and again, a News Corp IP address that showed someone who worked there had been checking what I was writing almost daily. I knew it had to be Steve.

From that point forward, as I sat in my gray-fabric-lined little box at the medical school writing about science grants while I watched Comedy Central in the background, I would make it a priority to religiously update my blog.

I treated it like a tryout session, an audition for him and anyone else who might be reading. At night, as I came home to my Gothic converted servants' quarters turned guesthouse in Humboldt Park where my husband and I were still living, my arms were filled to overflowing with stacks of celebrity magazines to stay current.

Daily, I searched to find a comedic angle on every fresh new pop culture obsession.

When TomKat was huge, I stationed myself on top of our orange velour couch, which we'd found outside a Dumpster, and basically read every article on Scientology ever written. Then I wrote a satirical "day in the life" story about the couple. Emboldened by the emerging linking economy, I forwarded the post on to Mark Lisanti at *Defamer*, whom I had never communicated with before, with the subject line "For your consideration"—and a day later, he linked it. Soon after that, I made up a fake Martha Stewart catchphrase for her new *Apprentice*-style reality show. Linked again! I watched as hits on my blog climbed into the thousands. And still, StatCounter showed that News Corp IP.

But then, just as quickly as my great career hope had arrived, Steve fell off the radar. Didn't write back to my pitches. Didn't run a sample thing I wrote for him. Nothing.

When last minute my dear high school friend Siobhan Foley changed her wedding destination from Ireland to New York, I took a chance and emailed Steve again in early August.

"Hey, Steve," I wrote, "if you're still alive, perhaps we can get together for a drink when I'm in New York Sept. 23–25 for a wedding."

Again . . . silence. By that point, I knew I needed to make dramatic changes in my personal life as my happiness and sanity continued to plummet. I made a resolution that I would:

1. End my marriage to James.
2. Move home to live with my mom, who said she was excited to have me back home in San Diego.

Unfortunately, that plan quickly unraveled, too, when . . .

1. My parents called to tell me they were getting back together after their five-year-long divorce.
2. Hopefully I could figure something else out?

A day before I was set to fly out to New York for my friend's wedding, I checked my email one last time. There it was. Steve.

"Am I too late for this?" he wrote. "I've been on jury duty and am seriously sorry and would like to see you."

While I had no hope that anything would come out of it, we made a plan to text while I was in the city. Emboldened by finally hearing back from Steve, I decided to test my cold-call-emailing luck and wrote a short note to the author Jonathan Ames, too. I had met him once after he spoke in Chicago as part of my friend Davonna's thesis showcase.

He was the closest thing to a real-life New York celebrity I had in my Rolodex, and I somehow thought meeting him might impress Steve and show him how connected I was.

"Hey, I'm in NY this weekend for a wedding," I emailed Jonathan. "Any chance of getting coffee or tea, or are you performing somewhere famous? That tall blond girl from Davonna's thing. Yep."

I made sure to send him a link to my blog—which featured all my romantic dalliances—to show him that I was single, skinny, separated from my husband after five years of marriage, and *very much* dating. On the blog, I wrote stories and showed pictures of nights out with suitors who ranged from guys who at first seemed un-googlable (savvy friends quickly informed me this meant they were just using fake names and, oh yeah, *married*) to headache-inducing frat bros driving Hummers to an older lawyer named Scott who took me out on his yacht.

Jonathan and I exchanged various emails, with him keeping me

up-to-date on why he probably couldn't meet up. Meanwhile, my
short trip to New York already felt like a small personal victory in
some minuscule way. I had arrived—at JFK International, almost
divorced. I turned on my phone and saw that Scott with the Yacht
had already called to say he missed me.

I settled into my college roommate's art deco apartment in
Park Slope, where I was staying, introduced myself to her two cats,
which I would be minding while she was away, and began franti-
cally reaching out to all manner of old friends and acquaintances.
"I'm in New York!" "What are you doing?" "I'm getting divorced!"

The next morning, the day of Siobhan's nuptials, I got Jonathan's
hypnotically lowercased invite: "going to a late party tonight in manhattan, but if you can't sleep, maybe when i'm coming back from the
party i'll call you and we could meet for a late drink or something."

I blasted the Strokes from my iPod, put on my cleavage-baring
black thrift-store slip dress, and blissfully attended Siobhan's vows
at St. Patrick's Old Cathedral in Little Italy, snapping pictures of
everything. The centuries-old weathered red bricks, stretched ten
feet high and permanently leaning, seemed to offer stark comfort
to my own teetering state of late. It wasn't long before I was partying into the night at the Prince George Ballroom, twirling around
the dance floor, drunk on sauvignon blanc. I checked my messages. One new voicemail from Scott with the Yacht. "Hope you're
having fun in New York!" I sure was. Now I just needed a date to
prove to myself I belonged here.

I grinned and texted Jonathan Ames. "Want to meet up?"

He did. I fell into a cab and instructed the driver to take me to
the Tea Lounge in Park Slope, chatting him up as he drove.

"Hey, do you know what my friends say about me?" I gushed to
the weather-beaten, old cabdriver, who had to suffer through all

my intoxicated rambling. "I'm the ultimate slumber party girl. It's really true, you know. I know how to create fun. Wherever I go, that's what I do. Ultimate slumber party girl . . ."

"Ultimate slumber party girl, huh?" he asked, glancing back.

"Yep," I said. "That's me."

I waited at the Tea Lounge and in walked Jonathan, hesitant and sullen. I ordered a Ketel One and soda and he drank a tea. I leaned in close, spilling all about my friend's ornate wedding along with the long-shot meeting I had coming up the next day and how weird it was to be getting divorced.

"And right now," I confided, "I'm dating this guy Scott who's so different than my husband, and I like how he makes me feel."

I paused, shrugged my shoulders, and added, "I'm dating *a lot* of guys right now."

Jonathan took my promiscuity show-and-tell cue and began stroking my hand.

"You are?" he asked.

"Do you want to go back to my roommate's place?" I asked.

He did.

We dropped onto the spare bed I was staying in and began kissing. He held my wrists and slapped me gently on the face, and I said I liked it.

"I've never really done that kind of thing before," I said.

"Really?" he asked. "That's surprising."

"It's hot," I said enthusiastically.

He slapped me once more. This time I changed the subject. "I'm meeting with an editor from the *New York Post* tomorrow."

"That's impressive."

"I'm a little nervous," I confessed, and then stopped myself.

This level of vulnerability always felt a little too real for me. I didn't want men to *actually* be able to see me. So instead, I slipped into a persona I discovered appeals to pretty much every man: The Whore.

"Lately, it's fun to play these different characters," I said. "Like, I could call you . . . No I don't want to do it. I'd feel stupid."

"Do it," he said.

I couldn't bring myself to say "daddy," so I went in a different direction.

"Do you think I'm a dirty little slut?" I asked.

He looked down at my face and said with the gravity of a judge, "Yes. You stupid fucking cunt."

"Whoa!" I said. "Hey!"

I shot up and immediately turned our light-kink sexual encounter into a college admissions exam. I told him how I got a 5 on the calculus AP when I was fifteen and even started rattling off my SAT scores.

"It's just bedroom talk," he said. "I was trying to please you by amping it up."

"No, I know," I said. "Just . . . wow. New York is really intense, huh?"

We didn't have sex, but stopped before.

A few hours later, as he grabbed his cap and bag to go, I still felt intoxicated with bluster and pulled out my Girl Scout–green American Apparel dress to ask him if he thought I should wear that to my meeting with the editor from the *Post*.

He looked at the microscopic outfit I was holding before him.

"That's a shirt," he said.

He left my friend's apartment, and I'm sure never expected to see or hear from me again.

After a few hours of restless sleep, I met Steve at a little Mexican place near where I was staying. My face flushed, I ordered a mango orange margarita and told him about the night's adventure.

"He's like the literati, right?" I asked. "I think he gets written about in Page Six sometimes."

Steve just looked at me, amused. I was such a dumb child—in the body of a thirty-year-old.

"Do you like working for the *Post*?" I asked.

"I do," he said. "I should have come to New York a long time ago."

"Well, don't worry," I said. "I don't expect anything. I'm going to move home to California and become a comedy writer."

"You should," he said.

"Besides," I continued, "I just read in *Bloomberg* that the *Post* loses fifteen to thirty million dollars a year."

I paused, then kept going, "I have a little tattoo that says that, actually."

This time Steve laughed out loud.

"So I suppose I couldn't interest you in a features-writing position?" he interjected.

"Seriously?" I asked. "Seriously?"

"Seriously," he said.

"Okay, so how many stories a week?"

"About one," he said. "More or less."

My brain was melting down. I knew I shouldn't appear too desperate.

"Can I think about it?" I asked. "I mean, I haven't written for newspapers in years."

"Yeah, but you can write," he said. "That's all that matters."

I smiled, my face glistening now with the confidence of not only sex and drink but also New York and career.

"Yep," I said. "That's all that matters."

And that was that.

....

NOW, TWO SHORT months later, I am face-to-face with Steve again, still unable to believe that he is taking such a huge gamble on me. I want instantly to prove myself to him and to anyone who has ever doubted me.

I want to conquer the city, the newspaper, the industry as a whole.

"So here I am at News Corp!" I say to Steve grandly, giving him a hug.

"Corp," he says, deliberately pronouncing the *p*—and correcting me.

I know that. Shit.

"So . . . where are you living?" Steve asks as he leads me through the security-guard-protected gates, the automatic metallic arms swooshing up when he presses his yellow badge down to the electronic red sensor.

"Oh—Brooklyn," I say. "Park Slope. With two lesbians."

"Nice," he says. "And Park Slope, that's a great area."

Walking into the building, past the giant Christmas tree on display in the lobby, I see the huge signs reading FAIR AND BALANCED and recognize faces I was watching on TV the night before. There's Greta Van Susteren, bitching someone out. There's . . . holy shit, is that Geraldo? That's totally Geraldo.

We take the elevators up to the tenth floor, and my swimming eyes absorb the electrified newsroom, with floor-to-ceiling windows looking down on Avenue of the Americas as put-upon reporters balance their phones with one shoulder while their whirring hands type at breakneck speed, scrambling to meet the day's 5 p.m. deadline.

"Mandy, meet Katherine Pushkar, my new deputy editor," he says. "You'll be sharing an office with her."

Katherine smiles up at me, kind and relaxed, and sticks out her hand to shake mine. She is in her midthirties, beautiful, with shoulder-length brunette hair and warmth that radiates. She swoops her hand around her to welcome me into what is not so much an office as a converted coat closet, but I have never felt more grateful. It is a room to call—at least partially—my own.

"Call HR, get all the paperwork taken care of," Steve says, "and Katherine can get you set up on the computer. I've got to go deal with tomorrow's cover."

When Steve retreats into the newsroom, I can feel my nerves starting to rattle. Katherine whips around.

"I'm really glad you're here," she says. "I don't know anyone either. I just came over from *TimeOut*."

"Really?" I ask. "Oh that's so rad."

"Rad?" she repeats.

"I'm from California," I say. "So yeah. You're definitely rad, dude."

Within the next hour, I make my way up to the fifteenth floor to meet with a tiny white-haired HR lady with huge black fashion eyeglasses to fill out a stack of forms. I look them over and realize that for the first time since I got married in 2000, I will now be marking "single." Emergency contact? I have none. After running through the options (my ex-husband? my new roommates? my editor?), I finally scrawl my parents' number in San Diego, 2,433 miles away. Screw it. If something happens to me, *they* can deal with it.

I hand the forms back. Then it's off to another floor for my photo ID. The bored office worker snaps my picture and prints out my canary-yellow ID badge. I hang it around my neck. In the picture and on my face right now, I am beaming with pride.

. . . .

I TAKE THE F train home that night, interrogating strangers on the subway to look for any anecdote I can cannibalize for content ("Hey, so, what are the latest trends? Got any celebrity gossip? Oh, you just want to be left alone? Sorry about that."). Everywhere I go, I am a heat-seeking missile on the prowl for story ideas, rumors—any kind of dirt. Until I arrive at the Seventh Avenue stop in my new yuppie neighborhood, which is the epitome of spotless—a health food store and yoga studio on every corner.

My ID is still swinging around my neck—I can't bring myself to take it off just yet. I walk up the stairs to the million-dollar brownstone, another small victory thanks yet again to a cold-call-emailing session.

Sex, job, and shelter. What couldn't a confidently worded query to a stranger do?

Write it—and they will come. Or maybe you will.

Juanita, a fellow Northwestern grad, had received my forwarded email plea a few months back when Steve sent my official offer. Turned out she and her girlfriend, Lola, had a spare room, which they were looking to rent for $895 a month. She sent me pictures of their mind-boggling Park Slope paradise: teak bathroom decor, movie-studio-quality views, and a state-of-the-art stainless steel kitchen that looked straight out of a TV commercial for high-end cookware. Was I interested? Yes. Yes, I was.

"You're back!" Juanita cheers when I walk through the door, and I see that a dinner party is in full swing with their friends—most of them coupled up—huddling around the kitchen to roll homemade sushi.

"Drink?" one of their friends asks, handing me some sake, and I accept the expensive miniature wooden cup so as to not seem weird. Every day I write in my "morning pages" long screeds about how I thought maybe life would be better without alcohol, but when push came to shove (it seemed impossible that you could actually *choose* not to drink), I didn't want to be the weirdo who didn't know how to have a good time.

"Not enough sex scenes!" one girl complains as someone pulls up an on-demand episode of *The L Word* in the background, and I introduce myself around the party. One girl wearing Ray-Bans and skinny jeans scopes me out and says she'd like to get to know me better, touching my arm, leaning in close. I have never been straight-up hit on by a woman before, and it is exhilarating and alienating all at once.

I concentrate most of my energy on just sipping my sake rather than downing it, like I want to so badly. The partygoers scream with laughter, repeating inside jokes and whooping at inappropriate revelations. I don't feel like I click with anyone the way I did with Katherine at work. Juanita and Lola are a power couple, whose careers are taking off. It's hard for me to distinguish between the Showtime series playing in the background and the who's-broken-up-with-who small talk being made over yellowfin tuna and rice rolls around me.

"I think I'm just going to go back to my room." I check out early with a smile and collapse onto the inflatable air mattress that is to be my bed for months to come—until Juanita spies a Craigslist freebie posting about an IKEA wooden-slat queen left on the street a few blocks over.

I shuffle my body around awkwardly, trying to get comfortable on the balloon-like structure that is my bed, finally give up, and pick up my computer. I need something familiar. Determined to make the kind of connection I didn't at the party, I email a friend from Chicago a rant to try to soothe the emptiness that lingers in my gut.

"So these girls are ridiculously rich," I write, feeling guilty as I covet everything around me, and wishing my hosts' opulent lifestyle extended to their guest bedroom as well.

"I mean, whatever . . . I get along with them fine, and this'll be fine and it's cool. It's just like this entire 'Don't forget to squeegee the teak in the bathroom!' lifestyle is pretty bizarre. We all just drank some hot sake. 'Should we do the sake hot or cold?' the girls debated as if their lives depended on it. The loneliness, oh the loneliness."

I hit "send."

But the grossness in my gut is still there.

I text Scott with the Yacht that I am getting acclimated, and he writes, "Miss you here in Chicago."

But I still can't bring myself to text or call my ex-husband, James, the one person who knows me better than anyone, while also never knowing me at all. How could he? I didn't even know myself.

He certainly knew who he was, though. His idea of a hot date was to bring me to an International Socialist conference. The day of our divorce, when the *Post* job became official, James whispered to me at the courthouse, "Now when anyone asks why we broke up we can just say it's because you took a job with Rupert Murdoch."

James was so angry and so liberal.

I used to love that about him.

. . . .

ON THE COMMUTE from Brooklyn to Rockefeller Center the next day, I whip out a notebook and attempt to do what I started doing two years before: writing my stupid morning pages.

Not stupid, *obviously*, as it resulted in all of the stream-of-consciousness insights that led to me figuring out that an emotionally abusive marriage wasn't for me, but it felt so indulgent.

I have countless notebook pages that just begin, "What do I want to say?" The hardest initial part is getting past the self-hatred that leads your body to nearly seize up in disgust that you do not have a perfect narrative outlined to a T. That you are raw, earnest, scattered, and scared. As I ride on the train, surrounded by sunglasses-wearing strangers, I peruse old pages. The journal now reads like some kind of Mad Libs tale of separation, reconciliation, divorce, and hopefully—potentially—rebirth.

March 5, 2005

1. *My marriage is ending.*
2. *This is a good thing.*
3. *My husband is masturbating in the next room.*

May 28, 2005

Today, I almost died, crashed my car. But then I didn't. And it was good. I asked James, "Do you want to be my husband?"

"I am your husband," he said.

May 30, 2005

Ah yes. And then there's a day like today. Kicked pillows, James knocking over a glass of water, ruining the print I bought him from the girl he fucked when we were separated. I don't think I can handle this.

November 13, 2005

I'm going to look back on these days and wonder. Last night the clouds floating past. So much happening. Man, I'm so glad I took an axe and chopped my life up.

December 5, 2005

So here I am in Park Slope. My sister says, "You're a single woman with a good income and no family." Except . . . that's something that I may always be.

Now I stare at the blank page in front of me and try to plunge in. The feelings are the hardest part, so I attempt to snatch at them, without thinking, as misguided and unformed as they might be.

December 13, 2005

Um hi . . . So I'm fucked-up and angry and sad. That's the only way to describe myself right now. I'm okay but I'm worried about so many things.

I glance around at the businessmen reading their newspapers. That's what I should be doing. Not this journaling crap.

Here I sit on the subway car on the way into work, and it always feels like the battle against the fifteen-year-old me . . .

That's a strange thing to write—*the fifteen-year-old me*. I didn't expect that to come up into my consciousness. My memories stop me in my tracks as the train keeps rolling into Manhattan.

One summer in 1990 I was assigned babysitting duties for my niece and nephew while my uncle was dying of cancer in Portland, Oregon. While I mostly just played nanny, one day a handsome man in his twenties rang the doorbell and invited himself in.

"Hey, I'm Jake," he said.

Turned out we were distantly related, and he'd heard I was in town and figured he'd introduce himself. He said he knew how hard it must be babysitting all day and that maybe one of these days he could show me Portland, and we could have some fun.

A few weeks later, he showed up again.

"I'm going to have a few friends over, and Mandy can come," he told my aunt.

"I want to go!" I begged her.

"I might have a beer, though," Jake said responsibly, "so Mandy should probably spend the night."

When I entered Jake's wealthy suburban home, it was clear this was not just a few friends. The place was overflowing with frat bros and margaritas, and I was never without a drink in my hand. I was suddenly beautiful, desirable, attractive—and so much fun.

My face flushed, I flirted and talked to Jake's friends. Until, that was, they each found out how old I was.

"You're fifteen? No way."

"Way," I said, giggling—so excited by their interest.

I went outside, woozy and laughing as I took a cigar from one of the guys who was smoking, chomping it in my mouth, flopping into a plastic patio chair, swaying forward sloppily.

"Look at you," Jake said.

Look at me.

Hours later, I stumbled upstairs to Jake's parents' bedroom to pass out. I was wrecked. I couldn't see, nor could I walk. I was wobbling and trying hard not to puke as I threw off my clothes onto the floor. As I stood in only my skirt with my top now off, Jake walked into the room.

"Oh shit," he said, looking at me.

Oh. Shit.

I don't remember the sex—except in flashbacks. A hand on his muscular back. The sheets. Going in and out of consciousness. And the next day, his boxer shorts crumpled up at the bottom of the bed like a murder weapon.

I took a shower, a sense of dread creeping over me. It had happened. I was no longer a virgin.

Jake drove me home in silence. Why hadn't Jake said what his friends did? "You're fifteen? Oh, never mind."

And he was family. Why didn't he take care of me? Why didn't he bring me back to my aunt's in the first place? I felt like I had been set up. No longer did it feel like a conspiracy we were both in on together. It just felt like a conspiracy.

"See you," Jake said, and I walked into my aunt's house, sallow and ashen, before heading into the guest bathroom. Finally, I was sick.

The next afternoon sunlight streamed into the Spanish-tiled white kitchen as I washed dishes and took care of the kids. I heard a car pull up. Then I saw out the window. It was Jake.

"I need to talk to you," he said, urgently.

"Okay," I said. "I feel really confused about last night."

"Listen," he said, "every family has skeletons buried in its closet . . ."

"What happened exactly?" I asked quietly. "I was so drunk."

"Nothing," he said, harder than before. "This never happened, and if you tell anyone different, I'll deny it."

I stood there dumbly, my hands still in green neoprene gloves with soap on them.

"I have to go," he said.

The first few days, I told my aunt nothing. I was quieter than usual, though, and I couldn't stop my obsessive thoughts.

"I have to talk to you," I told my aunt the next night after dinner. "It's about Jake."

I told her what happened in a monotone, not crying anymore, just wishing I could go back in time.

"Mandy, it's not your fault," she said. "He shouldn't have done that."

We arrived at the local hospital the next day, and a bald male nurse coldly took my inventory.

"Sexually active?" he asked, staring down at his clipboard.

"No," I said. "I've never even really kissed a boy until the other night. It was my first time."

"So you *are* sexually active," he said.

"I guess," I said.

"History of STDs?" he asked.

"I—no, that's why I'm here," I said. "I want to make sure I'm okay."

"Well, you might not be," he said, looking up.

I'm sure he thought he was doing a good deed by scaring the shit out of yet another slutty teen, but I was not his target audience. I didn't need any more scaring.

"Am I going to die?" I asked.

"We'll find out," he said. "You just don't know if you have AIDS until we test you. You can't just go around having sex without consequences."

He walked away, leaving me shell-shocked.

Meanwhile, my uncle was actually dying of cancer. My dumb teenage conception of death was proving to be as brilliant as my conception of sex. It happened. There was no going back. He was forty-one. He was gone.

Returning home to San Diego after that awful summer, I didn't tell anyone until I found myself in therapy—with a hip thirty-something woman named Janet. Filled with plants and copies of *Sunset* magazine, her office felt so safe, and she was so kind to me. I asked Janet if I could tell her a secret, but I made her promise she wouldn't tell anyone. It had to be just between the two of us. She agreed.

"Something happened to me," I said, "this summer when I was in Oregon."

I described in detail how I'd lost my virginity. It felt so good to get it off my chest, and I felt protected. But our next session, Janet was more serious than usual.

"Listen, Mandy, I know what I said, but one of the bounds of my profession is that when something illegal happens, it's my duty to report it, and I'm not going to tell the police, but you absolutely have to tell your parents," she said. "I'm sorry."

I felt the wind knocked out of me. I cried. I begged her not to make me. I was so angry. Opening up had been a mistake.

That night, I told my parents what had happened. I couldn't stop crying. I wanted them to see how bad I felt.

"Were you drinking?" my mom asked.

"Yes," I said.

They were both silent.

"Say something," I said. "Say something, please!"

"I'm disappointed in you, Mandy," my mom said.

My dad was just silent.

I felt so sick. So unprotected. So unworthy of protection in the first place. I ran into my room and hid underneath my comforters. I wanted to disappear. Just vanish from the earth and not ever have to deal with anyone's judgment again.

That event, and the butterfly effect around it, set off a sneaky domino-like psychological course that affected the rest of my life—and even my career.

Do you disapprove of me?

Do you think I have something to be ashamed about?

I'll give you something to be ashamed about.

All my fears felt confirmed. I was bad. I made men do bad things. I should be sorry. It was something I needed to destroy about myself. I should be able to see that.

There is a certain comfort in destruction. You know the outcome at least.

"Rockefeller Center!" The subway conductor's voice pulls me out of ancient history.

The F train jerks to a stop. The battle will have to continue another time. No time for fighting the demons of the past. Time to be someone else entirely.

. . . .

OVERWHELMED WITH THRILLING stimuli everywhere, I take in my new normal: human rush hour on crack, in the form of people speed-walking through the underground tunnels of Manhattan's nerve center. I make my way up to the tenth floor, drinking my coffee, determined to make new memories. My *Post* ID is swinging around my neck; I realize no one else wears them around the office, but I don't care. I'm too proud of the Lois Lane fantasy I am now living.

"My friend!" I cry with glee at seeing Katherine hard at work in our shared office/coat closet.

"My friend!" she says back.

Katherine helps encourage me that working for a daily is like riding a bike: You just have to climb back on. (Even though it feels like ancient history to me, I know that my clips from working at dailies—the *Washington Post*, the *South Florida Sun-Sentinel*, and the *Des Moines Register*—aren't so long ago.) She also gently tolerates my not-very-well-contained near-constant freak-outs about my body, my health, and my life in general. You see, the Divorce Diet is great for guys fetishizing me as somewhat approximating the shape and feel of a model, but it is not great for my actual health.

Thankfully, I am very busy. Work assignments come just as quickly as they go, twelve and twenty inches filed here and there on end-of-the-year best-of lists, new hot spots to visit in the city for the holidays—all of which I treat with the importance of Watergate. That is, in between making light conversation with Katherine about the excruciating details of my divorce/parents' remarriage/new city/new roommates/new job/hypochondria.

"I don't look like I'm dying," I ask by way of small talk. "Right?"

"Nope," she says cheerily. "But if you do die, could you file that New Year's Eve roundup beforehand?"

She makes me laugh hard, the one thing in life that has always made me feel sane and whole.

"Just tell me if I'm freaking you out," I say. "I realize I can be a bit much. Like if you need me to tone down the 'Do I look like I'm dying' questions to once an hour."

"Not at all," she says. "I think everyone pretty much feels like they're dying their first few weeks in New York. It's kind of part of the city's charm."

The mental turmoil of all my coinciding life changes has caused my body to shut down and the effects are showing. Every day, some mysterious new skin problem emerges. I haven't had my period in months, which has never happened to me before.

Honestly, when I got off the birth control pill a few months earlier—since I figured I'd be using condoms from here on out—I didn't anticipate the havoc that the change would entail. Huge clumps of cystic acne started appearing on my chin, small white dots appeared on my stomach, discoloration marked my forehead. And month after month, no period in sight. I began praying for blood spotting.

I spent thousands on doctors and specialists, and I finally had to accept that maybe there might be something to the "extreme stress" diagnosis I kept receiving. One doctor practically shoved antidepressants down my throat, but I googled the side effects and flushed them down the toilet.

"The worst part is I'm all skinny and hot now," I prattle on to Katherine. "But I have to put on like a pound of clown makeup to cover up my face."

"Yeah, but that's just a pain in the ass," she says. "You look totally fine. I bet you'll be dating some new guy in no time."

"Are you seeing someone?" I ask.

"I was seeing this one guy," she says, as she hands me some faxes to see if there is anything worth pursuing. "But he told me he wanted to 'branch out.'"

"Oh God," I say. "I hate that. I've just given up on men entirely."

"That's good," she says. "Giving up on men will help you file this hot breaking story on Christmas Web Santas."

"Oh definitely," I say. "By the way, you know who loves Web Santas?"

I open my email and click on a picture of Scott with the Yacht, who is now talking about flying me out to Arizona to take in the Fiesta Bowl. *"This guy."*

"Yeah, that guy is definitely all about Web Santas," she agrees. "Is that your boyfriend?"

"Hardly," I say. "But I might spend New Year's with him."

Before too long, Christmas is upon us at the office.

Katherine offers me a seat at the dinner table at her parents' home in Connecticut in case I get lonely, but I spend the day collapsed on the yuppie lesbian couch in Park Slope instead. I call twenty gyms near me because I figure since I don't have a boyfriend, I can at least work on a potentially tight body for the benefit of one— because I have awesome priorities. But all of them are closed.

"I think most people are with their families," one man says.

Yeah. I got that.

I hang out with Jonathan Ames a few more times, but I notice something. I don't enjoy it as much when I'm not tipsy. He's fine, of course. But there's no real connection. I hate that about daytime sobriety. It just makes you feel so present.

The only thing I have is my career—and I am determined not to screw that up, too. Which, by the way, a tip: If you suck at dating, you'll be aces at writing about it.

At work, I pitch a story about some new dating site that specializes in catering to hipsters and nerds. I find out that the Dungeons & Dragons contingent populating the user base is anathema to the most popular girl on the site. She is a textbook normal—like a Pumpkin Spice Latte–drinking, Delta Gamma kegger–level normal.

I interview her, write it up, and then share with Steve the story so far by putting it in his "basket," as we call the different file folders on our shared server.

He speed-reads, then comes over to my desk and stops me mid-typing.

"You see this?" he asks, pointing to one specific quote in the story where the girl is cringing about how the nerds on the site are attempting to romance her.

The quote is:

"This guy sent me a note that says, 'You would so be the perfect copilot for my Death Star cubicle.' I have no idea what that means. That's bizarre."

It is pretty funny—her utter disdain for the earnest gamer boys trying their best at romancing a Jennifer Aniston–loving mind. But the rest of my story is filled with tangents and quotes from her about the state of dating in general. It is all over the place.

Steve points again to that quote, in which she makes fun of the geeks wooing her.

"*That* is the story," he says. "Right there. Call her back and reinterview her to get more of that."

I do. With a sense of clarity from having a theme—a direction—I play the SAT "this is to this as that is to that" game with her to find out just how different she is from her suitors. I ask her, so if a guy is really into Dungeons & Dragons, what might be her poison instead?

"I don't know." She thinks it over. "Shopping? Like, yoga maybe."

And if a guy is into anime, she might be more into . . . "*Friends* reruns," she finishes.

It is gold. With that ten-minute tossed-off tutorial Steve has taught me what my writing—and maybe even what my life—has been missing: focus. I learn so much from that one editing session. You don't try to write the entire encyclopedia. You write the one entry that makes your heart sing. And if you're lucky, you do the same thing with the people in your life.

Later that day, at the copy machine, I meet a girl who is fretting over some papers related to her impending divorce.

"Oh my God," I tell her when she explains what she is doing. "I just got divorced!"

I say it like I have just found out she is my long-lost identical twin sister. Can you believe this luck? *How many more of us could there be?*

Then, before she has a chance to say much more, I pull out of my pocket a prayer I copied down a few weeks prior when I was staying at my great-aunt's in Ohio, during my cross-country trip to New York.

"Here," I say, shoving the prayer into her hands. "Take this. It really helps. I have another copy, don't worry."

She laughs and smiles at me.

"I'm Mackenzie," she says, introducing herself—and I realize she is Mackenzie Dawson, whose hilarious stuff I have been reading in the paper lately. Then she looks down and reads the prayer.

Do not fear what may happen tomorrow;
The same everlasting Father who cares for you today will take
    care of you today and every day.

He will either shield you from suffering or will give you unfailing
  strength to bear it.
Be at peace and put aside all anxious thoughts and
  imaginations.

—St. Francis de Sales

"Thank you," Mackenzie says. "I really like this."
"Let's be friends," I say.
And we are.

. . . .

I HAVE ONLY been at the *Post* a month before I decide to get out
of town.

It takes only that small amount of time for me to see precisely
why and how dating in New York truly sucks. Mackenzie, Katherine, and I bond frequently over this fact.

Anyone who's ever watched an episode of *Sex and the City*
knows this fact already, but when you experience it yourself, it's a
whole different ball game. Single, not-entirely-awful men in New
York act like chicks. They are that rare and precious commodity,
seeking to be wooed and convinced and courted, and they know it.

"So it's not just me?" I ask Katherine and Mackenzie over coffee as we sit together in the mint-green third-floor lounge. We
are surrounded by both wizened old newscasters bemoaning the
liberal media's so-called War on Christmas along with young up-
and-comers like Julia Allison, who shimmers and laughs, conduct-
ing a flirtatious preinterview before making rounds as an expert
on Fox.

"It's definitely not just you," they agree.

So I say yes to the chance to celebrate the end of 2005 on a fancy vacation with Scott, who bought me a ticket to celebrate the Fiesta Bowl with him in Tempe, Arizona.

I have just one rule for myself: I am not going to drink.

"Welcome to Phoenix, New York girl." Scott greets me with open arms when I get off the plane. I smile and kiss him.

"Thanks," I say, down now to 139 pounds and so proud of how prepared I am to play the part of the trophy girl with the eating disorder you fly out to see a bowl game.

When we settle back into his hotel suite, one of Scott's friends instantly offers, "Let me get you something to drink. You look thirsty!"

"No, no, I'm good right now," I say, just as I have practiced.

I hold out a long two days in Phoenix—even at the Fiesta Bowl itself, where Scott wins one bill on the over-under—until, halfway through a boring night at dinner, I absentmindedly finger Scott's martini glass and wonder aloud, "Maybe I should get a . . ."

Before the full sentence has even come out of my mouth, Scott signals the waiter.

"Can we get another martini over here?"

If there is one universal truth it is this: Everyone loves when a girl drinks.

A giggling drunk girl to a group of jocks and frat bros is as American as blue jeans, baseball, and apple pie. Because saying it's as American as slurred non sequiturs, bad sex, and the morning-after pill just doesn't quite have the same ring to it.

The next morning, my head pounding, Scott and his friends turn on ESPN and excitedly realize it is the national spelling bee championship.

"Every time it's on, I watch it," Scott says. "Every time."

His friends all join in the fun to roast the dorky girl on-screen. She's from some highlight reel they are playing—ticky, squirmy, uncomfortable, and unabashedly joyful in her spelling out of "E-U-O-N-Y-M."

Everyone is rolling laughing, imitating her unselfconscious, unfiltered existence.

"Holy shit, that girl is *rough*."

"Good thing she has spelling, because she is single for life."

"E-U-O . . . what a spaz."

I feel like I am going to be sick.

It hits me right then. I can drink a million martinis, shapeshift into another person for extended stretches of time, I can even weigh under 140 pounds—but I can never really assimilate. These are not my people.

"I'm going to go lie down for a while," I say quietly.

Scott enters our room and sits down beside me.

"What's going on?" he asks, placing his hand on my side.

"I just kind of wonder," I say, tracing the seam of the comforter on the bed, "about the casual misogyny of society, you know?"

He looks at me with his big handsome brown doe eyes, a placid smile on his face and speaks with total sincerity.

"What does 'misogyny' mean?"

I glare at him.

"You're kidding, right?"

He is not. Scott drops me off at the airport at the end of the trip, lends me his copy of *FHM* for the plane (so much for the "misogyny" speech), kisses me goodbye, and says, "I hope you got a lot of new material."

I nod. Once we land at JFK, I cast my eyes downward as I walk, trying to avoid people's gazes but several jovial strangers take my clownish red Ohio State sweatshirt as an invitation for small talk.

"Are you going to go back and celebrate?" an older man asks.

"Good job yesterday," a man in a suit says, patting me on the back.

"We are looking at one very happy girl right here," another says, pointing to me. "I can't wait to hear what Regis has to say about this."

I realize something: Never has the world so lovingly embraced my six-foot-two body as when I am wearing a sports team sweatshirt. Everyone finally gets it. *Oh, the giant girl—she's a jock. Yeah, that makes sense. I can understand that.* I think of the spelling bee girl they all laughed at on the trip, and I'm suddenly unable to stop crying.

Walking off the plane, I hurry to the first concession stand I see and order a green tea and a seltzer water. I collapse into a plastic booth, trying to hide from the eyes around me. I stare at my phone. I turn it on and off, on again.

Fuck it. I dial my ex-husband. I couldn't feel much worse.

"Happy New Year," James says.

"Happy . . ." I say, bursting into tears.

"What's going on?" he asks.

"Oh, it's just funny," I say, voice uneven, bobbing my tea bag furiously, "because I went to the Fiesta Bowl and I'm wearing this big Ohio State sweatshirt and I feel so completely sad but everyone keeps congratulating me."

He pauses.

"That *is* pretty funny."

"And . . . and," I sputter, "the guys I was with, when we were in the hotel, you know, on this trip, they turned on ESPN, and they were making fun of the spelling bee girl on TV. And . . . like . . .

I didn't say anything, but James . . . they couldn't see that . . . I'm that spelling bee girl, you know?"

He is silent.

"I know you are," he says.

I hang up the phone, softened but shattered.

Images flash through my mind, as they do every time I speak to James. The gold card he gave me for our anniversary that said, "To Mandy . . . who gave me a life." Our wedding vows written as we drove on the winding roads from the Grand Canyon past the Hoover Dam on the way to Sin City: "My love for you grows stronger every day." And then five years later, the VHS cassette of our wedding in Vegas thrown in the trash, on top of a greasy pile of chicken entrails.

That shakes me out of it. There is no going back.

I rip the sweatshirt off, throw it in the trash, and resolve that I need to find people in my life who can see me. People who can see through my own bullshit even when I can't see it myself.

chapter three

The New Normal

2006

Men are a waste of time. My career is not. This is my new mantra.

In journalism, there are the 5 W's: Who, What, When, Where, Why. Before applying that basic premise to my stories, however, I first apply it to the animal of the newsroom around me.

I notice quickly something that smart reporters do. You fake it until you make it. Big-time. This means that even when you don't have a definitive lead, you kind of swagger like you do. During the first phone call I make to an A-list publicist to inquire about a boldface-name client, I say semi-apologetically by way of introduction in whispery upspeak, "I'm calling from the *New York Post*?"

"You're who calling from what? Who? What do you need?"

This is not how things get done. Everything must be a statement. I am calling from the *New York Post*. You will give me the story. I am on deadline. Help me help you. I am a player. I deserve to be here.

Different stories I am assigned dribble in—lots of last-minute celeb feud roundups (Lohan vs. Johansson! Letterman vs. O'Reilly!) and then there is what is known in the field, or at any J-school worth its salt, as the "enterprise" story.

During my fateful Mexican restaurant brunch turned job interview with Steve a few months back, one story stuck out in my mind as the *Post* staple. Steve mentioned "huge Hummer strollers" as sweeping the city and this being a great get.

It has everything: rich, entitled parents; something absurd in proportion to its usual size; newness; and, most important, a photographic element that pops. The *Post* runs on pictures and "high concept" ideas. This is what publicists always get wrong. If you can't pitch a story in just a few words, your pitch is going to fail. You don't go with "new eco-friendly strollers that help busy moms on the go." You go with cognitive dissonance that grabs you by the eyeballs—or, even better, by the throat.

"Hummer strollers!!!"

You get it. Immediately. You can't *not* get it. So I begin the hunt for my own enterprise masterpiece. Since I am such an avid dater, I try to think of the most salacious story I can—either from my own experience or based on anything else I dig up online. I keep finding one phrase that jumps out as the ultimate outrageous you-immediately-get-it concept in the Rants and Raves section on Craigslist. It strikes me as the perfect *Post* piece: a phenomenon called, classily enough, "dinner whores."

One poster bitches about a woman ordering drink after drink on his dime, all the while exhibiting no desire to ever see him again: "What the fuck? Did she think I was some asshole?"

Yeah, this is my *Post* story, for sure. Now I just need to find women who will admit they are searching for guys whom they have no interest in dating—beyond the prospect of a gourmet meal and plenty of cocktails. While Katherine aids me in maneuvering assignments with everything from "you got this"–style encouragement to the much more practical brand of help like, say, telling me where the West Village is (west, it turns out), I use my evening hours to track down my dinner whores.

I have something on my computer I dub "source list" (as it rapidly expands, I change the name to "new source list," "hot source list," and, eventually, "BEST NEW HOT SOURCE LIST"), which contains the names of a hodgepodge of people I meet, from strangers on the subway to old college acquaintances. I email them all asking if they know any women who might fess up to the maneuver.

One after another, I make new friends who tell me their stories of suffering through boring-ass business guys who get them into Michelin-rated restaurants and how they feel no qualms about taking them for a $300 meal because the guy is getting their company.

But no one wants to go on the record.

Then I realize I've had the answer within me all along. Just like I was rediscovered through my self-published blog chronicling all my adventures, there have to be plenty of fame-seeking young New York women who would love to go on record who are self-promoting via their blogs.

I google "New York," "dating," and "blogspot," and a million combinations thereof and eventually hit the jackpot when I discover bellein-thebigapple.blogspot.com and a blond, bubbly young lady who after several emails back and forth eventually identifies herself as Brooke Parkhurst, a former Fox TV intern (who pals around with *Gawker's* favorite target, Julia Allison) who's just landed a literary agent who is trying to sell her book. This, I soon learn, is key. When someone has something they want to push, they will work with you. Big-time.

As I develop the story, I still fear everything will fall apart. Will Brooke and the other women I interviewed back out last-minute? Will the pics the photographer snaps not be *Post*-y enough? Will everyone realize I am a fraud and ought to be back in Chicago, still writing about science grants and languishing in an unhappy marriage?

Wait—no. That is my impostor complex talking.

Fake it until you make it. Fake it until you make it. Repeat it until you believe it. Tattoo it on your fucking forehead if you have to.

During these early days at the *Post*, I think a lot about a fellow intern I worked with at the *Washington Post* right after graduating in 1997, one of the biggest name-droppers I've ever met. His tales usually involved a celebrity or politician he had just lunched with or, oh, here's a funny coincidence, did you know the son of the newspaper's editor actually lives in his dorm at Harvard, too? But that guy, man. He had more get-shit-done confidence than any young person I'd ever met. He just did not apologize. He walked around the newsroom like he owned it.

I, by contrast, would go to intern parties; get drunk; look at my short, stringy, dishwater-brown hair in the mirror; then return to the party and proceed to kill the entire mood. Here's a good recipe for how to do that in case it ever comes in handy: Say a bunch of unfunny, radioactively self-loathing (beyond the normal level of light self-deprecation) bons mots like, "I look like a drowned rat."

Everyone will proceed to shift uncomfortably, staring down at their Grey Goose. The other intern, meanwhile, would find a way to work in that he had just grabbed a meal with David Foster Wallace.

So now, as I returned to newspapers after a long-ass, marriage-filled absence, that dude became my spiritual guide. Here's an actual non-sarcastic helpful trick: If you suffer from debilitating low self-esteem and crippling shyness most of your life, just pretend to be someone who has what you want instead.

It was actually the year 2000 when I first really tested out the pretend-to-be-someone-else trick, during my first major impostor-complex experience, after having been hired by an Internet company called MarchFirst to fill a questionable position called "content strategist." (I believe that job title went bust right when the economy did.) Formed a few months before the dot-com bubble burst, MarchFirst hired me after I rewrote my résumé enough times to make it look like I spoke Internet. My annual salary shot up from $32,000 to $47,000, and soon I was being flown from Chicago to Philly to talk to middle-aged chemical industry executives to justify my $200-an-hour bill rate.

My boss at the time was a perky blond twenty-seven-year-old named Stephanie, who gesticulated wildly in front of the ever-present whiteboard while using made-up words like *bucketizing*.

"We need to bucketize content!" she'd say, making exaggerated motions of what it would look like if content were physically plunked into imaginary buckets.

So on my business trips, wearing my cheap Clothestime business suit that I got dry-cleaned until it had holes in it, I just pretended I was Stephanie. I was scared shitless. Stephanie knew how to take that scared shitlessness—and just bucketize it!

Now, at the *Post*, I think back fondly to Stephanie, the confident intern, and every other prophet of big, brash, seemingly unwarranted confidence (not a dig—a necessity: Any performer you can stand to watch on TV for more than thirty seconds possesses it). And when Steve returns to talk to me about my pitch, I do not offer up the terror I feel inside. No self-loathing asides like "I look like a drowned rat" or "Oh God, my story sucks, doesn't it?" Nope. Just chill.

"I like 'dinner whores,'" Steve says with a smile. "It may take a little selling on the 'whore' part, though."

"Awesome," I say.

I turn to Katherine, sitting behind me, and grin genuinely. "Rad."

. . . .

MY FIRST MAJOR celebrity piece for the *Post* is a profile of Star Jones. As she prattles on to me in the pristine confines of the Core club about how she is an inspiration to victims of Hurricane Katrina, I see a dead woman walking. As she talks, she has no clue she is hanging herself with her own words. That's how tabloid journalism works.

There are a lot of sacrificial lambs—including one's own life relationships.

At drinks with Steve a few nights earlier, I related to him, all swagger, three drinks of merlot in, how I'd once identified the exact second I realized I would definitely not have sex with a guy: when I saw him rocking out to a jam band, a glint coming from the gold chain on his chest.

"Every woman does that," I explained. "Every woman has that moment."

"I love it," Steve said. "That's a story. 'How He Blew It.' That's the headline."

In the back of my mind, while I'm supposed to be focused on Star, I keep thinking about how I will soon be subjecting this jam-band-loving man (an extremely sweet doctor whom I have grown close to over the last few months) to the exact same exercise that I am about to subject Star: I am going to string him up by his words and actions. It fills me with dread and the feeling that everything is moving faster than I can control.

But "How He Blew It" is not right now. That is in the future. I need to triage my anxiety.

One foot in front of the next. I am writing tomorrow's features cover.

Inside the gorgeously swanky club, as I listen to Star go on about her cult of success, my eyes dart around. I'm looking for the focus (the one big idea) Steve taught me about, a way to connect her seemingly scattered, grandiose, and humility-allergic quotes. I have until 5 p.m. to file the story. I glance at my watch as she talks, and I see that it is almost 3:40 p.m. Shit.

I turn off my voice recorder, thank Star, and sprint off the elevator to find a cab to bring me back to 1211 Avenue of the Americas.

"How was it?" Steve asks.

"Great," I say. "She said she inspires victims of Hurricane Katrina."

"Hilarious," he says. "Go, write."

Back at my desk, the clock turning 4:12 p.m., my voice recorder to my ear, with forty-eight minutes to write the next day's cover story, I realize that the idea can be found in her book title itself.

Shine.

"Star Jones Reynolds is shining," I write in between scarfing jelly beans and sucking down a triple espresso. "Her hair is shining. Her lips are shining. Her bling is shining."

I play, rewind, and play again on my voice recorder any quotes that are usable, so terrified of even getting a single preposition wrong. I listen back to myself nervously asking about Howard

Stern's use of crack whores to reenact fights between her and Joy Behar.

Star's voice plays in my ears: "They're making their money. That's their jig. Their job. That's their gig. I don't think they want to be helped."

And then, as I type, I realize I can bring it all back around to the One Big Idea once more.

"Star lets it roll off her back," I write. "They're not shining."

Of course, Star did not know, nor did her publicist, that I returned from my interview to write the story for the next day's paper, a mocking layout already under way, peppered with preselected ridiculous quotes from her book ("As a Christian, I have to say, 'There's nothing anybody did to me any worse than they did to Christ.' So, if he can forgive so can Star.").

The next morning, I grab the paper and hold it to see if it is real. There it is. "Star Bursts: Star Jones Tells Fans How to Get Her Perfect Life."

On my way to the train, I check my messages. The first one is from her angry publicist. I feel bad, but I push the emotion away.

When I arrive at the office finally, I grab a cup of corporate coffee from the kitchen and join Katherine in our shared office.

"Nice piece," she says.

"Thank you," I say.

Star knows the game, of course. It was hit piece lite. Nothing truly eviscerating beyond her own lack of self-awareness. Plenty of book promotion for her. Besides, critical press tends to get more pickup.

Do I sound like I'm justifying? That's because I am. I fucking hate writing hit pieces. You're actually taught how to do them in journalism school. You're taught to weigh short-term versus long-term access. Short-term you can burn. Long-term you have to weigh the restriction of access that might occur if you offend your source.

I replay the publicist's message, "Mandy, I wish you would have told me the piece was coming out the next day . . ." and realize for the first time that I apply the same tactic to my personal life. If I realize that I can't stand someone, I let loose with burn after burn. One time I told a man right after making out with him that he had bad breath. I informed another man that he was full of shit and a waste of my time. What did it matter? I was never going to see them again.

Ducking out of the office, I go to the hallway and dial the doctor who is the inspiration for the "How He Blew It" piece I will soon be writing. It is no longer just a barroom conversation. There is a scheduled run-date and everything. As much as possible, I resolve to be more transparent and not to skulk around the sidelines of modus operandi.

"Tom," I say when my friend answers, "I need to tell you something."

He laughs—and it sounds like music—when I relay the story.

"That's why you didn't sleep with me," Dr. Tom says. "That's hilarious. And I'm honored. How many people get to say that they're the inspiration for a funny story in the *Post?*"

"Oh my God, you're the best," I say, a huge weight lifted off of me. "You're a literal angel."

"No, you're the best, Mandy," he says gently. "Now go write. I can't wait to read it."

A funny thing happens when you don't hook up with a guy— *and* you don't burn the connection. You can develop an actual relationship.

. . . .

NOT TOO LONG after telling Dr. Tom that I am writing about him, he calls me.

"I'm coming to town," he says. "No jam bands this time, I promise."

We make plans to meet at a bar off St. Marks Place, and when he sees my thinner-still frame, he looks visibly taken aback.

"You're too skinny," he says. "I mean . . . you look great and all, but I just want to make sure you're okay."

Ten months earlier, I had met Dr. Tom during one of the most important trips of my life: the one I decided to take without my then husband after we decided we were separating. My medical school PR job had a few notable perks, one of which was an annual conference gathering together university types around the country—always located in some fun vacation spot. In 2005, it was in New Orleans, months before Katrina. The city, always a hotbed of utter magic, felt like it was under an actual spell when I was down there—purple skies, strangers whispering secrets. Everything seemed to fall into place.

I had planned to go with James, until I realized that I was becoming the picture of a woman enabling her emotional abuser. Nothing physical, but the verbal abuse was beginning to take its toll. (Among his greatest hits: "You're not smart, you're not funny, you're not a good writer, and you're not pretty." "You are pathetic." "You'll always be able to find a guy to slap his dick in your face and call you a whore.") I told him I was going solo at the last minute, and it was the best decision I'd ever made in the course of our marriage.

It was the trip of a lifetime—a drunken one, albeit, but I woke up every morning and the coffee at Café Du Monde was sweeter, the breakfast at Le Croissant d'Or was tastier, and the nightlife at Jacques Imo's was pure heaven. That's where I met Dr. Tom, whom I sidled up next to at the bar, and we proceeded to spend the rest of the night together until I ditched him for a strip club DJ who lied to me and told me my stand-up was great.

In the months following, Dr. Tom became more than just a friend: He became a lifeline. As I grew skinnier and more alone in my life, my hypochondria, compounded by actual—but insignificantly small—physical anomalies, was magnified a zillion times by the fact that I was working at a medical school. No sooner had I checked my body for the hundredth time that day than I had emailed one of the medical school deans self-diagnosing myself with Crohn's disease. I would get back an email reply, immediately.

"You're fine, Mandy," the dean would write. "Stop googling."

Other times I would actually go up to his office and show him anything that seemed weird on my body.

"Still fine," he would say.

Dr. Tom bore the brunt of my anxiety's runoff, looking at picture after picture I snapped of my stomach and sent to him. Ever since my marriage had fallen apart, I had noticed tiny white spots that appeared there one day and were never medically explained (no, they were not tinea versicolor; believe me, I checked that out), and those, along with my insane period (marked by either constant spotting or long bouts of absence), consumed my every thought.

I was like the anti-sexter with Dr. Tom.

"What about this lesion? Hot or not?" I texted him.

My insurance was incredible, so I talked my way into test after test: a $1,000 allergy battery, an endometrial biopsy that almost

made me pass out, and a sonohysterography that was so excruciat-
ingly painful it inspired me to call my mom sobbing, thanking her
for suffering through the hell of childbirth.

In the midst of my hysteria, Dr. Tom never made me feel stupid
or annoying (which I most definitely was), and in one hilarious exchange, he assured me that I had passed one of the more important
informal tests of all. The fuckability one. The laughter he provided
in saying that gave me honestly the biggest relief of all.

Now, standing face-to-face with Dr. Tom once again, I am bom-
bastic as I assure him that my stick-thin body is totally healthy as I
do shot after shot of Maker's.

"Well, thanks for saying I look great," I say. "But don't worry.
I'm fine."

Dr. Tom is handsome, but we have the chemistry of brother and
sister. I love him in a way that you love the guardian angel who
slips into your life at a time when you need one most.

I sit down at the bar to meet his friends.

One of them, Adam Strauss, has recently started doing stand-up
comedy, so we agree to watch him do his set. He's fairly new to
performing, and as we sit at the table, it is clear he is warming up
on us.

"So how soon did Tom drop the D-bomb on you after you two
met?" Adam asks. "First ten minutes?"

I laugh. Not only does Tom have the D-bomb, for *doctor*; he
also has the H-bomb, for *Harvard*.

"Yeah, that sounds about right," I say. "Unfortunately, he had a
penchant for jam bands."

"You're killing me," Dr. Tom says.

Because I am eating very little during the day now, the shots I
am downing go straight to my head, which always makes me want

to drink even more. By the time Adam goes onstage, I feel nothing but pure liquid confidence.

"I wasn't going to do stand-up in New York, because I just wanted to concentrate on the *Post*," I whisper to Dr. Tom. "But fuck it, I think I'm going to do it tonight."

Placing my name in line to do a set, I try to sober up a little bit with a water.

I have been performing at open mics in Chicago for the past year since starting my blog, and I think about all my past shows. The very first mic I did in Chicago was run by a then unknown T. J. Miller, who introduced me and, after I did my set, told the audience and me, "My only advice for you is to try to be less attractive."

Yes, that I could definitely do.

I had also developed a pen-pal relationship with a young Kyle Kinane after joining a Yahoo! group dedicated to Chicago comedians. Kyle and I would email back and forth nearly every day for months (subject lines: "glad to hear you're not reproducing," "thursday morning coming down," and "am I retarded?"), and he gave me something I wasn't receiving from my ex-husband. Encouragement.

His lowercase stream-of-consciousness notes about the jokes I posted online and the status of his own life were like manna from heaven: "your blog is getting quite heelarious lately. well done. i've made a pact with myself that i'm not shaving until i'm not ashamed of myself anymore. last monday i got a citation for trying to sneak onto the train without having a ticket. this will be an amazing beard."

I try to summon up every tiny encouragement in my mind right now and cling to it like a life raft. But I haven't performed-performed in weeks since joining the *Post*.

"Up next . . . Mandy!"

Electricity shoots through my body.

I strut to the front of the tiny bar and survey the room. I feel a sense of nonchalance and attitude. I am just the right amount of drunk. Whenever I've performed before, I always overthought everything. I talked and delivered lines as if I was doing material. This time I delivered the whole set without thinking.

"I opened a fortune cookie the other day. It said, 'Give up.'"

Laughter.

"I was going to wash my hair with L'Oréal . . . but I realized I wasn't worth it."

More laughter.

"I'm writing a point-by-point response to *He's Just Not That into You*. So far all I have is, 'That's not what he said last night . . . when he was inside me.'"

The bar goes wild.

"Holy shit, that was great," Dr. Tom says, giving me a high five.

The booker comes up and gets my email. Maybe I'm not done performing quite yet.

I kiss Dr. Tom on the cheek, grab a cab home, and, before passing out, realize I need to work out all the nervous energy wracking my body. I do something I haven't thought about in years. Pulling out my cell, I dial a number I still know by heart. A phone sex party line that is free for women in Chicago. I discovered it the summer I interned at the *Village Voice* in New York in 1996, when I needed someplace to engage with those demons that have plagued me since I was fifteen.

Using a fake identity to self-flagellate sexually was my way to wrestle with the darkness. All those feelings of badness.

I record my intro message as I play with myself on my awful air mattress, sliding off it and falling onto the floor. "Hi . . . this is . . .

Crystal . . . and I'm feeling kind of drunk . . . and wondering if anyone wants to chat . . ."

Bing! Bing! Bing! Seven new requests to chat one-on-one.

"Hey, this is Bob, a fifty-six-year-old married man in Arkansas, have you been a bad girl?"

The pain inside me has found its flogger for the night.

"Yes," I say. "I am bad."

. . . .

ON THE SUBWAY the next morning, severely hungover from not just the alcohol but also the steep cliff-drop from stand-up to degrading phone sex, I check my email and see one new message from the guy who ran the open mic. He is putting together a show and wants to know if I'll be on the bill.

"Definitely," I write back.

I can't believe it. Just like that, in the span of one second, I have something to cling to: Hope. Excitement. A dream, even.

That day, at our Tuesday 11 a.m. pitch meeting I decide to suggest a story on the best comedy spots around the city—and I make up my mind to hyper-sell it.

Our pitch meetings are always a nerve-wracking process, with the possibility of having something shot down in a span of two seconds as seeming too weak, already done, unfocused, boring, or, in the most delicious smackdown of all (and a favorite of editor in chief Col Allan's): "Great idea. Tell them to buy an ad."

The ultimate symbol of approval from Steve, though, is "It's a talker," meaning, well, you know. People will talk.

One by one, every reporter sitting around the long conference room table takes turns pitching. Now it is mine.

I suggest a bunch of things scribbled in my notebook. "Haircut that changes your life?" Pass. "The reconciliation vacation—a last-ditch attempt to save a relationship." Maybe—find a news peg. "Replacement hotties—the next generation of young Hollywood set to upstage their older sibling stars?" Hard pass. "The detox-retox diet—the way pretty much every New Yorker lives." Approved. "The emerging 'fempire' of women in Hollywood?" Pass. ("All you have is the word 'fempire.'") "The blog girls primed for Hollywood, from Stephanie Klein to the Washingtonienne herself, Jessica Cutler." More reporting—and we'll see.

Then it came time for my big pitch—the only one that really mattered. "One more idea that I'm, uh, really excited about," I begin. "So I think the New York comedy scene is really having a moment right now."

Tip: If you are ever pitching a story to any publication on the planet, be sure to use the phrase "having a moment." Anorexia? Having a moment. Morbid obesity? Having a moment. Moments? Having a moment.

I continue: "There's a bunch of comics set to break out in a big way, like Aziz Ansari. Kristen Schaal. Nick Kroll. Baron Vaughn . . . I was thinking I could do a story roundup of where to check out tomorrow's biggest stars . . ."

Steve pauses. He knows I did comedy back in Chicago. He knows comedy is my big love.

"I could see that . . . for a Saturday cover," he says. "Talk to Katherine."

And just like that, my life changes again.

I now have a reason to contact every single emerging comedian who is breaking out and also an excuse to discover the best underground clubs. The most helpful person in all this proves to be a young comic named Liam McEneaney, who knows every single person in the scene.

"Talk to Aziz. Here's his number. Kristen Schaal? Sure, here you go."

He is beyond generous, and when he kisses me over Heinekens at 2A in the East Village where we've met to talk about my story, I realize, oh yeah, that's why.

You have to realize, this kind of attention is all new to me.

When I got married to James, I never wore makeup or watched my weight or dyed my hair or even got my eyebrows done. I wore clothes either far-too-old-for-my-age dowdy-professional or retro thrift, as if I hoped to seduce Eddie Vedder should I ever get a time-travel machine to 1993. I never played games at all with men. Ever. Unless the game was to act like the kind of nightmare who hysterically cries at the drop of a hat and relies on a man for all manner of self-validation, self-worth, and approval to fill that giant gaping hole inside.

But when James broke my heart, he broke all of my idealism as well. I pulled a complete one-eighty, a total George Costanza in terms of how I approached men, dating, and relationships. Had I made fun of *The Rules* before? Well, fuck it, this time, I was going to read it with an open mind. Did I never date conservative guys as a rule but instead gravitate toward anyone who would bring up Howard Zinn or Noam Chomsky within the first ten minutes of small talk? Well, why not date a union-busting corporate lawyer instead and "yes and" every Darth Vader illustrative anecdote he made over chardonnay as I fell down drunkenly on his boat?

Nothing mattered. The dream of true love was dead, and I was ready to position myself as a player. Now, sixty pounds lighter, hair much more bleached, makeup much more applied, clothes much more tweaked for sex appeal, ideology completely shredded, I was suddenly a piece of ass. And it was the strangest feeling of power, one I had never quite experienced before.

With Liam, I am open to romantic possibility, but after the one daytime date we have, seeing *Brokeback Mountain* in the theater, complete with awkward hand-holding, I realize I like him more as a friend than anything else. I so want to have that immediate-boyfriend-in-New-York experience, but there's nothing lonelier than trying to convince yourself that a friend is something more, when your heart knows differently.

Out at Liam's stand-up showcase one night, I meet Andy Borowitz, the humorist and creator of *The Fresh Prince of Bel-Air*, who has enough money to retire on forever but enjoys doing stand-up at small showcases in the city. He tells me I look ten years younger than my age, kisses me on the cheek, and gives me his number when I ask if I can ever use him as a source for a "future piece."

Ever the eager networking rube, I take this not-even-an-overture overture and leverage it with another pen-pal friend of mine, the then relatively unknown and future creator of *You're the Worst*, Stephen Falk, who had reached out to me as a fan of my blog a year ago. Stephen would check in from time to time to see how my New York adventures were going. He had heard national radio pickup in LA on my "dinner whores" piece and wrote me about teaming up to bring in one of my future articles to option to his agent.

So how do I respond to Stephen?

"Yeah, sure," I demur. "Maybe. I don't know. I just want to work for *The Daily Show* . . . Maybe sometime I could call you and we could chat. I also think the creator of *The Fresh Prince* wants to bed me so maybe that will take care of everything. Ha ha."

Question: Is it possible to die from literally cringing at yourself? Because I just did. A million times over. Why—specifically?

1. Because I idiotically didn't realize that Stephen was handing me actual gold on a platter (anyone reading this: Know there is no better way to "break in" to Hollywood as a journalist than to have an established screenwriter option one of your pieces).
2. Because I dismissively swatted his idea away like the moron I was.
3. Because I instead took the opportunity to go on about various flirtations that existed largely in my mind—as if that meant *anything*. Honestly, I think because I had never experienced this kind of male attention before, I actually thought this was part of my résumé.

Stephen writes me back, true to hilarious form, and says, "That's so funny. I got my first agent by fucking the guy who created *Head of the Class*. Sure, let me know what your schedule is and we'll set up a phone call. So official!"

After my article "How He Blew It" comes out, I receive an inquiry from a guy named John who says he is a movie producer who can get me into William Morris. Almost daily, I write him nauseating emails trying to represent myself as the Carrie Bradshaw/Samantha Jones ice queen I think he envisions me to be (versus the crumpled-up identity-crisis mess I actually am). In writing this producer (I just googled him now; his career consists of one low-budget film no one saw in 2010), I even make Dr. Tom out to be this dramatic Romeo because I know I need some kind—any kind—of Mr. Big figure in the messy shit show that is my life.

"You'll be pleased to know I had two heartwarming conversations with The Doctor this week," I email John. "For the sake of The Hollywood Ending, of course. Also got approached about doing a stand-up showcase in March. Should be fun."

My emails to John contain every excruciating nook and cranny of every development in my life. Someone wants me to write for a literary collection. Should I do it? My story for the next day's paper is about spooning positions people sleep in, so insert shitty joke here, keep an eye out for that one!

God, I feel so lonely and unhinged. Little do I realize, John is pretty much doing to me the same thing I am doing to everyone else: parlaying. Neither of us is a player (no matter how many times he talks to me about getting "Dane Cook or Jennifer Aniston attached"). But we just keep mentioning enough dribs and drabs to convince ourselves (and, more important, other people) that we are.

Here's how you parlay—in a nutshell. You try to pique the interest of someone else by inspiring the basest of human desires: jealousy that the other person is going to miss out on lightning. *I've got this BIG EXCITING THING going on, and this person and this person are interested, and boy wouldn't you be bummed if you didn't snatch this/me/it/whatever right up?* What I failed to realize at the time was this: It's not about the connections. It's only about the work. *Only.* If you don't have work that stands up on its own, you are toast. You are an embarrassment. You are as see-through as Saran Wrap.

The exact same theory applies to dating and romance. You want this guy and that guy and the other to be The One, but if you haven't done the work on yourself? World of hurt, baby. World. Of. Hurt.

Soon after John's inquiry, an agent from ICM named Kate Lee contacts me after I feature her then client Nick Kroll. True to form, I keep up my roll of great decision making.

Kate and I get together for lychee martinis and conversation (during which I make sure, of course, to relate every interaction I've ever had with anyone who has so much as glimpsed the Hollywood sign). Then I do a conference call with her and her team, who wisely tell me that no one has heard of this movie producer "John" I keep mentioning. For my grand finale, I tell her I am going in a different direction.

Brilliant.

Should you ever want to break into the entertainment industry, I'm about to save you a lot of time and tell you the only two words you need to know (which an executive finally told me years later): *deal memo*. Or here's one more: *contract*.

Everything else means nothing. It's just talk. Treat it accordingly.

In the midst of all this, Fashion Week descends on the newsroom. This is a time when the models showcase the upcoming seasons and every lifestyle editor wants to jump off a cliff due to the insane workload, late nights, and tens of thousands of photos filing in.

Steve says he has a potential assignment for me. Would I be interested in being body-painted nude while modeling a Vivienne Tam design and writing a first-person piece about it?

"Yes," I tell Steve. "But if I'm going to be naked in the paper, I'm not going to eat until it happens."

"You weigh like twenty pounds already," Steve says.

The day of the body-painting is surreal. While being brushed in oily black and red painted peonies, I scratch notes on my pad in pencil, including what is to be the lede: "My breasts look fantastic. That's what people keep telling me anyway."

The piece continues, "I am wearing nothing but a Cosabella thong and pasties. All of my bits have been shaved. I am so glad I went to journalism school."

When it comes to editing, Steve fights hard for every joke I write that the copy desk flags or red-pens. If you ever want to know what to look for in an editor, it's this: someone who is a writer first.

But Steve also has to fight for something else. During the painting process, I make a huge mistake. I never once ask to look at what the makeup artist is doing to my face. I am so self-conscious already, I don't think I have a right to demand to see what is happening. Someone says, "Fierce," at one point, so I think that's a good thing?

But when I finally go to a mirror I see it: I am nightmarish. The *Post* (like any mainstream media) relies on hot photos of hot women being hot. And I didn't look hot at all. I looked frightening—like a red-and-black Kabuki freak.

When Steve pulls up the photos in our system Merlin, I watch his eyes as he clicks through the hundreds of shots. Then I watch as he does what a good editor does.

He doesn't make me feel bad, but he is honest—and he saves the story. (In the words of one of my *Washington Post* mentors David Von Drehle, "Don't try to make an A+ story out of C- material." And that's what those photos were.) After he makes some calls, the publicist messengers over a CD filled with other art options of drop-dead-beautiful naked women covered in body paint that we can use for the cover—instead of me. Next to one of them on the features cover, I am inserted as a tiny little inset. "My Brush with Fame: The Naked Truth About Becoming a Body Paint Model."

It is humiliating, but it is also instructive. Never trust a makeup artist. Never trust anyone when it comes to pictures. If you think something looks weird, say something. Throughout a photo shoot, check in. Go with your gut. Need to start all over? Fine. Do it.

After the piece comes out, I keep up my aggressive parlaying streak.

I text Nick Kroll. Does he want to go to the body-painting-model-filled after-party with me? He is in LA. I call up Andy Borowitz, and he agrees. We walk through the party in the Meat-packing District as naked gorgeous women pose provocatively this way and that in silver, bronze, and gold body paint.

Outside the party, we pass by a newspaper box on the street. I put in a quarter to get out the paper and show him my piece.

"I got a few funny lines in it," I say, as I show it to him, proud of myself in a small way after listening to his impressive anecdotes.

I hold up the spread for him to see. He examines it momentarily.

"Yeah," he says. "That's not a good picture of you."

My heart sinks. I feel so stupid. Only I could be in the paper naked and look like shit. So much for the piece-of-ass trajectory.

....

PERFORMING STAND-UP IS never something I plan to do in New York, but that one drunken night out with Dr. Tom changes all that. When I am booked to do a show at a gay Thai restaurant in the Meatpacking District, I nervously prepare as best as I can, trying to build up the fake confidence that a real performer gains naturally by going up at clubs five nights a week.

Inside the venue a few minutes before showtime, I walk up to a young man whom I ask, "Hey, are you on the show tonight, too?"

He is.

"I work at the *Post*," I say, chatting him up nervously.

"Okay," he says.

Then, all of a sudden, he turns to me in the middle of my wandering spiel. His face pinches up. He asks, with disgust and disbelief, "Did you just fart?"

My face turns red, and then I laugh.

"Yeah, I totally did."

He pauses, stone-faced at first, then cracks up, shaking his head in disbelief. Onstage, I do not kill—at all. Halfway through my set, I look like a deer in headlights, and it shows. The young man I have been talking to before tears it up, however.

His name is Hannibal Buress.

"What are you doing now?" he asks me after the show.

"Nothing," I say. "Want to hang out?"

It feels like we are both just trying to figure the city out, and we spend the rest of the night together. We soon find out we have something in common: We both have Chicago roots. I went to Northwestern, and he went to Southern Illinois University, where he says that after the first time he got a few chuckles, he got that rush any new performer gets, where you feel like Chris Rock or something. Little does he know that he is just a few years from being in the same major leagues as Rock himself.

A few days later at the *Post*, I get a call from Hannibal.

"You going up anywhere tonight?" he asks.

I hadn't planned on going up anywhere again. But I meet him at a Lower East Side bar, where I get to see Eric Andre do stand-up in his earliest days of performing. Eric is modest about his talents, immediately bringing up that maybe Zach Galifianakis already has the music-and-comedy thing covered. Not a chance.

Hannibal calls me when he is hosting shows, and I get to do my own shitty stand-up. This sets my new intermittent pattern.

"What are you doing tonight, Miss Mandy?"

"Nothing."

"Going up anywhere?"

Well, now I am.

One night after a show, he says he has nowhere to stay so I invite him back to the lesbians' apartment to crash. We lie platonically in bed together, and he says after an awkward silence, "You're cool as shit." We make out for a little while, then fall asleep.

We text stupid shit throughout the day that makes me genuinely happier than most things in my life at the time.

Hannibal: *Was yesterday our first date?*

Me: *yes—only 29 more to go and then we do it.*

Hannibal: *Taxi!*

Me: *hahahahha*

Me: *I also like your ipod franz ferdinand joke—& I like that it tests ur theory of all u need 2 do is say franz ferdinand 2 hipsters & they laugh*

Hannibal: *I'm full of hipster references. I'm buying your hat today.*

But I never take him seriously. He is twenty-three. I am thirty.

Besides, it's also incredibly clear that we should just be friends.

Still, my phone chats with Hannibal are far smoother than my other attempts at connecting with men.

During one night out on the town with Jessica Cutler after profiling her in my blogs-to-Hollywood piece, we notice David Cross out at Three Kings, and go up to him and say hi. He has totally heard of the Washingtonienne's infamy in blog-land, and I offer to buy everyone drinks and expense them.

"Can you really expense them?" he asks, seeing through my bravado. "Because otherwise, I'm buying."

He talks about the crappy sound guy who screwed up his set with Jon Benjamin when the two of them danced around to "Let's Give Them Something to Talk About," and before too long we all move on to a place called the Magician on the Lower East Side.

Jessica doesn't have her ID with her, though, so she gets left behind. Inside, we meet Gavin McInnes.

"Wait, Gavin from *Vice*?" I ask after he introduces himself.

"That's the one," he says, smiling, as it's clear he's done many times in response to the question.

I have this theory that *Vice* is evil (old indoctrination from my husband), and after leaving the bar, walking with David Cross solo now back to his apartment, knowing what comes next, I tell him exactly that.

"*Vice* is evil," I say by way of small chat.

"If you think that, you can just leave right now," he says and stops walking.

Whoa.

I take it back, and we keep going.

Back at his apartment, I make myself comfortable on his couch, then we kiss for a little while, and all I can think of is the many images of his face in my head from watching *Mr. Show*. Am I in a sketch? I cannot believe this is happening. There are few greater gods in comedy to me than David Cross.

We take a break, and I pick up the *Wonder Showzen* DVD he has lying out.

"I've never seen it," I say.

"Best show on television," he says.

"Oh, hey, I've got an idea, why don't you put on MTV?" I say. "I can dance sexy."

He gives me the kind of look that a man gives when he fears you might actually be a crazy person. This makes me nervous, which inspires me to keep talking, change the subject, really open up.

"I probably shouldn't have sex," I continue, filling the silence. "Because I just got my period for the first time in like six months. I'm so excited."

His face has now definitely changed. I am for sure a crazy person. What is happening? Why can't I stop talking?

"Can I use the bathroom?" I ask, trying to make him forget all the weird shit I've just said. I go into his bathroom, look at the chipped toilet cover, and think to myself, *This is David Cross's toilet seat. He's just like us.* I splash water onto my face and try to will myself to stop saying stupid things.

I am literally the worst starfucker ever. I am a self-cock-blocking one by virtue of the insanity coming out of my mouth. I return to his living room. I sit on the couch. I keep to my pledge of silence.

"Hey, it's getting late," he says, and it is—it's nearly six in the morning.

"Okay," I say. "Do you want my number?"

He replies, with a distinctive question mark in his voice: "Sure?"

I jot my still-773 digits down on the back of my business card and leave it on his coffee table.

Then I stumble in as dignified a manner as I can muster out of his place, beeline straight to a bodega that is open, get a pint of double-fudge ice cream, and eat the entire thing on the cab ride home.

So begins a pattern. My deeply destructive binge-and-fast cycle.

Since my period is so erratic, I finally go to yet another doctor, who tells me plainly what is wrong.

"You're anorexic," he says. He is not amused by my recounting of the Divorce Diet.

I deal with his diagnosis by getting wasted and sloppy drunk during the evening, then telling myself that eating a ton of food is actually good for me.

But once I open that dark Pandora's Refrigerator Box, I can't seem to close it.

The Divorce Diet had been something I could follow and contain like an inner pain that you starve and deprive, but when I begin to fill it up with one little bite of ice cream—just like with drinking—I can't seem to stop. So many late nights, I come home and raid the lesbians' refrigerator, sampling cereal and jars of olives, until I finally visit the twenty-four-hour bodega in the wee early-morning hours, loading up on cookies and candy, stuffing them in my face until I feel satisfied to the point of pain and disgusted with myself to the point of incapacitation. Sometimes, I even chronicle the wreckage in my diary: "6 mozzarella sticks, 1 diet cola, 1 16 oz. Tasti D-Lite with 2 toppings, 3 bowls of Lucky Charms, 1 pint of Chunky Monkey." Looking at it now, it makes me want to puke all over again.

No one at work seems to "get" my pitch for this story: "The only person who knows the darkest secrets of your soul is the bodega guy at three in the morning."

The next day, like clockwork, I wake up after a binge a few pounds heavier and vow that even though I don't want to be anorexic, I don't want to go back to my nearly two-hundred-pound weight from when I was married. So I pledge not to eat at all.

But everything changes when nighttime comes around,

and, with nothing in my stomach for the last eight hours, I get hammered—and the binge-eating cycle resumes.

Anything to blunt out what I am feeling: fear, uncertainty, self-hatred, and not feeling like I have anyone there for me who cares.

By the time April arrives, I am so unmoored that one afternoon, without planning to, I log onto a travel agency site and book a last-minute trip to Florida.

I have no one to see. I just know, as Dr. Tom advises me after my last update, "You need to get the fuck out of Dodge."

So I do—appropriately enough, right after writing my "reconciliation vacation" piece, which I finally get into the paper after DJ AM and Nicole Richie take a trip together that I can use as a launching point for the story. I have no real purpose attached to the trip, but Fort Lauderdale is a place on a map. I know that.

When I arrive, I hail a cab and ask to go to the coral-beachy hotel I booked as part of my weekend package. But the cabdriver gets lost—really lost—and after he finally gets sick of trying to find the hotel, he just drops me off on a street corner somewhere. Not quite sure what to do, and having ruled another cab out of the equation, I decide to hitch a ride from a couple twenty-something guys driving a beat-up red Chevy who make room for me to sit on the lap of the tattooed skinny one in the passenger seat.

"Nice car," I say.

"Thanks," the one in the passenger seat says, blasting Ol' Dirty Bastard on the stereo. "It's all we've got."

"So, what's your story?" I ask. Because this is something I know how to do. Interview.

They tell me about getting off of meth and starting a new life for themselves, and I stare dazed out the window. We pass a sleazy nail salon, a happy-ending place, and a shop with a sign that says U WILL STOP SMOKING.

I ask them if I can bum a Newport. I hate being told what to do.

When I finally arrive at my hotel, I lay out my notes for my never-ending hopelessly doomed rom-com treatment of "How He Blew It" and turn on the TV. I know I should be so grateful for all these opportunities coming my way, but all I want is something real. And I don't know how to give that to myself.

So I head outside and realize that while I never considered hitching as an adult before, since I've just done it, why not try again? Some red-faced guy with frosted tips on his hair picks me up and looks at me strangely. I tell him to take me where the action is.

"Yeah, I'll do it," he says, with a look of concern it seems he is not used to giving strangers, "if you promise to never hitch a ride again."

"Fine," I say. "Whatever."

He lets me off at a beach bar, and I drink Sex on the Beaches like a fucking tourist and smoke Camel Lights, watching the tanned, swaying women dance with the old Hawaiian-shirted men who stare lustfully into their blank, drunken eyes. I try my hand at flirting with a group of businessmen, but the sadness and alienation in my affect blinds like a "stay away" flashlight.

"You're weird," one guy says.

"You have no idea," I reply. "Buy me a Long Island iced tea."

"No," he says.

"Whatever," I say. "I'm leaving. This place sucks."

I keep my promise to the giver of my last hitched ride, find a cab, and ask the driver to take me to the best nearby restaurant. He drops me off at a local Olive Garden. I sit there by myself, reordering more breadsticks and swallowing whole my lasagna until I feel nothing else inside. I am full to the point of throwing up, but I order the cheesecake, too. Feeling physically uncomfortable and bursting from my jeans, I head back to the hotel, where I sink into the Jacuzzi alone, admiring my increasing waistline in my bikini and sinking underwater.

Numbness. That is a much better feeling than depression.

This vacation is no better than fucking Dodge itself. I don't know how to have fun without chaos or self-loathing. The most enjoyable part so far has been hitching rides from strangers, knowing I could be murdered.

It made me feel alive, like there was a possible dangerous end.

chapter four
....

The Gossip Girl

2006

Back in New York, during another one of my binge-and-starve cycles, I go to a party—again at the Magician—with a few comedy writer friends of friends, and find myself talking to a bearded comedy TV producer whom I stand next to as a girl comes up to us with a giant black eye. She says nothing about it, and when she finally leaves, the producer comments on it.

"Well, that was the fucking elephant in the room," he says.

"Maybe that's the new thing," I say. "Chick punching."

He laughs. Dark.

Cut to three or four or fifteen Stolichnaya and sodas later: Everything blurs into black and gray until I am back at his place getting fucked. The sheets are so crisp and downy. I remember that.

The next morning, I take my cue that he has no desire to ever see me again—he is extremely cold and quiet—and I leave to meet up with a friend of mine whom I offered to show around the *Post* newsroom.

I am still a little drunk from the night before, and as I take her around to point out the old newspaper covers on the wall ("look, it's 'Headless Body in Topless Bar'"), everything still seems to sparkle with the go-go-go energy of alcohol and sexual attraction and keeping up with the comedy writer boys. I've managed to compartmentalize the morning rejection.

But when my friend leaves to go back to work, I go to the empty bathroom and look at myself in the mirror. What even happened to me? What is happening to me? I feel sick. I lean over the toilet and try to make myself throw up. I can't, but I do manage to shoot the blood vessels out around my eyes through my half-assed bulimia.

Then I sit on the toilet experiencing a feeling worse than ill. It's like I can sense something foul and sick rotting in my body. Squatting down on the bathroom floor, I reach into myself and discover it: a disgusting bloody-stringed tampon lodged deep inside. Revolted, I extract it carefully.

Since I don't remember the sex, I suppose it makes sense. How *could* I remember I was wearing a tampon? The producer guy had fucked it all the way inside me. I was that drunk.

Vile. Finally, I am sick.

I retch all over the *Post* bathroom and realize right then and there that I need to turn this ship around. For what it's worth, I make a promise to God that I will not have sex until I am in a serious relationship again. I just can't keep doing this.

For years, I will wonder who exactly this bearded comedy guy was that bleak night. I don't blame the man or even think he did anything wrong. It's not like that.

There's a psychological phenomenon called "repetition compulsion theory," where you keep subconsciously re-creating a traumatic event in your life—for me, getting blackout drunk and having sex—trying to somehow gain control over that which initially wounded you. Animals do this, too. It is the most primitive of reactions. One psychiatrist explained it to me as an attempt to master the original wound with a similar experience. But all it really ends up doing is cementing the trauma until it is part of you.

....

AFTER THE TAMPON exorcism at the office that day, I return to my computer and google "New York therapists" and make a few calls until I find a woman who takes my insurance. I make an appointment, and two short weeks later I am in to see a female therapist in her dimly lit West Village apartment.

The therapist is in her fifties, with long gray hair, and she is as tall as I am, which is unusual.

"So, I've been having these alcoholic blackouts," I tell her.

"How many?" she asks.

"Four, five," I say. "A lot, I guess. I mean, everyone drinks in New York. That's just how it is."

"Okay," she says. "Well, why don't we start with your family history . . ."

So begins my least favorite part of therapy. The "tell me your story" part. I don't want to sing for my psychological supper. But I do, as I always do with therapists, so many hopes and expectations placed on this stranger who you are paying to care about you for fifty minutes.

Here is my therapist elevator speech, boiled down.

"I shouldn't exist," I begin, ever dramatic, like I'm doing a performance at the Moth.

The fact that I do, I explain, feels like an unforgiving miracle at times, whispering in my ear: Don't be average. Don't be normal. Don't give up.

"My dad never gave up," I continue. "Because my dad is a hero."

Then I get to the good part.

"Let me tell you about my dad," I say, because I think relaying all the historical details will explain me, or make it all add up.

On June 15, 1968, after three weeks in the bush as a marine and an NFG (New Fucking Guy) in Vietnam, my twenty-one-year-old father had his world blown apart when he caught two AK-47 rounds in battle near Khe Sanh. The bullets went through my father's right eye and the right corner of his mouth, forcing bone and fragments into the prefrontal area of his cerebral cortex, leaving his nose hanging in front of his mouth, his left eye dangling out of its orbit, and his right eye obliterated.

The other men in my father's unit were instructed not to go back for him. "Stadtmiller's dead," they were told. "Move on." But one fellow marine ignored those orders: Al Fielder, a black man from the South who'd taken a liking to this privileged white college boy, and he searched until he found my father, who was praying at the bottom of a hill, head in his hands, saying, "Please let me die, please let me die, please let me die."

Because my father was too big to carry, Al instead screamed at him to get him to safety, "You call yourself a fucking marine? You call yourself a man? You fucking pussy! You're pathetic." The verbal assault worked. My father crawled up the hill to the waiting helicopter nearby and was flown to the closest medical ship. No one expected my dad to survive the night, let alone the thirteen hours of surgery required to save him.

"Over his lifetime, he's had more than one hundred and fifty operations," I tell the therapist as she listens raptly.

What remains of my father is less than 5 percent vision, a patch-work of scars across his sewn-together flesh, a nose built with bone from his left hip, and an unpredictable brain injury that manifests in wild swings of temper.

"I just can't fucking take it!" my father would yell throughout my life. "I just can't fucking take it!"

Sometimes, I think about the speech that Al gave my father as he lay dying on the hill and the aftereffects of the war on my childhood. I would hide under the covers as a kid, rocking myself, praying, "Please let me be, please let me be, please let me be," as my dad would erupt in one of his erratic house-shaking furies.

My dad gave me a master class in how to alienate people—and how to reel them back in. He didn't just have "no filter." He had no filter, no sight, and no inhibitions, all these having been ripped out with a surgical hacksaw.

From birth, I absorbed how the world reacted to him and how he lashed out in return.

"There was always a scene," I tell my therapist. "I always de-fended him. Life always went on."

"Childhood by fire," she observes. "Why don't you tell me about your mother. Did she meet your dad after or before he was shot?"

"After," I say, somewhat bitter over the therapist's predictability. That's the first thing people always want to know.

Then I go on.

"Actually, you know," I tell her, "my dad did a lot of the caretaking when I was young. Because my mom was mentally indisposed."

"Mentally indisposed?" the therapist asks. "How?"

"Obsessive-compulsive disorder," I say. "And depression."

Diagnosed in her young adult life, my mom's OCD manifested in her scrubbing her hands with dish soap for ten minutes at a time under the sink faucet, afraid to touch things because she might get infected.

It is no small miracle that my mom nursed me until I was two and a half years old, considering there were a few awful times when she was worried her dirty baby might be too contaminated, and she could not hold me at all.

Sometimes she warned my older sister and me that she needed to be left alone so she could "go crazy" at the kitchen sink. My mom would then make a loud noise, guttural, like a monster, growling, "SCHHHHHHHHH," as she washed her hands, scrubbing them furiously until they were pink and raw and clean.

"What was the noise she made?" the therapist asks.

"I don't want to repeat it," I say. "That's nobody's business."

My mother's particular brand of OCD expressed itself in extremes. So either all of the underwear in the house was ironed and folded or nothing had been cleaned for weeks.

My blind dad took care of my obsessive-compulsive mom, and my older sister took care of me. When we fought, we were sent to the back of the house, where my mom told us to "work it out."

My sister did exactly that, kicking me in the crotch and punching me in the stomach until I was good and sorry.

When my mom took me to a psychiatrist as a child, I did a mental dead man's float in the shrink's shabby beige office. I knew loyalty and secret keeping. And I feared that if I acknowledged just one drop of the pain and fear and anger I felt, my whole world would come collapsing down.

"I tried to protect my family," I tell her, "because somebody had to protect somebody in my family, but a lot of times I failed. Especially my father."

"How so?" she asks.

"Let's see . . ." I begin.

There was the time my dad was swinging me around in the expanses of our living room as I cried out in glee, and he cut it too close—it all happened so fast. My head smashed into the U-shaped corner of the sharp archway, which just barely missed my right eye, and the blood came pouring out. Later, in the emergency room, stitches being sewn near my eyebrow, my father hysterical and upset, I told him I was sorry, it was my fault, I didn't warn him fast enough.

"But it wasn't your fault," the therapist says.

"It didn't feel that way as a kid," I say.

I would do anything to prevent my dad from getting upset. Because with one false move, I could sense it coming: An anger explosion would come raining down on everyone. A string of curse words, yelling, throwing, mewling, sometimes a fist through the wall, culminating with one final come-to-Jesus howling-at-the-moon proclamation, his catchphrase if you will: "GODDAMMIT, I JUST CAN'T TAKE IT!"

It wasn't until years later, during a stray neuroscience course, when I was toying with becoming a teacher, that I learned that what I'd always thought was his "personality" was partially a function of damage done to the prefrontal lobe when he was shot. I read the story—as anyone who has ever taken a neuroscience class has—about Phineas Gage, the railroad foreman who suffered an iron bar through the skull. The man's personality completely transformed after the injury, with him becoming "fitful, irreverent, indulging at times in the grossest profanity . . . impatient of restraint or advice when it conflict[ed] with his desires . . . obstinate, yet capricious and vacillating, devising many plans of operation which are no sooner arranged than they are abandoned . . ."

You get the idea. Welcome to my childhood.

My mom, on the other hand, offered her own case study in brain science.

Because of her OCD, she often became preoccupied with whether things were "infected" with shit. So giving baths was pretty much out. Because we had tympanostomy tubes in our ears as kids, we weren't supposed to get them wet, so my dad used a wooden board that he would take turns laying my sister and me on in the bathtub to shampoo our hair.

The older we got, the weirder it got. At eleven and eight, respectively, my sister and I were too old to be running around naked in the house, and my parents definitely shouldn't have been naked themselves, but there they were. Doors were always open, and we could see as my dad changed in front of us. My mom, meanwhile, would be in her threadbare white underpants, trying to figure out what clothes she could stand to wear. I look back at pictures of this time, and I see my sister and me posing with our towels open by the pool making kissy faces. It looks like we're getting groomed to be sold into sexual slavery.

Of course, we were just the children of naïve hippies. Nothing more.

"But it sounds like it was a hypersexualized household," the therapist says.

"I just don't want to criticize my parents," I say. "I love my parents—so much."

Then I am quiet. Then I am crass. Crasser than my father even. Crasser than even ol' iron-in-the-skull Phineas Gage.

"All the same," I practically spit, "I wish I didn't have such a clear picture of my dad's dick in my mind. He was blind. We were not."

The therapist looks a little taken aback, but she asks me to continue.

"Was your father ever sexual with you?"

"Oh my God, no!" I say.

But, I confess, there was always that sexualized electricity in the house—where that energy just seemed to be swirling around him. Maybe it was the women he flirted with, who always seemed to be so enraptured by the alpha-war-hero energy he put out. I remember one woman who would call our house frequently, and when I answered in my clearly teenage voice, she would speak breathlessly, as if she was in the middle of masturbating, and simply say, "Jerrrrrrry."

I hated her so much. "YOU WANT TO TALK TO MY DAD?" I'd say, my voice pinched with anger. "IS THAT WHAT YOU'RE SAYING?"

Cheating happened early in my parents' marriage. My dad would always employ various "readers" to help with his paperwork, and, as my mom candidly told me, one time a reader was doing a lot more than reading. My mom heard the sound of my dad's belt unbuckle. My mother went in, mortified. My father said, "We weren't going to have sex."

This all happened in what was to be my room—before I was born.

"So you have resentment against your father," the therapist says.

"No," I say. "Yes. I don't know. Sometimes. The resentment is muted out by overwhelming love. Does that make any sense?"

As I grew older, I could feel the way my dad's friends looked at me without my father's knowledge. At the LA premiere for a documentary my dad was featured in called *Vietnam, Long Time Coming*, one of the high-ranking officers talking to my father began stroking his finger slowly along my shoulder blade as my dad stood there, continuing to tell his stories, grinning and rhapsodizing, with no idea what was happening.

Even earlier at that same movie screening, a woman got up to speak after the movie, and since it was a pretty heavy film about disabled veterans, she figured she would tell a lighthearted anecdote to cut the tension. In front of this packed auditorium, which included me and my eighty-something-year-old great-aunt, she smiled and proceeded.

"To lighten the mood," the attractive woman said, laughing, "I'll tell you what Jerry Stadtmiller told me right before the plane took off from LA to Vietnam. He turned to me and said, 'Don't feel too sorry for me. I've got a fourteen-inch cock.'"

I slunk down into my seat, so embarrassed.

When my father, who became a licensed massage therapist during one of his many careers, told me as a teenager that he could no longer give me massages because his shrink had told him it was "inappropriate," I felt ashamed. I know it wasn't his intention—my dad was simply doing the responsible thing. But everything was always so confusing. I was bad? I was inappropriate? I was sexually desirable? Why was he giving me massages in the first place? Why was he telling me any of this?

Let me be crystal clear right now, as I was with my therapist: My father never did anything unseemly with me—*ever*. Both my parents are wonderful human beings. But there were things lacking in my childhood—namely, boundaries. They were raised with none themselves. It makes sense, in a way.

"Do you still talk to your parents?" the therapist asks me.

Every once in a while, I tell her, but our calls usually go something like this . . .

Me to my mom: "A doctor told me I was anorexic."

Mom: "Well, Jane Fonda was anorexic her whole life, and she was a successful actress."

Me to my dad: "I think I may have a drinking problem."

Dad: "I find having a drink at the end of the day really takes the edge off."

They don't read any of my stories in the *Post*, and when I try to talk to them about it—about what it's like to have to write a cover story in under an hour that the entire city will be reading the next day and how much pressure that is, my dad responds by bringing up a really great email he wrote someone recently.

I feel so dismissed when they act like this. I don't feel cared for or nurtured or seen.

Moods and loyalties changed often with my parents growing up, and they still do. Like unwitting practitioners of the 48 Laws of Power, my parents embodied Rule 17 to a T: "Keep others in suspended terror: Cultivate an air of unpredictability."

Because there was no status quo in our home.

When my dad first received his Purple Heart, he threw it in the trash. Twenty years later, he became active with veterans' groups and reversed course, getting a new one to display at home. One week we were religious (my sister was born on a day my dad was feeling Catholic, so she was baptized at birth). The next we didn't go to church anymore.

Years later, on another religious upswing, my parents decided on a nice Lutheran church, and at eight, I was excited to finally be saved. In fact, I so couldn't wait to be the embodiment of a good Christian congregant, I signed up to be an altar girl. On Christmas Day—the most important Mass of the year—I stood in front of the entire church, and when I couldn't get my oversize altar girl lighter to work, I just stood there, paralyzed and weeping, until I was pulled off the stage, Catholic *Gong Show* style.

During the sermon that night, the pastor bellowed, "I think we can all say we're grateful for little Amanda, the altar girl who tried so hard to light the candles tonight."

After the service, my dad took me aside and congratulated me.

"Look at it this way," he said, laughing. "Pastor Dave only mentioned three people in his sermon tonight: Jesus, Mary, and little altar girl Amanda."

I laughed, too, and this lesson registered in my brain: Laughing at pain meant you didn't have to deal with it. When everything was wrecked, nothing was. When the worst had happened, the worst was over.

"So, you use humor," the therapist observes. "Humor is deflection."

I can feel the rage boiling up inside of me. This always happens with therapists. Because I can't take looking at it—any of it. My childhood makes me feel so many toxic and conflicting emotions, it overwhelms me. It causes me to shut down. It makes me want to drink. It makes me want to overeat. It makes me want to fuck.

After I am quiet for some time, the therapist changes the topic. She brings up the subject of the *New York Post*, where she saw I put down that I worked in my inventory.

"Does that mean you agree with its politics?" she asks.

I hesitate, looking at her. *What?*

"No," I say. "Don't worry. I'm a liberal."

"Oh good," she says, and I hate that. So much. If I were a conservative, would I be less deserving of her help?

"Now, how many alcoholic blackouts have you had again?" she asks.

I don't need this shit, I think. I never see her again.

. . . .

AS A THIRTY-YEAR-OLD woman, I am all about laughing at pain.

I do not want to look inside myself while working at the *Post,* so instead I look everywhere else. Every day is not only heart-racing ("You're going to the Dakota because Jared Leto is re-creating John Lennon's murder—get reaction!"), it is also the most fun at a job I've ever had.

You want extremely dark comedy to get through crushing pain? Working at a tabloid, you have it in spades. "Oh yeah, I think I just felt another egg die," one female reporter would joke. Another would go darker still, with the line, "Don't worry, you'll be spared"—meaning, if someone comes back for a shooting spree. "Best to get a picture of you on file," one editor suggested, "in case you die or something."

It is honestly the perfect place for me.

So many share the same wonderfully warped sense of humor befitting a city as warped as New York. The closest I've ever seen to anything capturing the pitch-black, anything-goes barbs is in the most brutally funny episodes of *Veep.* When daily suffering is coming at you nonstop just by virtue of the daily suffering of the news cycle, you either laugh or you cry. We choose to laugh. A lot.

Mackenzie emails me helpful updates about how many times the word *perv* and the word *fiend* have been used in *Post* headlines as the year progresses. (In case you're wondering, in 2006, there were 271 instances of *perv,* and *fiend* took the lead at 283.) When things are feeling scary, Mackenzie and I counteract our fear by going even more gallows, theorizing as to "who is going to finally murder me" among all the unsavory characters I either date or do stories about (like the former pimp who tells me that in every situation there is a pimp and a ho—and I make a point of implying that *he* is the ho in my story). Our conjecture is further supported by handwritten letters I get sent from prison, and some sweeter ones, like the one from the trucker who asks me for a picture, because the one he put up in his truck has faded with sunlight.

I and my closest friends at the *Post* develop a language all our own (sometimes writing Ibsen-like non sequitur *Post* headlines when we shoot emails to each other, like "Sex Perv Fiend Tragic Tot Mom Slay?").

Other *Post* friends teach me "gossip math"—Paula Froelich, specifically, is so helpful. (She also writes about it in her excellent book *It!* if you want to go deeper.) The lessons include:

1. "Two items for a favor." Meaning, if you want a shout-out for your event or client or whatever, you best have "paid your rent" in passing on some juicy dirt to help Page Six out first.

2. "Don't try to sell a favor as a scoop." Meaning, if you are a reporter or a publicist, don't try to pretend a plug or an item that benefits *you* is somehow *really* benefiting the Page, and that you're doing them a favor. Nope. This is also known as "don't bullshit a bullshitter." (In discussing this principle one night with the *Post*'s much-storied columnist Steve Dunleavy, he suggests another good gossip corollary: Be incredibly careful with the assistant staff. Or as Dunleavy phrased it—with far more linguistic flair: "Never lose a number, kid. Because today's junior cocksucker is tomorrow's senior motherfucker.")

3. Last, and most crucial of all: "Do not ever double-pitch." Meaning, only pass along exclusive info to one publication. If you double-pitch a story and both

newspapers end up using it, you will be blacklisted—
sometimes for life.

Equipped now with a knowledge of how the gossip game works,
after writing a piece declaring that we are currently living in "The
Golden Age of the Insult," I decide to request a press pass for the
William Shatner roast in LA. I can't exactly write another story,
since I've already covered the topic in the paper, but I might be
able to submit a gossip item and get it published, which would val-
idate the trip beyond mere stargazing from the sidelines. There's
just one problem, though: I've never even had a proper introduction to Page Six editor Richard Johnson, and I know he's far too important to be bothered by some lowly features writer like me. But
I still decide to go for it—nervous, stumbling, and overthinking—
cold-emailing him like a slavish, wide-eyed farm girl, asking essentially: *Dear Mr. Johnson, if I were to file a gossip item, do you think
you would, um, maybe, possibly, pretty please consider using it, I'm
so sorry and thank you so much?* I don't quite realize how out of
my depth I am in contacting the man who helps puppet-master
the entire gossip stratosphere. So of course, Richard ignores my
first email. And . . . my second one, too. But finally, after one last
note, I somehow manage to sound slightly *less* like a malfunction-
ing robot, and he responds to say yes, he will use something I file
if it's good.

I cannot believe my luck. *I am so psyched.*

When I'm finally out in Studio City, cattle call–style checking in at the not-glamorous-at-all asphalt-covered CBS lot where
the roast is held, I get to experience firsthand all the celebrity-
gossip sausage being slung. Cordoned off with the rest of the
braying media zoo behind the constructed-that-day red-carpet

step-and-repeat, my eye is immediately drawn to the painfully high-def smears of peach-, chocolate- and vanilla-colored makeup melting on the faces of minor celebrities everywhere I turn. It's educational—the way a steamroller is educational in teaching you all about the fine art of getting run the fuck over. My favorite part of the spectacle is the hush-hush theatrics of publicists approaching you before the star arrives, whispering their advance-prep essential-detail notes with Tony Hale levels of obsequious devotion. Seriously, even if the publicist is representing someone as obscure as Offensive Female Stereotype #9 on *Drunk Housewives of Embarrassing County*, a good flack will still solemnly deliver to you all the pertinent details (did you know so-and-so has their own lip gloss line now?) in the same exaggerated hyper-confidential tones of reverence normally reserved for Kennedy Center Honors.

Attending the roast itself is equally shudder-rendering and insanely entertaining. After a few hours of taping, it becomes pretty clear pretty quickly that comedian Andy Dick is beyond wasted. Out of nowhere, he leaves his dais post to just straight-up, unprompted, lick the faces of Farrah Fawcett, Patton Oswalt, and Carrie Fisher. Throughout the night, his performance is riveting and off-kilter, with the kind of too-delayed timing that betrays a very serious level of pregame beforehand.

So, when the show is over and the after-party starts, I know Dick is the interview to get.

When I see Andy walking past a gold-tinted-rock-star-glasses-clad Patton Oswalt, I bob and weave in between agents and handlers to approach him, immediately identifying which outlet I'm with and asking if we can talk. As the sounds of "Brown Eyed Girl" bleat in the background, Andy first tries to lead me off to a restricted-access area where it would just be the two of us, but a security guard turns him away. "You can't go in there, Andy."

Finally, he leads me to his dressing room, where two guys and a girl are waiting.

"I work for the *New York Post*," I repeat when he asks again why I want to talk.

"Oh shit, buddy!" one of the guys yells.

"Oh no, oh no," Andy says, looking me over. "Page Six . . . how old are you?"

"I'm thirty," I say.

As I stand there in the entranceway, Andy opens the bathroom door, unzips his pants, pulls out his penis, and starts peeing in the toilet.

"She'll put this in the article!" Andy's friend yells. "She's going to put this in the article!"

"Don't," Andy says, coming out of the bathroom. "I'm fucking serious."

"You haven't been nice," his friend says. "You guys have been mean."

"I'm always cordial," Andy says. "I'm a nice guy."

"One time, buddy," his friend says. "You hit on the fucking reporter one time, and they fucking hammered you."

With a perfectly timed pause, Andy replies, "I'm hitting on the reporter now."

He walks over to the couch to chat up a bubbly young woman with a plunging neckline and ample cleavage sitting there, grinning from ear to ear.

"Did I do good tonight?" Andy asks.

"Yes, you did," she says. "I was jealous you didn't lick my face."

He stares down at her breasts. "Are those real?"

"Mmm-hmmm," she answers.

I realize I have only a few minutes to get a quote before this potentially turns into a full-on orgy.

"Did you party before going on tonight?" I ask.

"Nothing," he says, glaring at me. "I always perform sober, and then when the show is over I have a cocktail or two to five."

"We have low tolerances," his friend says, laughing.

"How did you like my sober performance?" Andy asks.

"I thought it was funny," I say.

"Really?" Andy replies. "Do you want to do some blow then?"

"No," I say.

Things are getting out of control quickly.

Andy continues, "I went onstage and did my bit real funny and whatnot, and then after that I had a couple—just two vodka cranberries—and then that gave me the courage to talk to Farrah. And me and her have a date. On Tuesday, I'm going to fuck the shit out of her."

"Put that in Page Six," his friend shouts.

"Put that in Pages Six, Seven, and Eight, you fucking bitch, that's how big my dick is," Andy seethes.

Trying to combat the situation with logic, I return to his offer minutes before for me to do cocaine.

"Why did you ask me if I wanted to do blow?" I ask.

"I don't have any," he says. He combats me with logic of his own. "You look like a fucking coke whore."

"I do?" I ask.

"Yeah," he says. "Do you want some? Do you want some? Do you want some?"

"No," I say.

"Well then, I guess I was wrong, you're not one," he says. "I love coke whores. They're so easy. I guess you're not as easy as I thought. What do you want? Do you want me to fuck the shit out of you? What's your problem? You want me to fuck you. Give me a kiss."

"No, no, no, no," I say squirming away from him onto a chair.

"I think you want to fuck me," he says. "I think you want to fuck me."

"No," I say, and at that point, he reaches over and feels my breast.

I am half frozen, half clinging on to my voice recorder for dear life.

"Then what do you want?" Andy asks. "There's nothing dirty here."

"He hasn't even puked himself, look," his friend says.

"I'm not the fuckup you think I am," Andy says.

"Then why are you, like, pulling out your penis and, like . . ." I begin. This enrages Andy.

"Oh, that's good," he says. "Good try, lady. You're in my room, and I have to pee. I don't close the door, and you know why I don't close the door? BECAUSE IF I CLOSE THE DOOR PEOPLE THINK I'M DOING DRUGS, YOU FUCKING BITCH!"

"I think she broke in," his friend says.

"I'm going to pee again on you if you don't fucking . . . for real, dude," Andy says. "You need to loosen up. You need to fucking help me out. You're either on the team or you're off the team. You're either on or you're off. I'm not a come-and-go kind of guy . . ."

"He's a come-in-your-face kind of guy!" his friend yells, high-fiving him.

"Ow," Andy says. "My broken finger. I'm a come-in-your-face kind of guy. Yeah."

"So, when you were licking everyone's face . . ." I say.

"I was doing it because I was desperately trying to tie the show together like a fisherman with tuna," he says. "And you're a little piece of fresh tuna . . . But thanks for asking. Do you want me to lick your face now? Do you want me to lick your cunt?"

I take this all in, looking for the Big Idea.

"Whose face did you like licking the most?" I ask.

"Yours," Andy says, lunging toward me and licking my face. "Yours."

At this point, I am heading toward the door to get out of there.

"I love her, I don't want her to leave, don't leave," he says to his friends. And then to me, "Don't be a fucking pussy, don't puss out."

I turn the voice recorder off, and as I am walking out, Andy leans in to try to kiss me one last time. I ward him off, but not before he bites me on the right hand.

The door shuts. I look at the teeth marks on my hand. No skin broken. That's good, I guess. I stand there, stunned.

What the fuck just happened?

I walk, dazed, past the security guard and into the after-party, where I first run into Jeffrey Ross.

"Andy Dick just bit me," I say.

"Better get tested," he says. He isn't smiling. He knows I'm not joking.

I bum a Marlboro Light, type up my notes, and email Paula Froelich at Page Six the details. Short, straight, to the point.

The next day, it's the lead item in the gossip section—"Comic's Worst Gross-Out Ever"—and is picked up by outlets around the world. Childhood friends I haven't talked to in twenty years are calling.

"Turned out great," Richard Johnson emails me. "Thanks."

. . . .

I WATCH AS savvy industry people piggyback on the gossip item (not quite a feeding frenzy, but a feeding snack, to be sure). The entire experience gives me a chance to see firsthand how the tentacled gossip industry operates. Ryan McCormick, a publicist who is running New York's Funniest Reporter contest, places an item in Page Six that Andy Dick is banned from the festival unless he wears protective headgear. Howard Stern asks for the audio, and when I turn it over, they talk about it for days on air, with Artie Lange observing it sounds like a "pre-rape tape." When I walk into the *Post* after returning from the trip, executive editor Steve Cuozzo looks at me with wry amusement. "You're famous," he says.

I'm also asked to do shows I've never done before, including one with Nick Kroll and Julie Klausner at Mo Pitkin's. I decide I'll do a reenactment, and I get Nick and Julie to act out the parts. Nick looks at me after it's over, and, I think comparing it to my very mediocre stand-up, says, "That was funny."

Sure. When you have Andy Dick writing your material, no problem.

Which is where Dick is right to criticize me as he's done in numerous interviews about the incident. I do have a conflict of interest as a performer myself. In fact, I thought he was hilarious even after assaulting me. I suppose it's lucky for him I did. Any other reporter would have filed charges after being groped and bitten. I just lambasted him onstage.

The way Andy dealt with the incident? Rehab and carrying around a notebook with an unsent letter to me in which he referred to me as a "dried-up cunt." I learn all this from reading the *Washington Post* article profiling Dick and listening to his livid appearance berating me on *Howard Stern*.

After performing at the sold-out Mo Pitkin's show with Kroll and Klausner, which was hosted by Michelle Collins (now of *The View* fame), I'm approached by a small bald man who is in the audience. It is Moby. Turns out, he has stories of his own about touring with Andy. There are many, but the most notable portions:

1. Andy once took a dare to defecate on a cake, then actually followed through.

2. At one point, Andy made himself comfortable on Moby's bed, where he proceeded to have sex with a man, who Moby said was straight but just liked being with celebrities.

3. During the sex, Moby caught a glimpse of Andy's penis, which he described as being the size of his forearm.

4. Andy once replaced the champagne in a bottle with his own urine and served it to several unsuspecting guests.

Moby and I spend the rest of the night chatting at the bar, and I notice how celebrities are instant status boosters. A younger comic who has treated me like shit every other time I talked to him suddenly acts like I am his new best friend. Sipping my Smirnoff and soda, I tell Moby one of my dumb stand-up jokes: "I'm not really a starfucker. I'm more of a star-spooner."

He politely laughs. We exchange numbers, and I proceed to

send the following ingenious text messages to him as the night progresses, and I get increasingly hammered.

12:28 a.m.
All right, well very nice to meet you sir.

12:34 a.m.
Um that's me call me if u want

12:36 a.m.
Ok tried ur # but no cigar am headed home almost

1:18 a.m.
Am about 2 pass out near the slope?

1:20 a.m.
Gotta confess it would be fun to meet up but almost nearing my end of the night

1:24 a.m.
Well its 124 and I'm abiut to sign off. . . . fun 2 meet u!

1:30 a.m.
Tempted 2 call u 1 more time

1:46 a.m.
&Allright just woke up roommates r u in brooklyn even?

1:50 a.m.
Wacky good night, Moby. Good luck w ur evening's conquests

The next morning I wake up to the horrors of my cell phone. But—to my surprise, there is a single late-night email from him. "Hi from moby is this you? Moby"

"ha yep . . . reading through my novella of text messages I RULE," I write.

"yes. you do rule," he writes. "i concur. g'night, moby"

He sends me funny non sequitur emails from time to time, like, "do you know about the 2 different types of nyc fire-escape? and why nyc has water towers? i can be pedantic, if you like, and tell you about them. i'm going to go sit on my roof and read and drink tea."

Since I spent all of 2004 in a shitty marriage and a shitty job, blasting Moby's "South Side" in my office alone late at night, it's a strange feeling. I tell Mackenzie this in the *Post* bathroom one day and another reporter overhears and interjects super dismissively, "Congratulations, you've been hit on by Moby. You're officially a New Yorker now."

"Does that mean you have?" I ask.

Her face turns crimson. I guess she is not a New Yorker yet.

"I mean," the reporter says, "if you want to fuck him, fuck him."

I don't, really, but I do want to go on an actual date with him, which we do soon enough.

We meet at the vegan hot spot Candle 79 on the Upper East Side one night, and the conversation is nonstop. Some people are like scorpions, he says. You know they are going to sting you, but you befriend them anyway. He says fame is like a drug, and that he was really addicted to it at first. He says one of the main headaches of being rich and famous is getting hit with petty lawsuits—like for around $9,000—where the litigants know it's easier just to pay out than fight it.

I tell him I'm considering writing a book about douchebags.

We walk across a misty, dreamy Central Park to the $4.5 million prewar penthouse he is renovating in the twin-towered El Dorado building near West Ninetieth Street. To get to the "sky castle," as he calls it, we have to take an elevator up to the twenty-ninth floor, then walk up two flights of iron stairs guided only by the light of his phone. Caring for a dream home is like caring for a child, he tells me.

When we reach the roof, staring down at the swirl of traffic lights and cars below, Moby leans into me and says, "You have a very patrician neck."

Then he sniffs it. For a while. Gets a real good whiff. This is new. Moby pulls back and looks pleased with himself. He must know no one has ever done this before.

"In your book about douchebags," he says, "are you going to say some guy sniffed your neck?"

I laugh.

"No," I say. "I don't know."

"You have beautiful hair," he says. Then he smiles and says, "God took my hair."

Pointing to the softness of his sky-blue cashmere sweater, Moby says he can warm me up and rubs my arms. I'm super nervous and try to think of something to say to fill the silence.

"You could never feel sad up here," I say.

"No, not sad," Moby agrees. "Maybe forlorn."

On the cab ride to take me home, he directs the driver which streets to take ("At the right time of night, this one is like butter"), and tells me to buckle my seat belt. He says how strange it is no one does that in New York. The closest we get to being physical—outside of the sniffing—is a light kiss at the end of our night.

When I reach the lesbians' brownstone in Park Slope, I race upstairs to Lola and Juanita, who are awaiting details. I tell them everything.

"Congratulations," Juanita says. "You just had your first lesbian experience with Moby."

Other hangouts with Moby are decidedly non-dates. He invites me to a fund-raiser he is doing with the Roots at Crobar, and I run into Michelle Collins, who invites me up into the VIP section with Julia Stiles and Drea de Matteo. When Moby finally comes upstairs, I say, by way of seduction, "I hear you hit on all young writers."

"I like smart people," he says.

When he emails me with pictures of screaming fans at his concerts, I tell him this is like the celebrity version of a dick pic. "What's a dick pic?" he asks.

Another night, he joins me as a plus-one to an event at Dangerfield's comedy club on the Upper East Side, where Jerry Seinfeld and friends are feting a new documentary about Rodney. We drink Manhattans at the bar, talking about the awesomeness of the old-school vibe of the club, but when I say I am going to get some quotes for Page Six, he takes off. Now on a singular dateless mission, I walk up to Joy Behar and explain who I am.

"I know who you are," she says with a half smile, and I figure she must be referring to the Star Jones piece. Behar continues to eye me suspiciously, but Susie Essman jumps right in with an anecdote, telling me that Rodney Dangerfield was the only comic who told her to make her act even dirtier.

"Rodney called me up one day out of nowhere," Susie says. "'You got to be the female Andrew Dice Clay, that's the way to make you a big star.'"

Susie turns to Joy and says, "He was supportive of women comics."

"Yes, he was," Joy says. "He also wanted to fuck all of us."

When Moby says he wants to see me at the "reporter battle," as he calls the New York's Funniest Reporter contest I get asked to compete in, I give him the details, but the night of he doesn't show.

But I don't care, because I'm more focused on the stand-up itself. Thanks to Ryan the publicist's girlfriend, Sharon Simon, who mentored me before the show, I now have a secret weapon: information about how to not completely suck at stand-up.

Simon, a very funny stand-up comic with years of experience, listened to me patiently as I complained. "It's like, I do the same jokes, and sometimes I'm terrible and other times I do really well, but it's the same material."

"Okay," she advised. "That's actually pretty easy to fix. Tell me, when do you do well?"

"When I'm in the moment, when I'm just talking and being me."

"There you go," Sharon said. "All you have to do to put yourself in the moment is immediately comment on something that's happening at the start of your set, and everything will come out more naturally after that."

It was like the lesson on writing that Steve gave me. One moment, one thing determines how the rest flows. Find something that anchors you, that is naturally your voice, and the rest of what you say will follow.

The night of the show I follow the delightful Robert George, a wonderful op-ed writer whom I work with at the *Post*. He has just done his set, in which he talks a lot about being both an African American and a conservative.

When I am called up onstage, I remember Sharon's words, and

I say, without hesitation or overthinking, the first funny thing that comes to mind.

"I don't mean to sound bitter," I say, as I pull the mic off the stand, "but all these other reporters are stealing my 'what it's like to be black' material."

Huge laugh. And I am off, with the rest of my jokes flowing with the same ease of rhythm as the first. At the end of the night, the judges deliberate and then come back with their announcement: I won!

Mackenzie and Steve are both there to cheer me on, and it is such a high. But then . . . I get some whiskey in me. Afterward, walking through a drizzling rain, I go to a sleek new comedy club in the Meatpacking District called Comix and drink so much Jameson, I have trouble standing up. To my left is Eugene Mirman. To my right is Todd Barry. I have no idea what I say to them, but I'm sure it's a disaster. Tig Notaro is extra nice and maybe even a little concerned. Around 2 a.m., some cheesy grandstanding guy comes up to me, swoops in, and kisses me—and I go along, then stagger out. Not too long after, I end up making out with a second guy, with a shitty knockoff Morrissey hairdo. When we stop kissing, I start to cry and tell him about my promise not to have sex because of God and the last terrible one-night-stand tampon-fucking incident.

He writes me the next day.

Subject line: Nothing better . . .

. . . than making out with NY's Funniest Reporter nestled on a centuries-old couch in a deserted bar in the West Village at 3:10 a.m. in the morning. Did I forget to mention that afterward, she happened to cry a river and confess her sexual frustrations? You look so lovely rain-soaked and uttering such passionate murmurs in my ears . . . Don't be a stranger and surprise . . . surprise . . . A guy in this town actually followed up on his intentions. Call me.

Reading it, I feel like such an asshole. I hate hooking up with guys when I am blind drunk. It's so completely depressing and the opposite of what I want out of life. And as much as I want to make a random emo dude my savior, his email completely turns me off. Or maybe it's just me that turns me off. Whatever it is, I don't want anything to do with it.

. . . .

THE MORE I drink, the more I think about my earliest experiences with alcohol.

The first time I tried to get some, I was thirteen years old, and I walked with purpose into the dingy liquor store up the street next to the 7-Eleven on El Cajon Boulevard.

I plucked out a pack of Seagram's strawberry wine coolers from the fridge, carried it to the counter, and hoped that it would work like how cigarettes do. If you're tall and confident, you're good to go.

"How old are you?" the clerk asked me.

"Um," I said, figuring this was a test where you had to give the right coded lie. "I'm fifteen?"

"Come back in six years," he said.

"I'm twenty-one?" I tried again.

"Come back in six years," he said.

But the answer to finding alcohol came soon enough. One

day when I was babysitting the kids who lived up the street whose parents had all the dirty channels and kept expecting me to get their weird *Twin Peaks* references, I executed what seemed like a flawless plan. I brought tiny empty shampoo bottles with me; then I pulled down from their liquor cabinet the bottles of Kahlúa and brandy. I poured their contents into the barely rinsed out containers of Pert Plus and watched as they bubbled over.

I kept my contraband inside a pink-and-silver starry music box that my mom had ordered me from one of those special mom catalogues. Of course, like every other kid on the planet, instead of putting nice things in there, like barrettes and shit, I put in cigarettes and alcohol.

Later, in my parents' guesthouse, I pulled out my spoils to show my two best friends, Karen and Maureen. We gulped down the bubbly concoction: part liquor, part anti-dandruff hair care solution.

"It . . . tastes . . . really bad, Mandy," Karen said.

"Like soap," Maureen said.

"But do you feel it?" I asked.

Because I did. A rush of confidence. A warmness in my chest. Pink cheeks and excitement. For the first time in my life, I felt like I wasn't the bad person I thought I was. I had finally found the answer to all my problems. All I had to do was get more.

. . . .

AS AN ADULT, I can have all the alcohol I want, anytime I want it. Which, when you have no boundaries, is a dangerous combination.

Of course, sometimes it comes in handy. Like on satellite radio.

One of the more memorable moments in all the Andy Dick fallout comes when fellow *Post* reporter Reed Tucker asks me to do a guest spot on his radio show with Lazlow Jones, the tech genius who's the voice of *Chatterbox FM* in *Grand Theft Auto*.

It's an aggressive shock-radio environment (I've listened to enough Sirius and XM ahead of time so I won't flinch if I'm called a "hole"). And when Lazlow asks me about Andy Dick right down to the specifics of what female scent I might have emitted, I enjoy the opportunity to be unfazed and play ball.

"My website is actually myvaginasmellslikerosepetals.com," I riff, and it gets a nice laugh from the room.

I find out afterward that Jim Norton listened and dug my appearance. We begin an email and text friendship, including me asking him for direction in some of the sex-and-dating articles I'm writing. (Jim: "I give pervy advice." Me: "What? No, I can't imagine." Jim: "I know it's shocking." Me: "Shocking, disappointing . . . so many emotions.")

Norton is headlining a show for the upcoming New York Comedy Festival, which I'm previewing in the *Post*. During the festival, I see as many shows as I can, and when I go backstage at Town Hall to ask Howie Mandel a question, a gorgeous raven-haired woman follows me out.

"Excuse me," she says. "I wanted to ask if you'd like join me for a drink at my club."

It is Caroline Hirsch—the legendary namesake and owner of Carolines on Broadway. I nod yes, and she welcomes me into her chauffeured town car. As we ride the few blocks up to the Times Square staple, she speaks of the old days when Letterman and

Leno were friends. I follow her downstairs to the velvet-covered, rainbow-lit room and we join Howie Mandel at a table. He does a fist-bumping hello, and I remember how he speaks openly about his obsessive-compulsive disorder.

"My mom has OCD," I say. "So I totally get it."

"Oh wow," he says, the same way I react when I find out someone else is divorced. "What does she take for it?"

I rattle off meds and feel like I'm living in bizarro-land, where I'm suddenly reaching into my TV screen, having conversations with people I've watched and admired from the sidelines for years.

On Friday, I see Jim Norton perform, and at the after-party at the strip club Headquarters, I sit down next to a tall, good-looking guy in a nice suit.

"So, what's going on in your life?" he asks.

"Well, I've been kind of depressed lately and calling phone sex lines," I say.

He laughs.

"That's refreshing," he says, and introduces himself as Jonathan Brandstein, Norton's manager.

"So where do you live?" Jonathan asks.

"Park Slope with two lesbians," I say. Then I add, "I pay my rent in pussy."

He laughs, and I mumble, "Just kidding."

Jonathan then says one of the most profound things anyone has ever said to me about comedy: "Don't step on the punch," he says.

And I get it. *Own it.* Just like in writing, in comedy—and in romance. We are both not filled up on strip club food, and when I mention I've never been to a Gray's Papaya, he insists. We travel

outside, and he tells me hilarious celebrity stories, like how Richard Grieco supposedly likes to pretend to read Nabokov in bars to
pick up chicks.

As 3 a.m. nears, he grabs me a cab.

"You know something I like about you?" Jonathan asks as the
taxi pulls up. "Your height. That's very *Our Bodies, Ourselves* of
me, isn't it?"

"Wow," I say. "Nice reference."

He kisses me good night, and in the days following, I tell Norton about my crush, who texts me asking if Jonathan and I are in
"looove."

"Not quite," I text back. But I do like him.

Over the next few days, Jonathan asks if my job will be sending
me to Las Vegas for the upcoming comedy festival there.

"No . . ." I say, "but I could probably go for fun."

We make last-minute plans for me to join him on the trip, and
I arrive in Vegas complete with an overpriced $800 Cole Haan
leather jacket I've put on my charge card to give me a confidence
boost. Jonathan takes me back to his room, offers me a drink, and
we both kind of laugh uncomfortably.

"This is kind of weird, isn't it?" he asks.

"I'm not going to sleep with you," I say, "just so you know."

"That's fine," he says. "I wasn't expecting that."

He sneaks me into the greenroom, where I stand next to Sarah
Silverman and Jimmy Kimmel, who are cozying up to each other;
then I get a few quotes from Ray Romano for Page Six about his
wife being horny. I walk around the party and begin talking to
an older man bathed in the light of a tiki lamp hanging above.
Jonathan whispers to me, "That's George Schlatter, the guy who
founded *Laugh-In*."

George takes one look at me and says my height reminds him of an old vaudeville joke.

"Here's what you need to tell guys," he says. "You say, 'It's easy . . . you make two trips.'"

After the festival in Vegas, Jonathan and I talk fairly regularly. But then the calls become less frequent. When one of my friends suggests I play hard to get, I don't answer. Then, when I call him back a full two days later I can't reach him. Then I don't hear from him for days upon days.

I start to regard my phone as this thing of dread. I turn it off, then obsessively turn it on for a few minutes, then back off, then just hide it.

During that time, I hit upon a discovery. I can simply change Jonathan's name in my cell phone. From Jonathan to the catchy "Was Lucky That He Even Knew Me and Would Be Lucky if I Even Picked Up the Phone if He Called Again."

I tell the secret to my girlfriends, and they start doing the same. One friend changes "Richard" to "Doesn't Feel the Same Way." Another updates "Robert" to "Lives with Girlfriend." My friend can't help but be tickled when his latest text to her pops up as: "Lives With Girlfriend: *What are you up to?*"

When my phone does finally ring and the long acronym WLTHEKMAWBLIIEPUTPIHCA that I've entered for Jonathan comes up, I am pretty chill, I have to say. We decide it's better for us to just be friends.

Which is lucky, because Jonathan is the big brother I've made out with a few times I never had. When I start dating a comedy writer, Jonathan gives me all manner of advice. Mostly to just be myself and not play all those stupid phone games again.

The comedy writer is fine and all, but after I take him to the absurdly lavish News Corp Christmas party at the Hilton, I mention offhandedly my awful night where I blacked out and hooked up with the comedy TV producer.

"So you don't really know what he did to you," he says. "He could have fucked you in the ass with a razor blade for all you know."

I slink away and tell him that incidentally I'm "off" sex for a while. He breaks up with me shortly after that.

. . . .

CAROLINE HIRSCH SENDS me a bottle of Veuve Clicquot after my New York Comedy Festival coverage and an invite to her club's holiday party. I have a great time, and Norton suggests I text Jonathan inquiring as to his dick size, which is always a good look. But somewhere between my first glass of cabernet and my tenth one, everything gets fuzzy.

I remember instructing the cabdriver to stop at McDonald's so I can get fries. Then at a bodega so I can get a Chunky bar. And I definitely remember the cabdriver screaming at me when I realize I've lost my wallet to get the hell out of his cab.

The next day, I scrounge five dollars in quarters from the lesbians' change drawer to take the subway in to work, and, not really knowing who to call, I reach out to an uncle who I know is a minister.

I cry and talk, cry and talk. He asks me if I will agree to accept Jesus Christ as my personal lord and savior.

"Sure," I say.

My uncle shares with me passages of scripture from the New Testament, like "The man without the Spirit does not accept the things that come from the Spirit of God, for they are foolishness to him, and he cannot understand them, because they are spiritually discerned."

That sounds good. I ask him if maybe he will call me every day to check in.

"Oh well," he says, "every day might be kind of hard."

"No, no, don't worry about it," I say.

Awesome. I am just as needy with him ("if I accept Jesus as my savior, will you be my friend?") as I am with guys I'm dating. I feel like I'm just good for a one-night thing, either with Jesus or with sex. Still, I'm grateful for the talk and I don't mind the foray into spirituality either. Overall, my feeling about religion is this: If it works, it works. Even though that conversation doesn't quite lead to a long-term personal connection, I do appreciate the notion of welcoming God more into my life, no matter how bumbling I am in the application of it. Prayer is calming and focused and love. And—when it works, boy does it work.

Being alone does have *some* upsides, though. For my final story of the year, Steve agrees to let me do a piece where I go out on dates with all the randos who contact me on MySpace. The news peg? Social media folks are *Time*'s "Person of the Year."

While I'm writing the first draft of the story, Steve comes over to my desk and says, "It reads too much like a stand-up comedy routine."

I always forget that he can get into my "basket" (as our personal or shared server files are called, with editors able to read ours, but reporters unable to read editors'), and so Steve is reviewing as I am writing.

Steve looks at me uncertainly, and my heart sinks. I don't want to disappoint him.

"Go deeper," he says.

To do that, I focus on my favorite person from the story, forty-eight-year-old George Jack.

"We meet in Union Square," I write of George Jack, who I realize upon reflection might not have been using his real name. "And it's kind of like *Sleepless in Seattle* except that he lives in his parents' basement in the Bronx and I want to kill myself."

But then I get more honest, less jokey, at Steve's prodding.

"Let's be fair. George is pretty cool," I write. "He says he likes me because I'm not fake like some of the women on there. He tells me some ladies will try to get him to pay for their journey to America. I'm not like that at all, and I feel really great about myself. We part ways, and he tells me when he will be online next. The schedule depends on when the computer store is open. George isn't ashamed, and I kind of respect him for it."

When the piece publishes, I'm flooded with email from people all over the world who connect with the loneliness and the desperation. But the best email is from George himself.

> have merry xmas and thanks to myspace, me and my ex are probably getting back together and yr article sealed it ty george.

I am still single at the end of 2006, but at least George isn't.

chapter five

The Dating Column

2007

I welcome in the New Year with comedian Julie Klausner at a small dinner in Chinatown then a "Get Lucky in '07" party in Greenpoint. After taking a few long drags of a joint with repeats of *Intervention* playing in the background, I walk stoned and blissed-out in the rain to find the subway. On the F train home, with the mellow numbness of the buzz kicking in and the orange-and-cream colors of the seats fuzzing around me, I have a moment of clarity.

I keep waiting for my life to begin. I keep waiting for everything to be okay. But what if I stopped waiting?

Gazing around the rattling subway, soiled newspapers and trash everywhere I look, I sit down, close my eyes, and imagine myself on a ride at Disneyland. I repeat to myself the question: *What if I just decided everything was okay right now?*

Waking up the next morning, the feeling hasn't totally vanished, and I start enjoying how different things look. Maybe the fear that constantly wracks me could be processed as something else: excitement.

As part of my "everything is awesome" initiative, I decide I am going to be the best me possible—by trying to fix all my physical imperfections. So when a doctor I barely know says he is willing to give me a free laser treatment on a few veins near my ankles, I'm stoked.

I originally met him during my piece on the "detox-retox" lifestyle in New York, and a friend told me I should talk to this guy because he partied the hardest. I left the doc a message at the time, and he called me back.

"*New York Post*, Mandy speaking," I answered.

"You just feel like the coolest person in the world answering that way, don't you?" the doc said derisively.

"Oh hey, hi," I said. "Yeah, I was wondering if I could talk to you for—"

"Do I want to be quoted in a story about getting fucked up all the time?" he cut me off. "No."

But we kept in touch, and when the opportunity for the free laser comes up, I am excited to try it. In his posh office now, he looks over my chart.

"You've had a pectus excavatum?" he asks. "Interesting. Can I see?"

I lift up my dress, and he gets a nice long look at my breasts and the surgery scar from when I was nine.

"Very nice," he says, and I realize I have just shown my tits for the sole purpose of him wanting to see. I'm there for my ankle. Not my chest.

Pretty soon, he fires up the laser and goes to work on my ankle. It feels like I am being shot, and afterward, I stare down, and a huge red welt appears.

"That's normal," he says.

And I nod. But as weeks go by, it doesn't get any better. It gets worse, in fact, and I think about how much the increasingly ugly tissue reminds me of the pectus excavatum scar he had unnecessarily asked to see.

The scar from my childhood still haunts me.

I was just nine years old when I stood naked for another creepy physician who conducted a full examination, breaking down what was wrong with me.

"Well, do you see right here?" the doctor pointed out to my mom, touching my undeveloped breasts. "Her chest, it's concave. Now, you wouldn't want her to be embarrassed when she goes swimming, would you?"

No, no. We wouldn't want her to be embarrassed about that.

To counteract the very slight chest concavity that no one would have ever noticed in the first place, major surgery was required. In the next few weeks, I was anesthetized and laid out on the operating table, my chest was cut open, the ends of my ribs were removed, and my sternum was broken then straightened out, with a metal bar put temporarily in place.

I look at pictures of myself before the operation and it still blows my mind that this was done so that I could feel *better* about my body. Pictures of me before the surgery show a twinkling light in my eyes that just went dark.

My surgical scar after was hideous: bulbous, jagged, thick, inflamed, and deformed. It never fully faded. It just grew uglier, hardened and ropy, like I had been soldered back together by a drunk welder's apprentice.

I've learned as an adult: Pectus excavatum surgery is not recommended if you have no symptoms, like decreased lung capacity.

Failing the bathing suit competition at the Miss USA pageant is not actually a medical symptom.

"Who did this to you?" I've had other doctors say to me since.

I just shake my head when people do. Because I don't want to talk about it.

Honestly, it wasn't even the surgery or the ugly scar that fucked me up the most—it was the abandonment that came with it. That first night in the hospital, I was in so much pain, I kept crying out to my mom to comfort me. By that time, she was on heavy drugs for her OCD. She was passed out and couldn't hear me, no matter how loud I yelled. I just kept calling for her.

"Mom . . . Mom . . . Mom."

That experience stayed with me, psychically and emotionally. It was such an ugly slash and for the rest of my life, anyone who ever saw me naked seemed to react with this barely contained sharp exhale of disappointment. Like I had an *Alien*-style creature thumping out of my chest that I hadn't told them about. "What's—what's this?" men would ask, touching it, mildly pissed, filled with buyer's remorse.

For a long time, I wanted to write up a simple-to-read, handily illustrated pamphlet that explained the situation beforehand so that I would never have to hear that fucking exhale again.

That way, at bars, I could just slide my disclaimer on over: "Hello. We're enjoying a drink together right now but in the event that you see me naked later, I want you to know exactly what you are in for, because I can't bear to see the look of disappointment on your face."

And now my old chest scar has new company. The ankle disfigurement never goes away.

. . . .

WHEN *VANITY FAIR'S* Graydon Carter announces the opening of a new ultra-exclusive restaurant called the Waverly Inn, everyone in New York is abuzz. Press is not allowed to report (which, of course, is a surefire way to guarantee press), so the Sunday editor, Lauren Ramsby, wants me to go undercover.

"I want a nice, great, reported read," she says. "Not just opinion, but tell readers what it's like having spent a week there. Do they let in Wall Street VPs for the first seating? Do Barry Diller and Diane von Furstenberg come every Thursday? Is someone palming twenty dollars on the way in? Really just a fly-on-the-wall thing, but an aggregated, authoritative look at what's going on."

I have a week's worth of expense budget to spend at the Waverly, but it's seemingly impossible to get a reservation. Even getting the secret reservation number is a challenge. Corynne Steindler, a junior reporter for Page Six, finally hooks me up, but she warns I can't say it came from Richard Johnson. When I call, a man answers and immediately asks who I am and where I got the number. "I'm a model?" I improvise. "I got it from . . . friends?" He hangs up.

One of the first nights there, I wait at the Starbucks around the corner until I hear from the paparazzi that Gwyneth Paltrow has just arrived. I show up a few minutes later and meet Mackenzie at the bar, where we work very hard to act unimpressed that *SNL's* Maya Rudolph is incognito next to us in a bulky sweater and Paul Rudd's ice-blue eyes are betraying his identity above his thick beard.

Despite the celebrities everywhere, I'm more interested in Rick the busboy. Not only is he cute, I may be able to get his number and turn him into a spy.

When our table companion asks Mackenzie if I am really going to get Rick to divulge information using flirtation as a motivating factor, Mackenzie responds, dry as ever: "Journalists are emotional prostitutes. Didn't you know that?"

Another night, I go with Page Six's Corynne, and we recognize then *Men's Health* editor in chief David Zinczenko sitting with Richard Johnson. We go over to say hello. I tell David I wrote about his book a year ago (in which I also mercilessly made fun of it).

"You wrote that fucking article," David says, glaring.

"What?" I say. "I was nice."

I'm such a pussy.

Corynne then takes me to Bungalow 8, where, once I am inside, I suddenly understand what people mean when they talk about secret celebrity worlds. In one corner, I see the club's owner, Amy Sacco, holding hands with a cornrow-bedecked Axl Rose, jumping up and down near a giant indoor palm tree. In another corner is Mary-Kate Olsen, alternately chain-smoking and making out with her date.

On my way home, I call Jonathan Brandstein at 3 a.m. "I keep seeing all these celebrities," I slur, "and it made me think of you."

So classy.

My very last night at the Waverly, before I'm about to leave, I befriend a young man and a blonde I recognize from around 1211 Avenue of the Americas. They are both determined to keep up with me as I try to set a world record for alcohol consumed—bottle after bottle of Bordeaux and endless amarettos on ice—on a single expense account.

Before too long, the man suggests we all go to his place around the corner. The girl and I are the best of friends at this point, building buddy co-conspirators. We move to the second location, and it is not long before we are having what I would characterize as the world's most tepid orgy (because I'm still not having sex). But when my phone calendar reminder interrupts us, I realize, *Oh shit, I have to leave to go meet Rick the busboy.*

I sneak out, stumbling to the Blind Pig, where I meet up with him in his metallic studded silver '80s jacket. He is so eager to meet me. He thinks this is a real date. I am a terrible person.

"I'm actually a reporter with the *New York Post*," I say.

His eyes narrow for a split second. Then he recovers.

"I knew something was up, with you there every night," he says. I pull out my sketch of banquettes, and he helps me peg celebrities to tables and tells me the deal—reluctantly. "Graydon is the only person who has a fixed table," he says, and then explains the rest of the seating-chart hierarchy in this Darwinian little clubhouse.

After we're done, I resist the desire to fool around with him, and excuse myself to head out to the nearest cheap pub I can find. I order a Philly cheesesteak sandwich to try to sober up. Minutes later, I am puking it up outside on the street corner. A man and his girlfriend begin talking to me, making sure I'm okay. I guess at some point we exchange email addresses?

The next day I wake up and find, along with my scratched-on-a-napkin notes from my meeting with Rick the busboy (and the phone number of a doctor named Knut, who says I can call him "cunt"), my now-cracked BlackBerry. I check it. There's a new email. It's the guy who talked to me when I was puking in the street.

"I don't know if you remember me, but we met last night/early morning. Hope to hear from you soon."

Wow. That's a first. I drag myself out of bed, somehow make it to the office—and who is the first person I see? No, it's not the woman who said she works in the building with me. It's the *guy* from the tepid orgy.

"So," he says, "is that like a typical night for you guys?"

"Wait . . ." I say. "You work in the building?"

"*TV Guide*," he responds. We exchange cards.

It is the single longest elevator ride of my life.

. . . .

MY PIECE ON the Waverly Inn—"Secret Scene of the Inn Crowd"—is a big hit when it runs, and it's fun beating other publications, who soon follow suit with their own Waverly insider pieces.

But the best part is impressing Lauren, the Sunday editor. We keep talking after it publishes, she puts me on a few other long-range stories ("50 Most Powerful Women in New York" and, later, even a Michelle Obama profile), but it's the small talk that leads to a dating column.

I tell her about my never-ending ridiculous attempts to try to set my friend and editor Katherine up (of course, Katherine needs zero help—and is within a year married to an amazing guy she meets at one of music writer Mary Huhn's parties, but she endures my efforts). My latest matchmaking attempt for Katherine involves setting up a joint date with a guy who works in media whom I'm not interested in, but I tell him about this great girl I know. Would he want to meet *her*? We agree that the three of us will get together at Jimmy's Corner and see if anyone likes anybody.

Of course, after more than a month and twenty emails going back and forth trying to schedule it (at one point, Katherine even writes "witty repartee totally tapped out"), the date is a failure. Not because we're fighting over the guy, but because both of us exchange a secret glance within the first few minutes communicating the exact same thing: *This guy is the reason women give up on dating entirely.* He's not even a bad guy—at all. He's just so boring. Once you reach your thirties, a fifty-minute date can feel like a lifetime, where the biggest thrill is silently inventing what your excuse is going to be to leave.

I email Lauren all this, and she writes back, "Sounds like it's time for a new dating column!"

Immediately, I begin pitching her—the way I've been pitching Steve for months now. I have endless ideas. "Who Is on Your Secret Husband List?" "The New Intimacy: Using Your Real Email Account." "Googlebating: aka First-Date Oppo Research." (Oppo research meaning "opposition research," a term for the practice of political operatives gathering dirt against an opponent. The fact that I regard men as the "opponent" kind of gives insight into my fucked-up perspective on dating at the time.)

To support my campaign, I try to show all the editors how fascinating and bizarre I am. Boundaries? What boundaries? I have plenty to write about because I take all comers for fodder. Standards start loosening, men who are "jokes" are suddenly entertained as prospects again (I call this an "unjoking"). I'm still a youngish-looking thirty-one, and I am determined to exploit it.

I spend weeks trying to think of names for the column. My sister helpfully offers up "Penises on Parade." Mackenzie suggests "Love Patrol," with me in a cop uniform winking. My dad suggests "Mandy's Place," which leaves Steve in hysterics ("See you at Mandy's place!"). My contribution is either "Daddy Issues" or "I Was Going to Call My Column 'I Take It in the Ass' but I Found Out It's Already Been Done by the *Wall Street Journal*." But it's a consortium of editors who settle on About Last Night.

I still have not had sex for a year since swearing it off. This promise I made to God is starting to get old.

One night out with work friends, I am pounding back a record level of whiskey sours, which brings out a rollicking level of libido.

Before heading home, I hit another bar by myself and keep drinking, Bombay Sapphire and soda water.

I still have in the back of my mind good ol' Rick the busboy and his awesome '80s studded silver jacket. My texts with Stephen Falk kind of tell the story of the night.

Me: *I just came 2 a bar & some strangers are hitting on me. And I am drunk & akone. It is pathetic. Fuck. I have not dared look at who is hitting on me. Fuck. I am a caricature. Fucj fuck fuck fuck fuck fuck I'm scared 2 look. Fuck*

Stephen: *Do you need to call? Are you ok? Who are you with?*

Me: *I'm ok sorry I just really need 2 get laid. Maybe I will xall fone sex that won't be awkward at all. Tonighr I found out this girl I rthought waas my firnd hates me this is the besst txt message of all time. I'm floating, floating into the pancake place. See here's the thing I miss being regularly fucked. I know its not coy & um well anyway bye. KIT. Bye.*

Stephen: *Stop. I'm going to call you in a bit.*

Me: *ithe busboyr is coming over hoorah cobgratulations*

That's right. I finally reached out to the busboy I had crushed on weeks earlier. Before Rick arrives in Park Slope, as I walk home, I call Kyle Kinane in LA, rambling on, talking about all this self-created drama, crying and knocking over the TV on the shelf near my bed. "Stadtmiller," he says, "get it together." Then I call Stephen, telling him I am now playing with myself, surrounded by the scattered CDs of the Richard Pryor box set I had ordered along with $500 in other comedy albums I bought when I bombed onstage recently.

"Mandy unhinged," Stephen says. "I like it."

When Rick arrives, he takes a look at me, smiles, and says, "You are crazy."

I do not disagree.

The sex is pretty great (I suppose any is when you haven't had it in a year), and he does something no guy has ever done before, which is finger me in the ass, which provides the biggest orgasm ever.

I wake up the next morning, rub my eyes, and see the condom wrapper lying next to the world's sweetest postcard my mom has sent me that says: "Love from California, Hope your writing is in high gear!"

Boy, is it ever. I stumble out of bed and run into my roommate Lola. Do I tell her? I should tell her.

"I slept with the busboy," I tell Lola confidentially.

"Yes," she says, with a huge look of amusement, standing next to her hot-pink espresso maker as Juanita comes out and joins her. "We know."

"Oh God . . ." I begin.

"That's all right," Lola says. "It sounds like you had a really—"

"Please," I say. "That's okay. So sorry, so incredibly sorry."

"We're going to do a reenactment tonight," Juanita says.

I email the two of them from work that day. "You're getting 'I'm sorry I fucked the busboy so loudly' apology roses! What's your favorite color?"

"Yellow," Lola replies.

When the lesbians are gone for a few nights, I invite Rick over a second time, and to my disappointment, he does not finger me in the ass again.

I tell Stephen how disappointed I am in this and that I am considering writing about it, and he responds, "Sorry, *Curb* already did Cheryl Fucks Graydon Carter's Busboy and Is Let Down When He Doesn't Give Her Any Anal Play episode. I think it won a WGA award."

The best part about the Waverly Inn story, though, is not Rick the busboy. It's that one of the nights I met a doctor at the restaurant by the name of Dr. David Colbert. Since we did not meet in a doctor-patient scenario, it is the blossoming of a friendship that I never anticipated. He tells me to feel free to come in sometime and tell him about my new weird scar that the freebie laser treatment doc provided.

When I'm in his office, though, I drop the act. Something about doctors and people in authority has always caused me to break down and cry. He is the gentlest physician I've ever met. He tells me I never should have had that laser to begin with. He helps me dramatically reduce not just the ankle scar but my chest scar too with Fraxel and never makes me feel like an idiot or a hysteric. Most importantly, he is the first person to convince me to see a shrink in a long time.

The last shrink I saw, the best thing I got out of the experience was the psych intake form (which revealed, of course, that I am very depressed). It consisted of 175 true-or-false statements that started off mildly crazy, like, "People have never given me enough recognition for the things I've done" and then just got crazier: "I watch my family closely so I'll know who can and who can't be trusted."

After the appointment, I proceeded to take all these statements from the psych inventory to mess with guys in sex chat rooms (and to use the resulting material to audition for a show called *Shelarious* for which Julie Klausner was helping to arrange casting). The results were for sure entertaining:

Robert_hard: *what do u look like?*
Sexy_lady: *I believe I'm being plotted against*
Robert_hard: *I have 8" and am stroking it*
Sexy_lady: *Someone has been trying to control my mind*
Robert_hard: *do you like anal?*
Sexy_lady: *I have not seen a car in the last 10 years*

Robert_hard: damn girl you makin me horny as a bitch, why you talking that wild shit

As entertaining as that performing experience was, in terms of *actual* therapy, I am not getting very far—at all.

I spill all of this to Dr. Colbert, and when he suggests I see his good friend and colleague Dr. Marianne Gillow, I tell her that because of my experience with my mom and how medication just kind of knocked her out, I'm definitely not going to take any psych drugs. She does something that I'll never forget. She tells me that she respects where I'm coming from and doesn't try to pressure me into anything. This makes me instantly like and trust her and want to maybe give Zoloft a try.

When I do, it's like another world opens up to me. That crippling anxiety that has plagued me all my life is lessened so much. I'm able to give myself more of a break. And thank God I do, because the men I'm meeting for About Last Night require more self-esteem and resilience than I ever could have mustered otherwise.

The column affords me the perfect way to superficially seek love while never exploring the more difficult questions about what true love for oneself and others really takes.

Before too long, I am writing off Brazilians on my weekly expense report. I have only one goal: Get good material. And I am determined to find all necessary, even if I put myself in danger during the process.

....

A HANDSOME, GREGARIOUS man approaches me at the Apple store one day when I'm taking my Mac in to be fixed. He tells me that I am charming and intriguing, and that he must get my number.

"You must see the TV show I host," he says in his heavy French accent, beckoning me over to a giant HD screen, which he tells me he owns one of at home. "Here, I will show you."

His name is Hugues-Denver Akassy, and he pulls up his website orbitetv.org on the screen, which features segments of him interviewing everyone from Angelina Jolie to Bill Clinton. He is a French journalist come to New York to bring his TV show to America.

When Hugues and I finally arrange our date, he meets me wearing pink gingham at what he calls his favorite "cozy little wine bar," Shalel, on Seventieth near Columbus. He asks for a table with the curtains closed so we can have privacy.

I start to talk about work, and he reprimands me, then orders a thirty-five-dollar bottle of chardonnay and a single appetizer because "we are not hungry." He asks me what I want most in life, but I don't know, so he brings it back around to love.

"Most men are shit," he tells me. "They just want to sex in your pants. And I can tell you are a woman of romance, style, complexity, and many passions. Is that true?"

"Sure," I say, nodding distantly and scribbling notes on my reporter's pad when he's not looking. "That sounds good."

We split the bottle of Hess Napa Valley, and without food in me, I'm rather smashed rather quick.

He literally grabs me and kisses me underneath the chandelier on the burgundy pillows. His tongue is all over my chin, but I'm trying to keep an open mind.

"We go for a walk in the park?" he asks afterward.

As we walk into Central Park past Strawberry Fields, he holds my hand. *This is nice,* I think. Sweet even. I like hand-holding. Then he begins kissing me by the water, and when he reaches down into my pants, I tell him, "No, no, too fast."

Then he does something I've never had a man do before or since. He pulls out his penis and places it in my hand.

"No, no, no, no," I say. "I don't want to. It's not what I'm looking for. I'm sorry."

We walk along, and when we are hidden behind a giant rock, he says, "We kiss?"

We kiss a little more, and then he whips his dick out again. I'm pleading for him to stop, and then I finally say, "I feel uncomfortable."

He seems to understand. I have, perhaps, hit upon the international safe word. But he is angry. He yells at me: "You are a sexy brat provocateur!"

We walk along farther, to a small stone house in the park.

"I want to show you a trick. It is nice. It is nice," he says.

He unzips his pants and puts my hand on his dick once more. I feel outmatched. I turn around. "Jerk off on my back," I say. "I just don't want to touch you."

He does, I close my eyes, and we walk away. I'm stunned and disgusted.

"Why are you so quiet?" he asks.

"It's just confusing being a woman," I begin.

"Let's not get into all that," he says, and then launches into the world's most boring story about his cell phone provider, and as we walk across the gravel, I am counting steps, grateful for the gift of disassociation.

"What are you doing tomorrow?" he asks.

"Busy," I say. I leave him, and walk zombie-like across the street to use the bathroom at the Sherry-Netherland to wash the come off my dress. I am so revolted with him and with myself. Why didn't I just get out of there? Why was I so willing to dispose of my own sense of safety in order to not create a scene or make a man angry at me?

I tell the story to Mackenzie, who cannot believe it, nor the insulting texts he sends me afterward when I say I don't want to see him ever again. He says I am a bitch, a typical American, etc. Not only that, but he's put me on his stupid fucking email newsletter, and every day I get some new message saying that I have not confirmed my membership with a donation to help Africa or something.

I finally write him back on a whim one day. I'm sick of his fucking newsletter with the tagline "Whatever You Can Do or Dream You Can, Begin It." I don't want to think about this guy ever again.

"Hoping you've been able to keep it in your pants!" I email him back.

He responds immediately in hilariously garbled English, "Ms. Stadtmiller: This letter is to inform you that our database indicates record of your email communications and profanity comments. You are also inform that due to your insanity and unprofessional conducts, you have been deleted from our newsletter list."

I forward it on to Mackenzie, "I've finally been unsubscribed—hooray!"

I write about him in one of my earliest columns and call him Mr. Whip-It-Out.

Three years later, I get a text from Mackenzie: "You know how I have this thing for remembering names . . . Wasn't that crazy whip-it-out guy named Hugues-Denver Akassy? Because he just got arrested for rape."

My stomach sinks. Holy shit. I contact Steve, tell him about what happened, and he has me write a story that ends up on the front cover of the newspaper: "A Date with the 'Rapist.'" The ejaculation-on-the-back part is withheld—for my sake and for the newspaper's. "Doesn't really pass the breakfast test," Steve explains.

But I am so glad it is deleted—because the next day, I am barraged with the most racist email I have ever received in my life. I've been put on some white-supremacist site with the headline "Unattractive *Post* Reporter Dates N—er Rapist." The disgusting emails and even letters pour in. I am a ruined, filthy, disgusting woman, my corpse should be spit on, they tell me. I am a race traitor.

But dozens of women also reach out, thanking me profusely and confiding in me their stories. The emails that I have quoted from Hugues in my story were used word for word and sent to them, too. His TV show does not exist. The footage of the interviews he got was stolen from *Charlie Rose*. These women's stories matched mine: charmed initially—and then things got scary. Stalking. Abuse. I'm floored.

Shaken, I call my father. We talk for a while, and I tell him how much all of this has upset me. I read him one of the letters from some deranged bigot railing at me, saying he wishes he could spit on my corpse because he is so revolted that I dated a black man. I'm crying as I read it aloud. I don't know why I am letting this into my psyche. I don't know why I am digging deeper into the wound, but I can't seem to stop. I want to show how alone and scared and alienated and attacked I feel. I want to feel protected. I want to feel nurtured and defended and tended to by my daddy, who will guard me from the evil in this world. My father listens patiently. He expresses his disgust. But I do not feel the concern I am so desperately seeking. Instead, I feel distraction, almost indifference, and a practicality that taps into something deeper, younger, rawer inside of me—it's an ancient wound, and I feel like a neglected, self-pitying child. Is he just purposefully being withholding?

"Please," I say to my dad at one point, "ask me if I'm feeling okay."

My father is quiet. And then he speaks.

"You sound okay," he says flatly.

Of course—I understand, my dad has been through so much. He sees the world through a lens of combat vet brutality. He is right, for sure. I do sound okay. Because I am breathing. Because my eyeball is not dangling out of my head. Because I am not being left for dead in the Vietnamese jungle. This too will pass. And my feeble attempt at trying to express my needs in this moment makes me wish I was a combat marine myself—and not his daughter.

When a Manhattan assistant district attorney gets in contact with me, I'm able to connect her with countless women, which is one good thing that does come out of the experience. But when I go down to talk to the ADA in a corporate conference room on the third floor with *Post* lawyers present, going point-by-point through what happened ("And what did you do when he pulled out his penis the third time?"), something unexpected happens.

I can't even speak in coherent sentences, my sobs choke me so much.

"I feel so stupid," I tell the ADA. "I said no, but I still let him do what he did."

"No. Don't feel bad," she tells me. "One woman resisted, and he punched her in the face."

It turns out he terrorized hundreds of women. I am one of the lucky ones.

Incidentally, if you've ever wondered how disassociation works, consider this: I only remembered stomach-churning details ("I want to show you a trick") from finding my original reporting notebooks. When I went to write this, I still could not remember it, even though I had just typed up the notes.

Pain is a funny thing.

Giving my testimony to the lawyers after the piece runs summons up every shitty experience with men I have had over the course of my lifetime, and suddenly, I am drowning. I feel so much grief for myself and how much danger I put myself in. There is no denying it. I devalued myself so much, and I lost myself in the process.

Later that night, after meeting with the ADA, I attended some stupid publicist party with one of the Real Housewives of New Jersey. I think the one who flipped the table. It is held at the strip club Scores. A shy young bleached-blond girl comes up to me and asks if I want a dance. She tells me it's her first day as a stripper. I see deep cuts on her arms that are probably not visible to most people in the strip club's flashing lights.

"What are those?" I ask.

"I used to be really depressed," she says, smiling at me with empty eyes.

I look at her, at the blankness in her expression, and my heart goes out to her in such a profound way.

"From one girl to another, will you promise me something?" I ask her. "You cannot tell these men about the cutting thing. Just say it was a car accident. You need to protect yourself, okay?"

She nods and proceeds to conduct her business. It's like I'm getting a lap dance from my goddamned psyche.

. . . .

THAT NIGHTMARE DATE is, thankfully, the extreme exception. You don't end up getting legally deposed after most dates—or having to compartmentalize the trauma they inflict on you in order to move forward in daily life. (One therapist of mine calls these incidents "little t's," and I find that such a spunky way to talk about trauma.)

My dating is now kind of a job—and it becomes hard to even keep track.

Winning the award for most bizarre date during this time is the lawyer who after a nice night spent walking around the city suddenly leans over to give me what I expect to be a kiss—then he bites me on the cheek. Hard.

"Ow!" I say. "Jesus. That's going to leave a mark."

"So, what . . . you're into tonguing?" he asks. "You're, like, into regular Midwestern mainstream stuff?"

Another man is serial-killer-level honest after six or seven drinks.

"I'll tell you exactly what I want," he confesses. "My fantasy is to find a woman who's indescribably hot, she's a total babe, but then she has this one single flaw. Like a withered hand."

I spit out my drink. Jesus.

"Yeah, you know," he says. "Something that makes her just insecure enough so that even though she's a total ten, I never have to deal with all that hot-girl confidence."

Oh my God. Dating is so dark. Determined to put myself out there no matter what, I join the dating site Nerve with the username "ucanttouchthis." Because "fucksalotofdoctors," "cuttingmyselftofeelalive" and "witheredhand4u" are taken. The pickings are slim—in the sense that guys have names like "rebounding_withbaggage."

But every few profiles, there appear to be *some* signs of life.

. . . .

"GREAT SMILE," READS the message from a man named Blaine, a spiffed-up blond who asks to meet for drinks.

"Thanks!" I message back, excited to have a new specimen to dissect.

I wish I could say I believed any of these online dating possibilities made me think true love was possible—but I'm a dating columnist now. My personal happiness comes last.

Blaine and I meet at the Library Bar, a swanky affair looking down on Manhattan. I stand up when he approaches the table. As usual, I am several inches taller. In this case, though, he is far blonder.

Blaine is a kind of New York dandy, with pink socks and a self-satisfied twinkle, which honestly, I would have, too, if I had his obscene amount of wealth.

He is a few years older than me, and he speaks with polite lock-jawed disdain. I'm solidly middle class, and when I'm struck by condescension all I want to do is ruin that person's day. It's as if the lyrics to Pulp's "Common People" are swimming through my brain.

Blaine is definitely not impressed by the fact that I write for the *Post*.

He asks me where I "summer." I have never been asked this question before, so I imagine that he wonders if I return home to California?

"New York," I say, straight.

He looks at me pityingly. We exchange numbers, but I do not ever expect to see him again.

When, a few weeks later, I get stood up by a motorcycle-riding

Spaniard one night, I text about ten million guys so I can have an instant revenge date. One of the people I write? Blaine.

He tells me to meet him at the Sherry-Netherland, where he's at a dance.

After many, many drinks, later that night Blaine spins me out on the dance floor, where I go careening to the ground and the night fades into laughter until he unlocks the door to his apartment, which is the size of the floor of the *Post*.

I realized he was rich. I did not realize he was this rich. I immediately fall off some steps that go up to his bedroom and laugh because it has to be hilarious, otherwise it will just be sad. The next morning, I wake up. I look around and tell him that his place is insane.

"Tom Cruise actually has a place in the building," he says.

"Wow," I say. "That's nuts."

After I write my "50 Most Powerful Women" article, for the July 4 holiday, the grand dame of hedge fund selection Lee Hennessee invites me to her insanely swanky Upper East Side penthouse party, so I ask Blaine if he wants to be a plus-one. He says it sounds like fun but to watch out because the cougars might be all over him. At the party, I end up spending most of the night talking to a charismatic female plastic surgeon.

"Maybe I'll get a boob job," I tell her. I'm saying it to pass the time. I could just as likely have said, "Maybe I'll have a heart attack," if I was talking to a cardiologist.

"No," Blaine interjects. "You're perfect."

We are soon talking to a red-haired children's-book author who has clearly undergone a lot of plastic surgery. She's telling us about her book *When I Grow Up*. When she goes to get a drink, Blaine whispers, "You know who that is? Tina Louise. Ginger from *Gilligan's Island*."

"Oh man," I say.

"I would have gone with Marianne," he says.

By the time we leave the party we are fairly wasted and go back to his apartment once again. When we wake up, with the morning sun streaming in, the mood is romantic. The mood is sexy. The mood is ripe for sweet nothings. He moves in a little closer.

"I'm going to get you," he says, touching me gently, "some upper-arm exercises." He smiles. "They're a little flabby."

My face betrays a look that I'm about to murder him.

"I mean," he backtracks, "you're perfect."

"What?" I say.

"You're an über-babe," he says. "You're an undeniable über-babe."

It's so funny to me, being out on these dates with men who fetishize skinny women. As we lie in bed, strategically placed above Blaine and me in his ridiculous loft is a giant art print of two naked porn stars giggling. They are airbrushed and gorgeous, with upper arms that are beyond reproach.

They will make much better companions, I think. As we lie in bed together, he continues to look over my body. He points to the scar on my ankle.

"It's healing," I say.

"I just want you to be perfect," he says. I lie there, pissed beyond belief.

I can't leave immediately, though, because I can't find my dress.

"Did we throw it out the window?" I ask.

"Maybe," he says.

I take some old sweatpants and a T-shirt and head out, infuriated. Soon after, I receive an email from Blaine telling me how much fun he had creating "some fireworks of our own" after the

July 4 party. I write back, "I had a good time, too. But that line about my arms was kind of a deal breaker."

He replies immediately, profusely, and sincerely—explaining that it was teasing payback from the night before, when I'd told him he had "man boobs."

Oh shit. I forgot I call everyone fat when I'm drunk. We talk on the phone and some of the night comes back to me. I also said, "You don't have herpes, do you?" and "You should send me flowers!"

Later that day, I get a call from the messenger's office. Flower delivery. From Blaine.

In the column, I call him Super Preppy. I send all of these About Last Night columns along to Alex Balk at *Gawker*, who links it, making fun of it as expected. The comments are, of course, savage. I summarize them and send a note out to my mailing list, "I've started a new man-hands, horse-faced Renée Zellweger with Down syndrome dating column!"

But I know the game. *Gawker* brutalizes you. Your site gets the traffic. Everyone is happy.

....

ONCE ALL IS copacetic again with Blaine, he surprises me by wanting to see me—a lot. When he is traveling for work down South, buried in paperwork, he writes, "A bold suggestion, why don't you come down to East Hampton? Weather is supposed to be nice, and it would be a good change of scenery for a summer weekend."

I take the jitney up, catching up on email, one of which is introducing Hannibal Buress to a few comedy folks I know. I've by now told Hannibal all about this new guy in my life, even showing him a ridiculously preppy picture of Blaine wearing blinding yellow trousers.

"Thanks, Mandy," Hannibal writes after I've made the introductions. "This almost makes up for you consistently going out with this weird-pants-wearing dude."

Kyle Kinane describes him another way. "He sounds like a villain from a bad eighties movie."

Blaine picks me up in his Jeep at the station, and we drive to his family's converted farmhouse in Amagansett, which has a long winding road to the main house. It is daunting. I've never been to East Hampton before, let alone to someone's regal country estate. The view from the living room window looks like a Monet painting, with a tiny bridge leading out to the water, trees and tall waving grass.

"This will be interesting," I say, trying to just be myself instead of someone who is totally out of her element. "I wonder if we'll like each other for a whole weekend."

"Maybe we'll kill each other," he says.

"Maybe!" I say brightly.

We sit on the window seats, looking out into the marshlands, drinking chardonnay. When Blaine goes off to run some errands, I am given the edict *"Mi casa es su casa,"* and I'm left alone to play woman of the manor. An hour later we are having cantaloupe and vanilla ice cream and zinfandel with his mother and her friends, which is surreal, to say the least. I'm meeting his mother?

"You're from San Diego," his mom says with an upper-crust lockjaw even more pronounced than Blaine's. "And what do your parents do?"

There are a lot of double-cheek kisses on the way out, and then we're off to another party in Bridgehampton. More zinfandel, more double-cheek kisses, and while I'm having fun, it's also a little bit like the episode of *The Sopranos* where Tony is invited to the exclusive golf club only to realize he is there as the circus oddity.

"What's the *Post* like?" everyone wants to know. "It's my favorite rag."

Soon enough, the frequency of dating Blaine has an impact on my life—personal and professional. I am all Blaine, all the time. When I get asked to do *Red Eye* on Fox, not only do I not know that you should always prepare a bunch of funny lines to say in advance, but I'm more concerned about getting my fake tan just right because I'm seeing Blaine later that night. I suck on the show and never get invited back.

But it certainly pays off with Blaine. He invites me to spend the weekend with him at, as he describes it, "the ridiculously, pretentiously named" William K. Vanderbilt Jr. Concours d'Elegance weekend in Newport, Rhode Island. I'm told to wear something dressy, preferably black or white, but he knows I'll be "stunning" in whatever I wear. The man knows how to lay on the charm.

I rent an insanely gorgeous long swishy black Christian Lacroix dress from a friend of a friend for $250. It's worth several thousand, but I don't ask any more about it for fear of psyching myself out completely.

When we go to the party, we arrive at a Gilded Age mansion, complete with a temple-front portico resembling the White House. Where have I seen this place before? Oh, that's right. In the movie *The Great Gatsby*. There's Tommy Hilfiger charming and captivating a circle of admirers. On the dance floor there's Byrdie Bell. It's also the first time I notice that Blaine definitely does not want to be photographed with me on his arm for the society pages. He conspicuously whisks me past the cameraman there to document the six hundred celebrants in attendance. *That's okay,* I think. We're very new to dating, and high-society people only want to be written about three times (birth, marriage, and death), so I don't think much of the snub. It smarts, I'll be honest, but who cares? What a fun escape into fantasyland for a little while.

"I like your confidence," Blaine says, and I see what he means when I look at a selfie I've taken of the two of us together at a table, with his lips planted against my cheek. I'm nearly unrecognizable from the miserable woman I was just a few years ago.

We spin around the dance floor, and I spend most of the night trying not to put my foot in my mouth (aside from asking one particularly buxom society girl if her breasts are real), smiling and nodding as much as possible. But unfortunately, the night doesn't end there. Back at the gorgeous waterfront house he's renting with some friends of his, we keep partying on the deck, which sits on the edge of the Atlantic Ocean. We even have our own sixty-three-year-old tuxedoed bartender named Bobby, who has been hired for the night to keep those drinks a'comin'.

"That's straight vodka," one of Blaine's friends says, taking my glass and pouring its contents out into the bushes. "Let me get you a real drink, darling."

He brings me a Smirnoff martini and makes the wry observation, "You're wearing a twenty-thousand-dollar dress, but you're with a ten-thousand-dollar man."

Zing. It's only a little while later I find out that this same friend warns Blaine that I am going to get him kicked out of all of his private clubs. And that he and his wife want nothing to do with me. In their defense, it is not just my plebeian status. I apparently say a bunch of insulting things when I am drunk—which I have no memory of doing.

Besides, maybe they are on to something. Because even later that night, when Blaine and I can't keep our hands off each other, as we are making out on the patio steps, a bleached-blond forty-something woman suddenly cries out, "I want my pussy licked!"

We are all about five drinks past smashed. Blaine looks not very interested at all. I shrug and say, "I'll do it," and proceed to go down on her as he watches the X-rated scene unfold.

Then I stand up, triumphant—and proceed to fall into a bush. My neck now looks like that of a slashing victim, and Blaine and I pass out on our bed soon after. I wake up, cringingly remembering the night before, and say, "Oh my God." I proceed to give what can only be described as an apology blow job and say how sorry I am.

"I thought it was cute," he says. "Don't worry about it."

Then he takes me to an exclusive beach club, where the first thing he does is show me a sign posted on the wall directed at anyone in the press that they are not to write about the club—ever. Yeah. Got it. Later in the day we go to brunch in town, and we run into the same bleached-blond woman from the night before. I give her my best dude "sup nod." Remember . . . from before?

On a casual sailboat ride later that day with some of his friends, a woman points out the largest house in sight and says, "You know that's Blaine's family house." Good Lord. It's the first time I really make the connection. Yeah, I am way out of my league here. On a positive note, I do not fall into any more bushes—female or leaf-bearing.

As the year progresses, so does our romance. Weekends in the Hamptons and Newport become the norm. And so does my observation of his patterns. Blaine keeps pictures of his ex-girlfriends up. "They gave them to me," he says. He doesn't throw anything away. He is a multimillionaire but is always stressed, and I frequently provide comfort and solace. He is incredibly paranoid about people finding out he is the one I am writing about in his column—that it could "hurt his career prospects . . ."

He didn't need to say the rest of the sentence. I knew how it would go: . . . *because he was dating such an embarrassing slut.*

Before he meets some of my colleagues he asks, "They know to keep my identity quiet? God, I feel like Deep Throat." If he feels like Deep Throat, I feel like Nora Ephron wanting to burn her ex-husband Carl Bernstein to the ground in her famous roman à clef *Lovesick* about what a bastard he was during their marriage.

The worst part is that Blaine isn't even a bastard. He just is terrified about me somehow sullying his rich-dude super-exclusive status or reputation. And I put up with it.

A few months into dating, we travel to Phippsburg, Maine, and spend a weekend at the Small Point Club, roaming the beach and getting to know his mother and her sisters. I wear a skintight white dress, and, ever the lady, not wanting to show any panty lines, I go commando.

The picture his mom snaps of us sitting on a wicker chair is so adorable, I proudly send it on to everyone I know. After I've sent it on to a good three hundred people in my address book, Mackenzie pulls me aside and says, "Hey, this is awkward but . . ."

"What?" I demand.

"You can see up your dress in that photo."

Fuck. Of course you can.

Among the many mishaps that befall me as the non-prostitute version of Julia Roberts dating Richard Gere in *Pretty Woman* are those that could only occur in the alternative universe of dating a guy like Blaine.

One day I'm heading down in the elevator and a member of the Strokes is in there with me. "Going . . . down?" he asks with a sly grin. Another morning Katie Holmes is breastfeeding Suri in the lobby. The most over-the-top experience, though, is when I walk out front and there is a sea of paparazzi, all waiting for the new power "friend couple" of Tom Cruise, Katie Holmes, and their besties, Victoria and David Beckham. One of the paps who I'm friends with even snaps a shot of me as I walk out of the building, and he emails it to me later. I'm wearing shades, a baseball cap, and a Burberry trench coat the lovely fashion editor Serena French has kindly gifted me from the fashion closet, which features our designer overstock. I look very on the DL, and it provides me another perspective on how the world might see me.

I look . . . powerful. Like I have my shit completely together. It's amazing what a photograph can show.

But there are also many evenings out with the *Post* crew, along with Blaine, where some of my true drunken colors start to come out. One night I fall off a stool at Langan's after "playfully" biting photo editor Dave Boyle's finger out of the blue, accusing one of the editors that his girlfriend is flirting with Blaine, and then on the way home demanding that Blaine have sex with me in the cab. Another night at the Soho House, I break a chandelier after a raucous evening spent screaming "vagina" and singing "Rock Me Ahmadinejad." What a nightmare person I am when I drink too much—which is most of the time.

The day after Soho House, Blaine says, "If someone didn't know you, they might think you're a little unstable. Surly . . . and unstable."

Yeah, I know. Believe me, I know. It's so annoying that other people don't seem to have the same problems that I do when I drink. But normal people drink. I know that. So I drink, just like everyone else. It's fun, except when it's not. I just have to remember to keep it to two or three glasses of wine a night. I don't know why I keep losing track.

I see some "doctor" during this time who bills himself as a healer, and I show him all my bruises from falling down. He tells me that I just need to "clean my blood" by detoxifying and not drinking for three months. *I can do that,* I think. Blaine is a little concerned, though. Am I done drinking forever? No, no, don't worry, I tell him. It's totally temporary. It's not like I'm going to retire from ever having fun again.

When we travel to Miami for Art Basel, Blaine gets recognized by a *Vanity Fair* reporter who asks, "Wait, are you Super Preppy?" He looks a little mortified, then shrugs and says, "I guess I'll have to get used to it." Later in the year, we travel for the holidays to a fancy party with his relatives, and even though I am on my best behavior, I receive two edicts passed down to me via Blaine: "Kindly do not write about the family." And, regarding my fitting in, "She's not even trying." Not long after this, I also hear back that his mother thinks I'm "a little strange."

My strangeness is only compounded by small chat with her. When I do a story about a bad-boy New Yorker for my column, revealing this guy's strange experiences with women, I quote to Blaine's mom one of the lines he told me, that he once spent the evening "somewhere with an industrial-size tub of Vaseline, a dead horse, and an underage Thai hooker." Blaine's mom laughs along with me, but later Blaine scolds, "That wasn't appropriate."

"But it's in the column," I say. "She'll read that exact same quote on Sunday."

"I know," he says. "But it still wasn't appropriate."

When Blaine and I make plans to fly to San Diego to meet my family, I think of all the stories he's let slip when he was drunk.

Like about one ex-girlfriend's family he met who was so crass and expletive-prone, Blaine knew it would never work.

I anxiously relay to my parents some of this "please do not embarrass me like that one girl's dad did" oppo research and beg them to be on their best behavior. My mom says not to worry, she plans to just "prostrate herself on the floor at Blaine's feet when he arrives," and I can't help but love her for it. My parents don't give a fuck. They never have. A huge part of me respects that.

....

TO SAY MY parents are themselves crass and expletive-prone is the understatement of the year.

When we were growing up, my parents let my sister and me curse as much as we wanted. They both swore in spades. As part of their therapeutic teachings, my parents studied at the Esalen Institute, birthplace of the human-potential movement, where they were taught "bad" words are "just words." As a kid, I was allowed to say almost any obscene word or phrase there was (I once named a cat that I adopted "Buttfuck" without even knowing what it meant), and I relished the freedom. Part of me just wants to list a bunch of swear words right here because I can.

My ever-irreverent father at one point started the tradition of referring to fellow blind folks as "blindfuckers." It somehow made the tragedy of losing your sight into this darkly comic absurdity—and banished the deep wells of victimhood and pity my dad never chose to live in. My mom followed suit in taking up his catchphrase.

"Daddy's going to his blindfucker training today at the VA, so you guys are going to be watching each other," she'd tell my sister and me, and we would nod, understanding. "It might be a while, because you know how those blindfuckers get."

My parents are a gotcha journalist's wet dream. They live their lives leaving a heavily bread-crumbed trail of self-indictments, and I've always loved them for their defiance. Who cares? You could get shot in the face tomorrow. Enjoy today.

"My dad is different," I warn Blaine over and over. *"So is my mom. But they are great. You will see."*

One of the more illustrative stories about my dad came early in my parents' marriage. Walking along with my uncle Bob and the rest of my mom's family in the airport, my dad accidentally walked head-on into a giant concrete barrier, smashing his head and crying out in pain. A major scene soon unfolded. He began yelling uncontrollably, his frustration morphing into a full, unbridled screaming session at the people who hadn't prevented it, and at the world in general.

"GODDAMMIT MOTHERFUCKER SHIT FUCK COCKSUCKER!"

This went on for a while. Later, on the plane, my uncle Bob came over to my father and said calmly, "You know, Jerry, I think we were with you. All the way up until 'cocksucker.'"

Humor, as it always does in my family, provided relief from the pain.

My dad never censored himself, including when he came to speak to my seventh-grade class about Vietnam. One of the kids raised their hands. "Mr. Stadtmiller, what do you think of *Rambo*?"

He paused to give his response the maximum impact. "I think it's pure shit."

"They are kind of unlike any parents you will ever meet," I repeat to Blaine.

I always tell the following story so people will know what to expect when they meet my dad. One time I watched from the sidelines as he chatted up his female boss and waxed on about how much the two of them had in common.

"We're both from San Diego, we both have no siblings . . ." He rattled off his list, and then his supervisor interrupted him.

"That's not true, Jerry," she said sharply. "I had a brother. He died."

Without pausing a second, my dad replied with a big grin on his face, "Well, fuck him!"

My dad could not see his boss's reaction, but I could. I stared red-faced down at the concrete.

Would I have laughed if someone said this to me? Absolutely. Jarring, fearless, funny, unexpected, a reprieve from the tragedy at hand. But most people are not Stadtmillers.

"They aren't really about fitting in," I tell Blaine. *"Never have been."*

Both of my parents worshipped at the altar of the taboo and the inappropriate.

My mom often gave jaw-droppingly honest—and specific— answers when I was a kid. In middle school, I once asked her, "What are you going to do today after the parent-teacher conference?" My mom replied casually, "I'm going to smoke a joint and masturbate."

After I went to mandatory D.A.R.E. training in school, I confronted my mom in hysterics. Whipping out my mom's marijuana from the refrigerator, I told her she had to throw it away or she was going to go to jail. I even threatened to call the cops, like the little snitch I was. But inside, I was really just scared. She finally relented. She even disposed of it across the street to ease my fears that the cops would catch her in the major manhunt I imagined would soon unfold.

As I write all this, I feel so guilty.

Do you know how terrible it feels to criticize your combat vet hero of a father and your emotional warrior of a mother? It feels terrible. But my parents taught me it is okay to recognize and name and examine your flaws and mistakes—and that those flaws and mistakes do not have to define you.

And for all those hypocrites who actively seek to string you up by recounting some hijacked, partisan, purely malicious curation of your worst moments?

Well, fuck them.

. . . .

I ARRIVE HOME in San Diego before Blaine does, and I do a thorough sweep of my parents' home for anything potentially embarrassing—weird New Agey magazines, crafting supplies, and the like. Meanwhile, my mom torments me by talking animatedly to her teacup poodle, Shady, who is dressed in a Santa outfit.

"Are you excited to meet Blaine, Shady?" my mom asks, glancing at me to see if I am reacting. "I know I am!"

I shake my head at first, but I can't help but laugh at everything my mom says and does.

My mom is honestly one of the funniest, most original, most guileless people I've ever met. She is dry as a bone and knows how to cut to the quick in every situation.

When I asked her what she got for Christmas one year, she replied, "Well, I got a twenty-five-dollar gift card that I resented." In a normal conversation (like that Christmas one), when I am busy journalistically extracting whatever gem she is uttering, typing into my phone, she'll say, "Why don't you tweet that, you cunt." There was the time I told her all about Pussy Riot, the Russian all-female punk band creating a stir overseas, and she observed, "My pussy is a riot." And when I eventually set up a Facebook profile for my mom, she absorbed my listing all the profile options ("Let's see, hometown . . . relationship . . . are you interested in men or women?") and my mom replied, deadpan as ever, "Women. It'll be a whole new life."

So, she is aware of how non-Blaine she is. And, more significantly, so am I. My love for her morphs into something like false concern. How will she be perceived?

"What is your poodle even wearing, mom?" I ask her.

"It's Shady's Christmas 'pretty,'" my mom says with a smile. And I can't help myself—I crack up again. I love my mom for being such an individual, so playful and silly but also so wickedly acidic in turns.

She is the exact opposite of Blaine's mom, who is steeped in propriety and controlled perception and by way of small talk asks me in a thick upper-crust accent, "Tell me, Mandy, are you in involved in supporting the arts?" I stammer in reply, "Um, I interviewed Jamie Foxx recently. How's that?" Don't get me wrong, Blaine's mom is cool and all—funny, intelligent, warm at times—but she's also a bit above reproach.

I look at my mom, and I love her, but I also wish I could quickly give her a makeover the same way I have fraudulently given myself one with the Lilly Pulitzer and Kate Spade costumes I am now wearing as if that's what I totally always wear, not just because I'm dating a guy I call "Super Preppy" in a newspaper.

I get a text from Blaine. "Just landed," he writes.

I nervously kiss my mom goodbye on the cheek, and we make plans to meet later for dinner.

When I pick up Blaine at the airport, my defensiveness is turned up to eleven. Blaine is a bit out of the loop when it comes to pop culture, so I play music on the radio, singing along, naming all the bands, trying to grab any bit of superiority I can.

"Do you know this song?" I ask, sort of ignoring him and driving straight ahead.

We arrive at a hotel that my dad has purchased a stay for us at with the thought that Blaine will reimburse him, but my dad has made the same mistake I often do about people with money. One of the reasons they've held on to it is that they are on the precipice of cheap. Blaine warns me more than once that he won't be my "gravy train." If anything, rich people don't recognize the meaning that a few hundred bucks can have to the middle class versus the chump change it is to them.

I remember once borrowing $20 from a friend to get through the week while I smiled, nodded, and empathized as Blaine talked about how annoyed he was at losing $20,000 on an investment.

When Blaine and I arrive at the restaurant my dad has selected, my stomach drops a little bit. My last dinner with Blaine's mother was at Jean-Georges, a three-star Michelin-rated restaurant, where she knew the celebrity chef personally.

The restaurant we are meeting my parents at is a literal piano bar. Like, a scene out of *Saturday Night Live*, Bill Murray-hamming-it-up-in-a-tacky-suit piano bar.

To add to this, my dad hands me a corsage like I am going to prom. It is so beautifully sweet and so horribly embarrassing I feel like splitting in two from the inner conflict of loving my parents so dearly and being so ashamed of them.

I feel like such a narc, such a sellout, such a dating-a-rich-guy whore that I actually have the gall to feel anything but adoration for my one-of-a-kind, well-meaning, utterly bizarre parents. What kind of asshole am I turning into?

"Nice to meet you," Blaine introduces himself, reaching across the table to shake my father's hand. Being blind, my dad sticks his hand firmly out in the opposite direction. That childhood feeling is rising inside of me. Of wanting to protect him. Wanting him to be someone different. Wanting him to be exactly who he is. Wanting to just disappear completely.

We settle in to order, and my dad turns to us and says thoughtfully, "Tell us about yourself, Blaine."

I suddenly catch a shared look with my mom, who knows how worried I am, how uptight, how afraid I am that everything is going to turn into a disaster. She tries to stifle it, but the shared knowledge is too much, and she lets out an inadvertent laugh.

Then I do, too.

Have you ever had one of those laughing-crying-fit epiphanies because you know you are not supposed to be laughing, it is the last thing you should be doing, and so it makes you laugh even harder? Yeah, my mom and I are in the throes of that.

My dad and Blaine both look so confused.

"Sorry," my mom catches her breath and apologizes. "It's just, no one makes me laugh like Mandy."

Blaine and my father eventually feel the infectious laughter and join in, and the rest of the dinner goes by without much of a hitch. There are no major tantrums, no swearing jags, no big scenes. Even my dad's guide dog is on his best behavior.

Later, relaxing in the hot tub of the hotel, Blaine expresses a sentiment that, depending on how you interpret it, could go either way.

"I'm really glad I met your parents," he says.

Except, I don't think he did.

I made sure of that.

chapter six

The Homemaker

2008

Everything changes with the New Year.

Even my roommates, Lola and Juanita, aren't who they were when I first moved in.

Lola is now pregnant—thanks to an international sperm donor flown in to make his deposit—but Juanita is moving out. Now, it's just me, Lola, and the twins she is carrying.

I don't mind, though. I love Lola. She's funny, kind, generous, and one of the most authentic people I've ever met. She rolls with the punches, and she can't wait to be a mother—even though the relationship with Juanita is not going where she expected.

Lola is an inspiration to me—not least because of how she manages to keep things friendly with Juanita. The two of them have a love for each other that makes me realize that the end of a relationship does not need to be terrible. You don't have to curl up and cry in defeat. It can sure feel like that at times, but if you've built yourself up strong enough, you can and will go on. You will thrive. You're stronger than your circumstances.

And I'm still not drinking. During this time, Blaine and I plan a trip to Brazil—led by photo editor Luiz Ribeiro—on which we are going to be joined by other *Post* friends, the most exciting of which is Mackenzie.

Another giant change is that Steve is promoted to editor of the Sunday paper and now Katherine is my new boss. One of the stories she assigns soon changes my life in a way I never could have imagined.

It's about radical honesty.

The piece is ostensibly about a new TV show centered around the concept, and will include an interview with the founder of the movement, Brad Blanton, and then a first-person documentation of my attempts to be "radically honest."

But it is Brad Blanton who blows my mind.

I talk to him on the phone, and he is unlike anyone I've ever interviewed. He will literally tell you anything that you want to know—including if he wants to have sex with your sister, the fact that he's let a dog lick peanut butter off his balls, even how much money he makes. This is the theory of radical honesty. He calls "withholding" the most pernicious form of lying. That is when you try to abide by the mores of polite society by not saying things like that you want to fuck someone's sister.

"Whenever something occurs in the world, there's always what occurred and then there is the story about what occurred, and then there is the meaning made out of the story about what occurred," he tells me in explaining why most communication—filled with all of its half-truths, twisted perceptions, and withholdings—is so problematic. "Most people stay lost in the meaning made out of the story."

It's true.

I don't think about reality: "I got divorced." I think about the story I tell about it: "My ex-husband betrayed me." And the meaning I attach to that: "I am unlovable. I am unwifeable. I am a failure. I am not worth it."

Brad also forces me to look at some painful truths about my own anger and discomfort. He tells me that you should just say what you are thinking about someone. I tell him that I hate when strangers start talking to me about my height.

"So, if someone says, 'God, you look tall,' do you get offended by it still?" he asks me.

"I don't get annoyed," I say. "It's just boring."

"Well, boredom is anger and you haven't expressed your anger sufficiently to all those people who ask you about being tall," he says. "You still have a lot of resentment about people—and probably some resentment about being tall. So when someone says, 'What's it like being so tall?' just say, 'Fuck you! Eat shit and die! And I resent you for saying I'm so tall.'"

I crack up. "Then I would appear like this easily hurt social leper," I say.

Then he reveals the real key, the real magic of what he is preaching.

"You're worried about how you would appear, see?" he says. "That's what you think your identity is. It doesn't matter how you appear. You'll appear differently in another half a minute anyway because people's registry of how you appear changes very dynamically. For a while, you appear to be a leper of some sort, and a little while later you'll appear to be someone who's very brave and willing to talk about things honestly. Later on, you'll appear as a kind of person to be trusted because you're not going to be withholding."

When I am assigned the piece, I assume it will be the usual "shtick lit" where you stunt it up and write the reactions. Instead, I find myself unnerved. Emotions are bubbling up.

Earlier that day, I bought a fancy $350 red coat from Ann Taylor to wear because the photos are to be in color, and one of the photo editors told me I need something to make me "pop" in pictures instead of my black overcoat. After I file my piece, I am exhausted, and Katherine joins me to return the coat to the store right before closing. We are walking in the rain, when I realize I left the receipt at my desk. But all the tags are on, and I bought it that day. I explain all this to the clerk at the counter, but she cops an attitude like a Soviet bureaucrat.

"No receipt, no return," she says.

"I really don't appreciate your shitty attitude," I tell the clerk, and now I am both livid and ashamed of my behavior. I hate myself. I hate everything.

"Are you okay?" Katherine asks, and I am embarrassed and confused. I can't see straight, I am so angry over nothing.

"Are you a manager?" I ask the clerk. I am now just gone completely, riding a wave of fury.

"No," she says.

"That's what I thought!" I snap, and I leave the store with Katherine.

"You're not crazy; she was a total bitch," Katherine consoles me, and I start crying at the stupidity of it all. I give her a hug good night, and walk away.

I trudge back to the office, now soaked in rain, seething with irrational rage and even more anger directed at the anger itself. It's like a cycle of shit.

I haven't let myself feel this way in a while. Only when I am drunk does it come out.

I sit at my desk. I text Katherine and tell her I feel sick, "like congealed lamb fat left over from lunch now in the fridge."

I keep texting. I say I miss being her friend now that she has been promoted.

I am . . . radically honest.

She is kind. Katherine is always so kind.

And I keep sitting there, unable to move. The clock says 7:55 p.m. It is me and my best friend, Angie, the cleaning lady, once again. I look in an email folder I haven't checked in ages. "Old Mail." Therein lie emotional land mines. The soul equivalent of photographs taken right before an assassination—or, in this case, a marriage's end.

In one email to my ex-husband, James, I tell him how some of my new friends remind me of him a little bit.

"They don't remind you of me," James wrote back. "They remind you of aspects of me. No one reminds me of you."

I keep wanting to scratch the pain.

Angie, the cleaning lady, maneuvers politely around me to remove my trash as I sit there, weeping openly. We talk all the time, but right now she knows to just let me be. I am having what Blanton calls "an orgasm of grief." I have several.

I pick up my cell phone, and I have no desire to talk to Blaine. I know he doesn't want to see or know about any of this weirdness. I know it is "a little strange."

Impulsively, I call James, and I tell him about what an asshole I've been tonight. I tell him about finding these old emails, about being reminded of our old life in our ridiculous run-down house in Chicago with the stripped old cars in the yard and the concord grape mini-vineyard that we lay under looking at the stars and how it felt like the Grand Canyon. I tell him how badly he hurt me and how I want to forgive him but that everything is so contaminated by anger.

He tells me how I hurt him.

"I know you didn't think you did, but when you said I was like an 'alien,' that hurt me," he says. "It made me feel terrible."

"I am sorry," I say, bawling. "I am so sorry."

He tells me about his girlfriend. I tell him about Blaine.

"You only call me when you want to talk about things that make you feel bad," he says.

"Do you . . ." I choke out. "Do you want to hear about things that make me happy?"

"Yes," he says, and I can feel that gentle connection filling up the space around me.

I tell him about the nice emails I get about my column from women who tell me it helps. I tell him about Comedy Central asking me to pitch a show. I tell him I am traveling to Brazil in two weeks with Blaine and some friends from the *Post*.

"There's nothing worse than feeling like you should feel happy about something and feeling totally unable," I say.

This is how Brazil has been feeling lately. Like a beautiful shiny golden thing completely covered in the rust of my mind, which says, *I can ruin this, oh, just you watch me.*

"I want to move on," I say to him.

"We were so young," James says. "We just saw in each other a sense of possibility."

As we speak, I see some of that rust disappear. I see some of the beauty of the luster return. There is always a sense of possibility.

. . . .

TWO SHORT WEEKS later, Blaine and I—and Mackenzie and several other *Post* friends—arrive in what is truly a Brazilian sun-soaked paradise. It is like we are walking around in a postcard.

We are staying in Arraial d'Ajuda, a picturesque district in Porto Seguro, Bahia, in a little resort three minutes from the beach by the name of Casarão Alto Mucugê. (You should actually check this place out if you're ever considering a South American trip. And tell Eloisa, who runs the joint, I said, "Opa!")

This is my first really big trip with Blaine, and I'm skinnier than I've ever been, thanks to that sketchy healer guy I've been seeing, who tells me to cut out not only alcohol but also sugar, flour, coffee—basically anything that gives you joy.

At the entrance to the main room of the gorgeous resort, I dance around with my arms outstretched, twirling underneath the Bahia sky, and it feels like I'm truly in nirvana. But my body tells a different story. My legs are covered in welts from bug bites, my face is overwhelmed with cystic chin acne, and my stomach is twisted up in knots.

One afternoon, Blaine and I go seek out a mud bath that supposedly has medicinal properties. We get lost. We walk seventeen kilometers. We ask a stranger, "*Onde* mud?" which we realize is the equivalent of a tourist coming up to us in New York asking, "Where mud?"

The man smirks at us like we're the stupid Americans we are. "I speak English," he says. "You want to see mud? There's a river a kilometer up from here."

We give up on the magical mud bath and now are simply determined to find civilization. We ask the man for help. "Ah, you want the next town," he says. "Trancoso. You've very near there. Don't worry. It is civilized. They will not attack you."

Sure enough, Blaine has something akin to Hamptons-dar. The next town is utterly posh.

After a forty-five-minute cab ride to take us back to our resort and a night of hanging out with our friends, finally, at 2:30 a.m., I start to feel internally what my outsides are showing. I'm lonely. I want to be radically honest. I want to connect.

"Do you think we're good together?" I ask Blaine out of nowhere.

"I sometimes feel like you're testing me to provoke some kind of reaction," Blaine says. "Listen, I'm used to dating the uptight Upper East Side kind of girls and you're used to dating angst-filled emotive artists. But maybe we can accept that dating one another is a good thing."

"Why do you think that?" I ask.

"You've got to be one of the more complex, deeper people I've known," he says.

I am quiet. "Thank you," I say.

Then I am quiet even longer.

"Where do you think this is going?" I finally blurt out.

"Mandy," he says, "I really don't have the mental capacity for this right now."

"Cool," I say, radically dishonest. "That's fair. Night."

The next morning, I wake up nauseated. I am violently ill, unsure why, but remembering how all my repressed emotions from childhood usually led to trips to the gastroenterologist.

"Just go ahead with the others," I tell Blaine. And he does.

I'm better by nighttime, and Blaine is sweet when he returns.

"I missed you today," he says.

I am tight. I don't want a repeat of the night before.

"I *really* missed you today," he says.

"*Onde* mud?" I ask him, and he laughs.

This is as close as we get.

The next morning, we lie in the hammock, and Blaine looks down at my expanding bug bites.

"It's kind of grotesque," Blaine says, touching one. He sees the sadness this elicits in my face.

"I mean," he says, "I wish you had those insect bites all the time, it would make me so hard."

He imitates a mosquito. "Zzzzzp. Who could resist this beautiful blond goddess?"

I laugh meekly, and then I try to go deeper.

"Do you feel a sense of possibility?" I ask.

"I do," he says. He kisses my neck and says, "Mmm. Tastes like bug spray."

I smile weakly and Blaine says, "I don't think people really know you. You put out this brash image, but underneath you're very different."

The next day, late at night, after having done the required three months of no alcohol that the healer dude recommended, I head with Mackenzie and Blaine to the small wooden hot tub overlooking the ocean.

I jealously eye the caipirinhas that Mackenzie and Blaine are drinking.

"Do you want one?" Blaine asks. "Or are you still off alcohol?"

"Yeah," I say, and Blaine calls the waiter over to bring me a drink.

We look out at the clouds shifting over the ocean like magic, changing the color of the water from dark blue to purple, and the plants look like the roots of ginger reaching up to strain against the sky.

"Beautiful," Blaine says.

"I can't believe we're really here," Mackenzie says.

"Neither can I," I say, and suddenly my first drink in three months is upon me.

It hits me like a wave of fluid relaxation. Everything is softer, fuzzier, easier. The water in the hot tub is bubbling, steaming, and the sky matches the swirly rising intoxication in my brain.

"Crazy to think this all came from an online date," I say.

And that leads us to talking about the hilarity of online dating profile headlines and how much they reveal about someone's psyche. We suggest how people might game their profile so as to appear to be catnip to the opposite sex. Mackenzie suggests that a man couldn't resist a woman's profile with the headline "Don't Want to Talk About the Relationship." And I suggest that for a woman, a man's headline would be "Can't Wait to Make a Woman in Her Thirties Feel Safe and Secure."

More caipirinhas are consumed. Everything blurs out after a while, but there is a lot of laughter. I don't even make any scenes. I do say at one point, *"Yo quiero comer penis,"* but nothing too insane.

See, I can definitely drink. I just need to be more aware.

. . . .

WHEN WE GET back from Brazil, one of the first problems I encounter comes in the form of the dating column itself.

When you write about your life, a big challenge is coming up with material. A lot of times the best stuff—the *real stuff*—is off-limits. I can't write about what it feels like to have Blaine edit my columns before I turn them in so that I can try to keep the relationship intact. I can't write about how I'm steadily racking up massive amounts of debt in an effort to appear to be a certain type of higher-society girl than I am. I can't write about how humiliating it feels when Blaine doesn't want to be linked to me on Facebook. I mean, I could. But I'm far gone at this point. I am in this, and it's fun to pretend to be someone else. It's fun to be the kind of girl who would date Blaine.

So, in attempting to write less about Blaine, I try to work the angles to write around him. I quote a psychiatrist at length as he "counsels" me, suggesting that I should not bring up my anxieties and insecurities but rather work against these baser instincts. It is basically the opposite of the radical honesty that provided me so much relief.

I tell the shrink about the sadness I felt in Brazil and the aftershocks that ensued—physical and mental—and he says, "Say you're on a vacation in Brazil and nothing has happened. Then do yourself a favor. Act against your feelings."

In my column, I write the lazy joke that, following this doctor's advice, if I were a cocktail it would be called "Faking It on the Beach." Because I'm pretending to be all chill even when I'm stressed. Other than that, the column is pretty tame.

But when the piece comes out in the paper and Blaine returns from the corner store with a newspaper and coffees, he looks pissed and embarrassed.

"That's quite a headline for today's column," he says.

I have no idea what it is, so I look down and see what he sees: "Fakin' It for Super Preppy on Doc's Orders."

"Oh, wow, huh . . ." I react, although, to be honest, I am a little less shocked than he is.

By now, I have a very jaded familiarity with the fact that the writer has no idea, no control, no ownership over what happens once she turns in her final copy.

"I mean, the story itself is just about pretending to be relaxed and easygoing even when you're freaking out inside," I say, freaking out inside.

"You know what it implies," he says, disgusted.

Of course I do.

I grew wise to this headline-switcheroo trick over time and even developed a warning speech for more sensitive souls wading into the murky thirty-six-point-screaming-font waters of tabloid journalism. For new writers, before they submitted pieces or agreed to be written about, I would tell little illustrative parables.

"It's like," I would try to explain, "let's say you turn in a thoughtful piece about not being sure if you want kids and how you're happy just being single. You have to be fully prepared, because the next day, the headline on the front page of your article might very well read, 'I'm a Dried-Up Spinster Who Will Die Alone . . . and I'm Lovin' It!' But if you're okay with all possibilities of what might happen when you relinquish your words, then proceed. Because the exposure will be great."

Most people proceed. Others back away slowly.

As for Blaine, he never wanted to be written about in the first place.

I start staying late at the paper on Friday nights to make sure I see the final pages that include the headline so no more embarrassment occurs.

But I should have listened to the speech I gave so many others.

Because while another column that I write initially bears a headline like "The Illusion of the Perfect Relationship" or something, that all goes out the window after I sign off. In the piece, I quote a man who confesses to being a serial monogamist who talks candidly about what happens when he notices a woman starts trying to act like a wife—doing all the dishes, making the bed with the TV remote perfectly lined up, extra dusting no one asked you to do. This serial monogamist tells me, "That's when *we know* we have you."

He says it happens in a flash, which he calls "going from being totally chill to being totally psycho in a split second."

It's a throwaway line, but a good quote, so I leave it in.

On Sunday, when I open the paper to read the piece, there it is.

The new headline screams: "How I Went from Chill To Psycho."

Great. This should go over well.

. . . .

WHEN I'M NOT writing the column, I'm reporting feature stories on illustrious subjects on which I am an expert.

Like an article about the dangers of "emailing while intoxicated" and a guide on how not to be what a *Bachelor* alum calls "that girl"—you know, the one who's drunk, weeping over past relationships, showing her panty line, all while skimming *Modern Bride* on the first date.

Of course, in so many ways, I am *that girl*. But why start being honest now?

When I'm tasked with writing an investigative story about what the *Sex and the City* movie has in store for viewers, I get to do some old-school tabloid reporting.

Using my paparazzi contacts from the Waverly Inn piece, I

track down a photographer who tells me he can get me pages from the script that I can use. He puts me through the wringer, though, and when we finally meet up, it's past midnight in a burger joint, where he continues to tease me about whether he'll give me the goods. We make some deals about his pictures being used in the newspaper at some point, and finally I leave the diner with the pages from the shooting script.

Now I have to consult with the *Post*'s legal team about whether or not we'll be sued depending on how I report the material. It comes down to this: While I can't say that we have the pages, I can give insight into what happens based on someone who is familiar with the script. This provides the *Post* with that very special legal protection of not appearing to have received stolen intellectual property but rather of having access to a person who is familiar with the stolen intellectual property in question.

Playing private investigator is my favorite part of *Post* reporting. It's fun to be given the challenge of getting information that is locked down. I also learn just how little I know about Hollywood. When a friend hooks me up with an interview with one of the actors in the movie (I label the actor an "insider" in the piece), I straight-faced ask this person, "Now, I've heard that some of these scenes are being shot to misdirect people as to what is going to happen . . ."

The actor interrupts my question—to laugh at me.

"Do you know how much it costs to shoot for five minutes?" the actor says. "It's like ten thousand people on the crew, and it costs a ridiculous amount of money to shoot. Anyone saying that full scenes are being shot just to throw off the audience, that's an absolute lie."

We're able to bill my spoiler-filled (and spoiler-warned, don't worry) *Sex and the City* preview as an exclusive, and in the final minutes before signing off on the piece, I go into my editor Isaac Guzmán's office, where he has a specially prepared cosmopolitan waiting for me that he made from his in-office bar. He knows I've worked my ass off, and it's an incredibly thoughtful gesture from an incredibly thoughtful guy.

Isaac also knows, as the guy who edits my dating column every week, just how unlike any kind of rom-com fairy tale my life is. Unlike Carrie Bradshaw, I'm essentially a joke, eviscerated on *Gawker* and an embarrassment to the guy I'm dating exclusively. It's not like in the movies where the guys are beating down your door. The guys want sex, and then they want you to disappear forever—or at least to keep your trap shut.

There's nothing so loathsome as being associated with female desire expressed and documented. That's how you *don't* get a husband, don't you know? The reality for most women who write any kind of dating or sex column is that there is no Aidan who tries to thrust the engagement ring upon you, but you in your freewheeling lifestyle of carefree fun and abandon can only bring yourself to wear the giant rock swinging around your neck fancy-free. Because dammit, you've just got to do you.

There's no Aidan, and I'm as far from that doesn't-want-to-be-caged story line as you can get. I can't wait to be wifed again, to be claimed. And in constantly vocalizing how no-pressure our relationship is to Blaine, I'm absolutely trying to appropriate a cool girl character like that—because I sure as fuck don't know who I actually am. I just know how good it feels when I receive approval—especially male approval—and my laser target of choice is poor Blaine.

So, most of the time my mental energy at the paper is consumed with About Last Night. Not even the column itself, but the stress around it that it creates for Blaine.

Whenever Blaine meets more of my friends, I try to ease his fears, but my passive-aggressive anger leaks out.

Me: "I do feel a little pathetic at a certain point saying, 'Please don't let it get out that this guy is my boyfriend.' Like that you're ashamed to be that person."

Blaine: "Listen, you know that I take our relationship highly seriously and am totally excited to be dating you. I am also excited for most of your friends to know my identity and really like meeting and hanging out with your friends. Just not sure if I'm quite ready to have the whole *Gawker* media circus thing."

But I do enjoy the status that dating (and writing about dating) a high-society guy affords.

Shallow actions bring shallow rewards. The slightly buzzed thrill of being swept in VIP to Skybar and the Reading Room in Newport along with the rest of the blue-blazer set, with Blaine at my side makes me feel like I've come so far. I am no longer the too-tall high school dork who screamed along to the lyrics of "I Don't Like Mondays" and tolerated the popular girls who would ask for homework help, then later pretend not to know me at parties.

When the sad reality is it is *the exact same dynamic.*

I am still the embarrassing secret. I am still gobbling up those little crumbs of love and attention anywhere I can get them, and then apologizing for the burden I am.

As the relationship intensifies, I realize it is time for me to finally unburden myself of my physical past. So I return to Chicago for one final trip to rid myself of stuff I've kept in storage. Going through boxes, I unearth an old CD that has a song that my ex-husband, James, wrote for me right after we separated. It was inspired by a story I told him about how a friend once told me, "Before I got divorced, I was getting a major operation. And to get through it, my therapist told me to say, '*I can do this.*' So, I did, and I didn't cry—not even once."

A little while after I told him that story, James showed up outside of my therapy appointment and handed me a mix CD that had this song he wrote called "I Can Do This."

I can't resist when I see it. I play the CD and listen to it once more.

"I can do this," the song begins with a soft, uplifting melody. "There is nothing to this. / I cannot find in myself. / When strength has deserted, hope seems unreal. / Take heart, in knowing / That strength is filling / A heart / Far from yours but filled by yours."

It's wrenching. Another ghost in a city filled with them.

On the flight back to Manhattan, drained and seemingly cried out, I check my email and see that I have a potentially interesting reader note in my "User Quarantine" folder with the subject line "Love reading you!" It gives me a smile. These notes from readers always make me feel so good. It's been a rough trip, so I decide I won't release the message just yet, but that I'll savor it later.

Once in Park Slope, I release it.

Subject line: "Love reading you!"

I click on the email to move it to my inbox so I can read the rest. Here's what it says:

"Actually . . . you are the fucking worst. You are the reason men think women are crazy. Your teeth are worse than Austin Powers and if I were you, I would have put a gun in my mouth a long time ago."

I just sit on my bed staring at it. Numb. I know I shouldn't let things like this get to me, but the extra effort of someone trying to make me think it was positive so they could maximize pain inflicted when they pulled the rug out to tell me I should commit suicide hurts even more.

Wanting some kind of comfort, and with Blaine on a trip to Europe, I call my parents instead.

I ask them if they've read any of my recent columns, even though I know what the answer is going to be. They haven't. Of course they haven't. I do feel worse. It's almost like I wanted to get there, to punish myself somehow.

My dad follows up our phone call with an email.

"Mandy," he writes, "we are being hypocritical to tell you we love you and in the same breath admit that we don't care enough to read your past columns. Whereas our intention is not to hurt you, I realize that we have not only hurt you in the past by not reading them, we are continuing to hurt you each day that we don't."

It goes on, and he apologizes and reiterates his love for me. But it feels like a punch in the gut. Physically revisiting this email from him (and of course, I have blocked it out of my memory entirely until finding it) inspires such sadness. It's like the embodiment of a lifetime of not being good enough to warrant attention and care.

How could I expect Blaine to want to be associated with me? My father doesn't even care enough to pay attention to what I'm doing. I'm not worth it.

But despite my wallowing briefly in self-pity, I resolve to not let myself go there fully. Because there is something else growing inside of me: resilience.

I take to my blog, and I compile a ton of reader emails that are kind, and I publish them with the email addresses blacked out and preface the entry by saying, "I never have enough time to thank all the wonderful readers, so I wanted to share some of their notes here."

It is my fuck-you to the guy telling me to kill myself. It's even a little bit of a fuck-you to my father. I'm not going anywhere.

. . . .

WHEN LOLA'S TWINS arrive, her luxury apartment now houses me, the Trinidadian baby nurse, the two baby boys, and Lola. The only thing we're missing is the international sperm donor, and we could have ourselves a reality show. It is about as modern family as you can get.

Looking back, I wish I never left—although I might never have found myself if I'd stayed.

The five of us live together for quite a while, and Lola's fraternal twins are the sweetest little creatures on the planet: crawling around, playing in their bouncy, loving on their mama, and just being so grateful to exist at all.

But word is soon passed down the newsroom grapevine that the *Post*'s music critic Dan Aquilante has an apartment for rent in the SoHo building he owns (he bought it for a steal back in the '70s, and if you get anything out of this book, let it be this: Invest in New York real estate). Inspired, I decide it's high time that I get a place of my own. Dan and I agree to $1,600 rent for the initial eight months and then $1,800 after that. I'm right smack-dab in the middle of all the bustling action of SoHo, and it feels like the height of luxury. The apartment is so nice, with a separate office in the back, a spacious living room, a kitchen, big windows with a view to the street, and exposed-brick walls.

Blaine calls it "cute."

As I settle into the apartment, I try to feng shui it according to one friend who's an expert on the subject. "Always shut the toilet seat," she says. "It keeps in prosperity that way." Another maxim is to put mirrors over the burner for "abundance." I learn peonies are good for marriage, so I buy an Isaac Mizrahi peony comforter, too.

The entire move is such a major undertaking, but I'm so psyched to finally prove myself a capable homemaker. Of course, I tell myself it is for me. But it's so obviously a self-imposed "look at how wifeable I am" display for Blaine. On my first shopping trip to Bed Bath & Beyond, I fill up two carts and spend more than $2,000 on everything from boot shapers to three kinds of wineglasses because I don't want Blaine to think I'm not cultured enough to know the difference.

The wineglasses never get used. The boot shapers get tossed in the corner. That's okay, though. Because I've just read *The Secret*. You have to spend money to make it. Besides, I'm not digging myself deeper into debt. I'm attracting things. With my *credit card*.

I call this *Secret*-ing yourself into bankruptcy.

Around this time, the other spiritual pop bestseller of the moment is *Eat Pray Love*. I read that, too, and when I spot that *SNL's* Mike Myers has a new movie coming out called *The Love Guru*, I pitch a trend piece on the topic.

To report "Feelin' Guru-vy," I reach out to several gurus, including Amma, the so-called hugging saint of India. At the end of my interview with her spokesperson, he tells me I should come meet her myself the next time she visits New York.

When summer arrives—and so does Amma—I do just that.

When I enter the Manhattan Center on Amma's first day in town, I'm dazzled by its top-to-bottom transformation into a sandalwood-scented bazaar, with kirtan devotional music piped throughout. When I go to receive one of Amma's famous hugs, she clutches me close to her bosom in what is called *darshan* (a Sanskrit term meaning "visions of the divine"). I lose track of time and feel all-consumed by a sense of love and acceptance I didn't anticipate. Amma releases me backward and gives me a playful smile, hands me an apple, and I am moved to the side, where chairs have been set up for people to meditate.

What the hell just happened? The little glimpse of peace I feel is like a rush of heroin to the veins. Is it cult? Probably. Maybe. Who cares.

As I explore, I sign up for healing treatments being offered. Spiritual acupuncture. Sound healing. Distance Reiki. Pranic healing. There's an Amma retreat coming up in Massachusetts for only $200 in a couple of days. Should I go? Yeah, I should definitely go. I sign up and fork over my credit card. When all is said and done, I spend more than $2,500 in a matter of days.

When I start going to the healing sessions, I fall even farther down the rabbit hole. I am going to be healed, dammit. I don't care what it costs.

. . . .

IF MY SPENDING on "spirituality" were the only thing that made balancing my budget hard, perhaps I would not have spiraled out so much financially during this time.

But from the very first day I arrived in New York, my almost daily shopping sprees to look like I fit in began. I watched as my savings account, which had started at $18,000, at first dwindled, then disappeared entirely, and then suddenly went into negative territory. As I watched my credit card statements mount, I told myself: *It's only a few thousand dollars.* When one credit card completely maxed out, I just applied for another.

These are all reasonable purchases, I told myself. The $150 bikini wax, the $600 facial lasering, the $80 nails, the $60 eyebrows, the $400 teeth whitening, the $500 hair, the $300 makeup, the

$200 perfume. When I travel with Blaine up to the Hamptons and Newport, I try to observe and write down the best brand names all the socialites are wearing; then I run out and buy these, too.

There are outfits for beach days (Scoop sunglasses, $200; Lilly Pulitzer beach dress, $200; Jack Rogers sandals, $80; Vineyard Vines tote, $100; Tommy Hilfiger bikini, $60) and outfits for brunches (Rag & Bone denim, $225; Barbour jacket, $200; Brooks Brothers shirt, $80; Ferragamo shoes, $350) and outfits for evenings (Kate Spade dress, $300; Gucci purse, $500; Tory Burch high heels, $250; Oscar de la Renta jewelry, $300). I won't even get into what a skiing weekend costs—just in accessories alone.

It is my desperate attempt to fit into a world that I very much do not. Instead, there is often tension—and the feeling that I am a very expensive liability.

One weekend, one of Blaine's friends drives me up to Newport before Blaine, who is finishing business in the city, and even though no one is home at the house where we are staying, the friend drops me off to sit on the steps, alone, in the dark, with nowhere to go.

I'm pissed at how I am treated, knowing that Blaine's friend never would have dumped some socialite girl on the curb like that. I drink even more than normal that night, starting out with a Dark and Stormy and working my way up to glass after glass of champagne.

Blaine and I are having dinner with a bunch of his friends, and one of them begins to tell me about how even though he is in his sixties, he dates girls in their twenties.

"Sometimes even younger," he says with a smile and a wink. I take this as a guy doing a bit with me, so I "yes and" him to the ludicrous extreme.

"You fuck kids?" I ask. "Wow, this guy fucks kids!"

The man laughs and raises his glass to me. We are all drunk, cracking up, in hysterics, being obscene, like a scene from *The Aristocrats*, when Blaine turns to me and hisses, "You need to tone it down."

I look at him, blind from the alcohol, and get up and leave the table. He comes and finds me, where I am crying in the bathroom, enraged. I say that I'm going to go back to New York.

"Oh, come on," he says. "You're acting like a hot mess."

"What does it matter?" I say. "Everyone's laughing."

"I don't care," he says. "You need to stop."

I go back to my seat and stare down at my food the rest of dinner. The next day I apologize, but I know that the anger is coming from somewhere else. What we're talking about doesn't have to do with one tasteless joke to an old pervert. Blaine doesn't approve of me in general—nor do his friends.

Every week the ritual of doing the column starts feeling like an exercise in self-immolation. I can never write about the issues that I'm actually concerned about in the relationship. His urging of me to exercise more, the little white lies I catch him in. And mostly, his pointed censoring of my writing, which even now fascinates me. It's so interesting to see what is shameful in someone else's eyes. What we must do anything to deny, lest the world know that sometimes bad choices and bad things happen. Blaine's editing notes read like:

- "What's the point of writing that you were so drunk that you don't remember having sex except to call attention to yourself and know that someone is going to read that sentence over seven times?"
- "Can you change 'porn fetish loop in your brain' to something tamer?"

- "Can you not imply that you went back to that guy's hotel room?"
- "Can you take out the nipples thing?"

Rather than seeing these issues as the problems they are, I decide that the column is the problem and that I must find a way to change it lest I ruin my secret relationship, which I hope against hope will someday turn into a legitimate public union.

One weekend just the two of us travel to Newport, looking at potential houses Blaine might buy for fun, and I feel a wave of smug confidence. He's taking *me* house hunting. Me. I'm like the best fake wife ever. I cannot screw this up. I need to take action right now to change the future of About Last Night lest I suffer another "Fakin' It for Super Preppy"–size disaster.

Inspired and overconfident, I email my editor Lauren, being sure to mention that we are just having a chill Newport house-hunting weekend together, NBD, what are you doing by the way? I suggest that I think it's best if we change my column into a weekly advice piece instead of a tell-all about my romantic life. Oh, the arrogance. There is no better way to piss off an editor than to assume that you have any say at all in changing the entire direction of something you were very lucky to get in the first place.

Lauren writes back to say we should discuss it in person. I forward everything on to Mackenzie, who asks if I will be okay if Lauren doesn't want it to continue. But I am in a delusion of my own making, and I hardly even think of this as a possibility.

"I'm sure she will be open to it," I tell Mackenzie. "I mean, I'm not worried."

But Mackenzie calls it. Lauren has no interest in anything other than what the column has always been. So we make plans to discontinue it after it has reached a year of running, and I will an- nounce the end of it within the pages of the *Post*.

It feels like a risk, but also like a relief. Blaine seems pleased at the idea of no longer being written about every week, but I notice he is also twitchy and stressed, as if I now expect something from him. Instead of expressing how I really feel, I provide nothing but reassurance to him, as always.

"I just think we should give this a chance, outside of the pages of the *Post*," I tell him, patting his hand as we share a bottle of prosecco. "Don't worry. *I don't expect anything*. No pressure. I'm doing this for me."

I am utterly and completely full of shit. I expect everything.

In my final About Last Night, I position it as the breakup that Super Preppy didn't expect—but the breakup is with the *column*, not him, do you get it?

....

ONE NIGHT AFTER many martinis, I engage in a long conversa- tion at Langan's with *Post* editor in chief Col Allan, and I tell him boldly all about *The Secret* and vision boards I have made to try to get Blaine to propose. (Oh, and I don't remember this part, but Mackenzie tells me later that I also apparently tell him that when I'm drunk I call phone sex lines. So that's good.)

"You should do a vision board for increasing the newspaper's circulation," I slur. "Seriously. I'll show you the one I made up with a bunch of engagement rings and stuff for Blaine."

Col chuckles, and the next day, I triumphantly bring my big dumb hot-pink floppy poster board into the office and ask his assis- tant to give it to him. Honestly, I have a lot of drinking regrets, but thinking about this grizzled, legendary Australian newspaperman receiving my ridiculous vision board covered in Tiffany rings and Vera Wang gowns still makes me laugh to this day.

But when Blaine comes home with me to San Diego for his second Christmas with the Stadtmillers, it provides me with a small revelation that is a wake-up call and counterpoint to any vision-board delusions. There is a moment late at night in our austere hotel room after we've made all the visiting family rounds together.

"I don't want you to take this the wrong way," Blaine begins, "but I have to ask because it's been on my mind. If we break up, you're not going to try to get revenge or anything, are you?"

It feels like a knife to the stomach.

"No," I say coldly. "Do you want to break up?"

"Not at all," he says. "I just wanted to ask because it was on my mind."

"Why would you ask that?"

"I just wanted to put my mind at ease."

Blaine's doubts make me see very clearly where all this is coming from. It's not even Blaine's anxiety. He's a fairly roll-with-the-punches kind of dude. It's coming from all those people around him who are *concerned about me*. And make those concerns known any chance that they get.

That will never go away, I realize, but there's nothing I can do about it. I've already given up the column. I've broached the idea of breaking up with him several times when he expressed doubts. And now here we are in San Diego with my family, and I see that all of that is fairly worthless.

....

IN ALL OF my stories for the *Post*, I cover dating and relationships so much that sometimes it feels impossible to not let them worm their way into my head—and stay there permanently.

That's the case with Sherry Argov's opus *Why Men Marry Bitches*. I hold on to the book, and the longer Blaine and I date, the more I find myself consulting its pages, wondering if there might be something to the advice.

One day, I find myself greedily flipping through the manual, perusing sections about the importance of interjecting the word *fun* into conversation as much as possible (a man's "favorite word"!), how *bitch* stands for "Babe in Total Control of Herself," when suddenly the headline of chapter 8 catches my eye: "From 'I Might' to 'I Do': How to Have the Delicate Conversations About Engagement and Marriage."

Whoa! Holy crap. Now this is exactly what I need. I just didn't have the right speech and talking points! That's all it's been this whole time. Above all else, the book advises, if engagement is your goal and it doesn't seem to be happening, you best make yourself scarce to your significant other when you're wanting him to pop the question.

When I finally gather the courage to try to casually drop some amalgam of all this advice on Blaine, I review my notes, and my spiel comes out like, "I'm having so much fun. You're so much fun. I love that about you. How fun you are. I don't want you to do anything you're not ready for, but we might want different things. I'm having a really fun time, and I mean, *I'll* be fine no matter what, but I want you to be honest with yourself about where you see this going."

I consult the book later after I've given my super-casual speech and see this warning: "A strong woman does not hint about marriage or ask, 'Where is this going?' Instead, she hints about the removal of herself from the relationship. *The word* marriage *never even comes up.*"

Oh, well, fuck it all to hell. At least I didn't use the word *marriage* specifically. And quadruple points to me for using "fun" four times. Men just love fun.

Blaine's reaction to all of this is to clear out a drawer in his giant loft where I can put three to four dresses and a few pairs of underwear. I'm elated, to the moon, until I tell my mom, who can't stop herself from being sarcastic.

"Wow," she says. "A whole drawer."

Oh, right. A drawer.

On Valentine's Day, I disregard the rules of the book entirely, and I just straight-up ask him, "Are you going to ask me to marry you?"

"Thinking about it," Blaine says.

I hear his words, I know what he means, and I don't like it. He's not even doing anything wrong. I am the one at fault for staying in this fucking thing. The problem is the power dynamic I've set up: He's not trying to prove himself to me. He's deciding if I'm good enough for him. Because, let's be honest, I don't think I'm good enough for him. Otherwise, I would have left long ago.

. . . .

NOW, IF YOU'VE cringed at things I've written so far in this book, prepare to have a full-on heart attack as you read the final plea I send Blaine suggesting he both launch a lifestyle brand based on the "Super Preppy" moniker I gave him in my dating column—*and* propose to me.

Yes, you read that right. I hold myself in such low regard that I think that I need to show him what an amazing limited-time offer I'm selling and to prove, once and for all, why I am indeed so wifeable. Because it can't just be that he loves me. No, I'm far too practical for that.

In fact, the two things are so completely intertwined in my mind, I can't even distinguish between where my relationship begins and my ambitious career striverism and potential to be a marketing "value add" ends.

The subject line to my email is a forward: "Fw: Superpreppy .com—Protect your brand today."

Because I have—wait for it—actually registered for him "superpreppy.com"—as some weird ultimatumish-y present. The idea is that since he is getting more into entrepreneurship, I suggest he can spin off a lifestyle brand based on the *Post* column name.

My email to him reads like the perfect sludgy storm of soul-dead, car-salesman-like career opportunism and my worst romantic hardball bottom-lining tendencies. It's enough to make you want to stab your eyes out via pure mortification by proxy.

Hi Blaine. This is an email that you are welcome to discard—but I had a realization tonight as I was whining to a friend about, "I just feel like it's now or never with Blaine . . ." and she was mostly quiet and said nothing, and then she said, "It's funny—because you guys are so sophisticated, but then in this way you are so typically male and female."

Maybe that's when it hit me. Is that I'm 33, and you are 39, and as much as romance is fun and stewing is fun and pining is fun and the titillation of will you/won't you is fun, I'm over it. I thrive when I have forward movement. And right now, I don't feel any. You are adorable for cleaning out that drawer. This email is a lot more than that drawer. It's a bunch of ideas.

You can ignore them. But I'm letting you know where I'm coming from. Because I have dreams. I have like recurring dreams about you proposing. It's making me crazy. And—dude—one thing to be clear on, I am fine if you don't—but let's decide now. Or soon. Let's—or rather, YOU—please, decide soon.

So, in the spirit of symbolic forward movement, I just registered the domain name superpreppy.com.

Here are a few ideas I have.

1. I think that you should propose to me.
2. I think you should do so soon.
3. I think we should meet with a media investor at your fancy impressive place, and he can meet you and be wowed by you, and we can say that we have some big news on the horizon and then he will have the heads-up to write the post when we are linked as being engaged on Facebook. You can then announce that you are launching a lifestyle site on superpreppy.com. It'll be like PerezHilton.com—for the preppy lifestyle.
4. If you don't feel comfortable being linked on Facebook, then I question you ultimately feeling comfortable being in the *Times* with me as your spouse.
5. I think that if we get married—possibly even as early as this summer (this would allow you to get my health insurance right away), we could plan to have a small garden wedding at your mother's house in E. Hampton with just your immediate family and my immediate family.

6. As I said above—re: all of this, if we break up tomorrow, that is totally cool. Seriously. These are ideas.

7. Ideally, I would like a Tiffany Setting engagement ring—no cheap flower-stand roses, please. (To use an analogy.)

8. I will happily sign a prenup agreement saying I want none of your money. As I said over a year ago, the only reason I even have you pay for dinner and drinks is simply because I cannot keep up financially with this level of leisure.

This is all. Thanks for listening—and thanks for the fun times so far.

Mandy

Are you dead? Did you die? Because I did, and I do every time I look at this hot garbage fire of an email. Every time I think I am done feeling physical revulsion, I slap myself on the forehead yet again. "You can have a site like PerezHilton! I want the Tiffany Setting ring!"

Soon after sending this, I go over to Blaine's place, and he tells me he thought the email was "funny." We never discuss it again. Maybe if I had about eighty more bullet points. That would have done the trick.

Not too long after, we go to Stratton, Vermont, to go skiing with all his friends. I go out and buy hundreds of dollars' worth of wintry clothes to try to look like it's not my second time skiing in my life, along with a pair of Timberlands so I don't wipe out in the snow.

As the weekend progresses, as per usual, there is a heavy amount of drinking. After five or six gin sours on the first night there, I'm nice and loose. By midnight, I'm suggesting a game of truth or dare in the hot tub and making out with one of the girls in the house who is a drop-dead gorgeous blonde and a hard-core Republican.

"It's so funny," she says the next day as we laugh about it over coffee. "I've made out with a girl one other time, and she was also a six-foot-two blonde."

"I guess that's our thing," I say.

While this debauchery is totally enjoyable, I also think I am impetuously trying to show Blaine what a cool, fun party girl I am, and how he will have the *best* time ever with me if he does decide to propose.

It's in many ways even more thirsty than that shit show of an email I sent.

Soon after, when Blaine and I go to another party in Brooklyn, we get incredibly drunk on draft beers, and a friend of mine from college, Katie, and I are dancing hot and heavy under the neon lights of the rave-like atmosphere of the Bell House.

As our dancing grows increasingly flirtatious and sexual, I ask Katie and then Blaine if they'd want to have a three-way. Everyone is on board. So we all pile together into a cab to head back to Blaine's loft, where I proceed to ravish Katie—which is pretty fun, actually—as Blaine watches and occasionally joins in.

Going full-on Caligula is always a good time, but let's be real, I know what I'm doing. I might as well start bringing in a cavalcade of porn stars to start pleasuring Blaine when I'm not there—that's how bad I want his approval and commitment and to "close the sale."

We go to East Hampton soon after, and my stupid non-ultimatum ultimatum is still hanging over my head like the sword of Damocles. I find myself unable to concentrate on anything.

"I want it to be summer," Blaine observes, without a care in the world, as the March winds whip around his sprawling estate.

"I'm sorry, what did you say?" I ask, not able to follow one train of thought for too long.

To combat this problem, I decide to do a detox. I don't allow myself any alcohol, caffeine, flour, or sugar like I did before in Brazil. Let's see how long I can go this time.

By the time Blaine's fortieth birthday rolls around, I feel slightly reinvigorated. The months-in-the-planning party is a formal affair with his relatives, closest friends, and, of course, his mother. I'm pumped to go, and when I do, I am seated next to an old family friend of Blaine's.

He's a lawyer, he tells me. I introduce myself, and he grins.

"Oh—I know who you are," he says.

I'm so thrilled. This means Blaine has been telling old family friends all about his awesome girlfriend!

"You do?" I ask, my eyes lighting up.

"Yeah," he says. "Blaine was going to ask me to draw something up to ask you to never write about him again."

I can feel the tears welling, so I stab my hand with my fingernails until it bleeds. I am not going to cry over this. The internal mortification is enough.

I confront Blaine about it later, and he says he's not sure what the guy was referring to—maybe it was something he mentioned when we first started dating? Which confuses me, because I was the one who tried to end it then, and he made a concerted effort to keep it going.

Unsurprisingly, this birthday evening humiliation—along with all the other little slights I've felt and enabled—feels like a death by a thousand cuts.

I revert to my spend-less-time-with-Blaine-to-make-him-love-me strategy. About a month later, when I am booked to perform at a comedy show with several friends, I ask comedian Jessica Delfino to hang out with me afterward instead of just heading straight over to Blaine's. I'm feeling amped, and the show was so fun it's like I'm on a natural high soon to be enhanced even further by many unnatural ones. This is the night I finally throw my "detox" to the wind. As we down our first of many martinis, I tell her we should take sexy pictures of ourselves sipping them, and I'll post them on Facebook to make Blaine jealous.

Jessica laughs—probably at the fact that a thirty-three-year-old has the emotional maturity of a thirteen-year-old—and we proceed to carry out my plan of attack. The second and then the third martini hit me hard, and I begin babbling on to Jessica about how I'm trying to spend less time with Blaine in order to increase my value—and that includes withholding sex.

"But I'm so horny," I whine to Jessica. "Maybe we could just go back to my place and fool around? You're a girl, so it wouldn't really be cheating."

Of course, that's totally cheating, but never mind that.

"That sounds really fun," Jessica says politely, while also slickly employing every man's favorite word. "But I can't because I have a boyfriend."

"Oh, I totally get it, no worries," I say. "I should just go over to Blaine's place, but I'm really trying to do better about making myself less available."

Still cruising on the elation of the show and now the solid in-toxication of a three-martini punch, I walk out of the bar to head home. I see two men on the street smoking, and I realize I should definitely bum a cigarette. I haven't smoked in years, but tonight feels like the night.

"Hey, got a smoke?" I ask. Looking a little closer, I realize, *Holy shit, these guys are hot.*

"We are pilots," they tell me in heavy accents, as they dispense to me many cigarettes and look me over, "visiting from Italy."

I have zero filter at this point, and I am 100 percent pure unadulterated id.

"Man, if I wasn't in a relationship I would totally go for you," I crow. "You guys are super sexy. Here, come with me, I'm going to introduce you around and get you laid."

They are charmed. I lead them up into Sixty Hotel in SoHo, a celebrity hideaway where I once spent the day staking out Paris Hilton with a tattoo-covered paparazzo I was profiling.

"You'll love this place," I say. "Let's get a drink, and I'll introduce you around."

As I nurse my fourth martini, I begin my totally-not-weird-at-all quest of hawking these Italian pilots' sexual wares to confused single women. The pilots finally put an end to the performance I am putting on and corner me in the middle of the bar.

"But," Pilot #1 says, brushing up against my arm, "we like you."

"I know, right?" I say cockily. "I wish I was single."

I wish I was single.

My heart is thumping. I sip my drink, nibble on my olive, and think about that statement, wishing I was single. Suddenly, I have the justification-for-cheating epiphany to end all epiphanies.

Aren't I, though—pretty much? I'm in a relationship with a fantasy lover kept in secret who is perpetually disappointed with my ability to be good enough for him. These last several months especially, I've been making a fool out of myself trying to change for someone whom I should have let go the instant he didn't want to have his picture taken in public with me.

You know what? I wish that lawyer family friend *had* written up something threatening me not to ever write about him again.

Fuck Blaine. And fuck me for having tolerated this for so long.

I look at these hot Italian pilots in front of me, with their black curly hair, olive complexions, and hedonistic smiles. I kiss one of them. Then I kiss the other. This shit is *on*.

We sneak to the back of the bar, and Pilot #1 (I find names so formal, don't you?) drapes his coat over my legs and begins to finger me while Pilot #2 kisses me in exactly the way I like. Kissing that says This Is Exactly What I'm Going to Do to You.

"Do you want to see my place?" I ask, and we walk to my apartment, where, all full of bluster, I show them a picture of Blaine, then turn it over, and we all proceed to: Tone. It. Down.

. . . .

FLUSHED, SWEATY, AND still very drunk, when my new pilot friends leave, I wake up to reality. Like, *reality* reality. Oh shit. That just happened. *Fuckfuckfuckfuckfuckfuckfuck.*

My entire "If you liked it then you should have put a ring on it" drunken epiphany I had earlier has transmuted into a dark pit in my stomach filled with fear, personal loathing, and regret.

I stand up and immediately fall over my plastic tower of CDs, bruising my leg badly and sending the jewel cases shattering everywhere. I find my cell phone and dial Blaine's number.

It is two thirty in the morning. "Hello?" he answers.

"I just had sex with two Italian pilots," I say.

"What?" he asks groggily. "Why are you telling me this?"

"I'm coming over," I say, and I grab a cab to head to his place.

I wave hello to the doorman—he's the third one I've gotten to know in our nearly two years of dating now—and head up to Blaine's apartment.

"So, do you want to break up?" I ask.

"I need to think," he says.

A small smile shows on his face.

"Maybe we could all get together and talk about it," he says with a wry chuckle. "Just you, me, and the pilots."

"Totally," I say, laughing. "Oh my God."

And then—as I sober up—I return to my ABC (Always Be Closing) Stepford Wife party line. So much for the "Fuck Blaine" independent-woman internal monologue I gave myself last night. Now I'm back to used-car salesman. Hey, I can still save this thing. We talked. We laughed. We bonded. No one said they wanted to break up. Maybe it's time to register him another domain name?

"You could propose to me," I say.

He looks at me quietly.

"Yeah," he says, "that'll be quite a story for our grandchildren."

Blaine and I have an already planned dinner with his friends that night—the ones I apologized to after saying mean things to them when I was drunk a few years ago. And the entire thing is bizarre. We are now fully playacting. Pretending that I haven't just sent a nuclear missile into our relationship.

After dinner, Blaine tells me he's going to go to Vermont for the weekend to go skiing.

I text Mackenzie, encapsulating everything down to one sentence: "I had sex with two Italian pilots last night."

"HOLY CRAP," she texts back.

Staring at myself in the harsh glare of daylight, I see what I don't want to about myself.

I am in fact even more chickenshit than Blaine in this entire scenario. I'm the one who didn't have the courage or dignity to end things earlier because I was in such a disgusting diamond-ring horse race mode. And when it doesn't seem like I'm getting what I want, I turn into a feral maniac.

When Blaine and I finally meet up when he returns from Vermont, within the first few minutes of talking at the Smith in Union Square, he says, "You know, you did hurt me. I think we need to take a break."

"Fine with me," I say, and I stand up instantly. I leave the merlot I've just ordered on the bar. I walk away, crying as I march through the East Village, logging onto Facebook on my phone, and changing my status to no longer in a relationship.

My self-awareness is sorely lacking. My entire problem with Blaine is that he's so afraid of what people might think about us dating, but what's the reality here? I'm the one hung up on perception. Status. Associative redemption. And I so care how I'm seen.

The very next day after we break up—I kid you not—my first assignment is to cover a wedding expo. A goddamned motherfucking wedding expo. I'm doing a video, and ducking into the bathroom frequently to fix the eye makeup I keep fucking up with unexpected tears every time I see some happy couple reminding me of what a complete failure of a human being I am.

A few weeks later, when I am gone at work, Blaine drops off a stash of my assorted belongings with a note that reads, "You are a fabulous, joyful person whose life is filled with nothing but happiness."

I feel empty reading it. So I have a long conversation with my old friend Hollywood manager Jonathan Brandstein about what I have done. He emails me a little bit later on.

"Mandy, you are a Kashmir Sapphire," he writes. "The famous sapphires of Kashmir are mined from a remote region high in the Great Himalayan mountains of northwestern India. Lying at an elevation of approximately 150,000 feet. These sapphires are so beautiful and rare. Today with the exception of estate sales, fine Kashmir sapphires are virtually unobtainable, mute testimony of the degree to which they are coveted. They are often categorized as a conundrum gem. They form an exclusive class of its own. And once they are cut, they make a beautiful jewel."

His note makes me weep. I don't cry because Blaine fails to see me this way. I'm crying because I can't see it either.

....

chapter seven

The Unhinged

2009–10

"Y ou seem lighter," Mackenzie says after the first week or so.

I definitely am—but there is an inner darkness that she doesn't know about.

My mission to de-Blaine myself results in a kind of twisted logic where I become determined to do the opposite of what I once did with him in my life. No one tells me what to do. Did he think I was embarrassing? Did he think I was unwifeable? Well, he doesn't know the half of it.

I'll show you fucking unwifeable.

It's not just Blaine either. One day I receive an email from a wealthy tech entrepreneur I had reached out to asking if he could set me up with any "nice guys." No, he can't do that, he explains and proceeds to shame me for everything I've ever written online.

"Given your proclivities," he tells me, "I'd predict you'll either never get married, or have N husbands."

It turns my stomach a little to read. So I tell him that I already have been married once before and indeed am a very loving and devoted partner.

Instantly, he replies: "I'd suggest you stay away from marriage going forward? :)"

Reading his words, I am livid.

I hate him. I hate Blaine. I hate anyone who has ever looked down on me ever. I despise the hypocrisy inherent in shame. *If I don't fit into a polite world, then I will live as impolite a life as possible,* I think. *I will ravage myself. I will dive headfirst into one seedy encounter after another.* And that's exactly what I do.

. . . .

MY LIFE BECOMES a cocktail of excess. And my coworkers start to notice.

One night after a rollicking evening on the town with a bunch of *Post*-ies, I lose all track of time around 2 a.m. I come to early the next morning. I wake up in a hotel room with a strange man I quickly remember I met the previous evening when I swerved into a Village diner, approached a booth of strangers, and swung my legs up onto the lap of the closest guy—and proceeded to eat all his onion rings.

Everything after that goes to black. At this very moment, though, I recognize that Mr. Onion Ring Man is now on top of me, looking positively gleeful, his shaggy brown hair flapping about as he thrusts inside me.

"You took a little nap," he informs me. "I had to wake you up."

Yeah . . . that's one way to put it.

On the way into work, I refuse to feel sadness or regret. No, this is just a crazy story. That's what it is. So I write it up and email it to all the coworkers I partied with the night before, telling them all about the "hilarity" of what happened after I left.

All jacked up on no sleep and a severe hangover, I'm greedy for even more reaction and jokes to be made, though. So while Katherine didn't go out with us, I forward on my witty little summary to show her what a hysterical maniac I am.

I just *know* she'll get a kick out of this.

Later in the day, Katherine walks over to my desk with a tentative smile on her face. She is kind as always, but there is a difference in her demeanor. It's like she's looking through me.

"Wasn't that crazy?" I laugh, all lazy and cool and smiling.

"Yeah," she says quietly, sitting on my desk, shifting uncomfortably, seeming more like a big sister than my boss or my friend.

"Hey, I don't want to be weird," Katherine begins. "I'm just, you know, a little worried. I don't want you to end up like Diane Keaton in *Looking for Mr. Goodbar* or anything."

The instant I hear the concern in her voice, tears well up in my eyes. Embarrassed at having blown my cover as the wild party girl who is having *so much fun*, I look down and brush them away. I'm crying because Katherine knows how easily I get crushed. She knows I feel crushed by someone winking at me the wrong way, breathing accidentally in my direction, and yet she's saying all of this anyway. She is saying this as a friend. She is saying this as a friend who doesn't want to see me die.

"Well, I mean, I'm . . . I'm sorry," I stutter. "I mean . . . I certainly don't want to worry you."

"No, that's not it at all," she says softly. "I'm just a little concerned. Just a little bit."

That's all she says, but it's something I've never forgotten.

I wanted so badly for someone to look at me the way that she did that day—to want to protect me, to care if I am alive or dead.

And when it happens, just that tender little scrap of love feels almost too much for me to handle without breaking down crying.

. . . .

NOT TOO LONG after my breakup with Blaine, when I realize that I can't stop looking at his Facebook profile, I decide to do a story on "stalking exes," where you keep looking at their social media to see who they are dating and what they are doing.

I interview and get to know the comedian Marc Maron for the piece. He shows me very quickly that I am not the only one to do this.

"After my divorce, I decided to do a Google research project, and the title of the project is, 'Who Is My Ex-Wife Sleeping With?'" Maron tells me. "And I googled her name and saw some pictures of my wife with a screenwriter, and within a half hour I found out he was Harvard-educated, comes from a rich family, writes for a TV show, and has a script deal with a major studio. All I didn't find was footage of them having sex, and stopping in the middle to turn to the camera and laugh at me."

Maron pauses. "I'm not saying it's not out there. I just didn't want to search anymore."

Not too long after that article runs, I have a killer meeting with an HBO executive and the idea of doing an exaggerated version of my life is tossed around. So I decide to film a reel to illustrate what that might look like, based on the two-pilots story. I call the project *Spinster*, and I ask Maron if he'll play my boyfriend in what I'm shooting.

It is an incredibly strange experience to act out a comedic vision of what happened.

"I . . . fucked two Italian pilots last night," I say to Marc, and by way of reasoning say I was pissed he wouldn't confirm on Facebook that he was in a relationship with me. "But I was thinking about you."

"Well, that's very flattering," Marc says. "So let me get this straight. When did this happen? Was I sleeping? Was it before I came over? Did you shower?"

"Oh," I say.

"Well, that's great," he says. "That's really . . . that's classy. It's coincidental, because I have to meet an entire Swedish flight crew. And I'm going to now confirm the relationship with you is not only over, I'm going to say, 'Fuck her.' That is: Mandy. And then in my status bar, I'm going to say, 'For fucking two Italian pilots at me.' Because that's what you did. You're basically, you're like, 'Look, two cocks. Bye!'"

During the course of several hours of filming, we shoot various establishing shots to set the scene of him as my fictional boyfriend, so we pretend to cook in my kitchen, hang out in the living room, and then "pretend" to fool around on my bed.

"That was really hot," I text him after he leaves.

"It was," he texts back, and we make plans for me to cab out to Queens.

I'm a little intoxicated when I arrive, but I listen to him tell me all about this new podcast he is trying to get off the ground called *WTF*.

When we go into Marc's bedroom, we are able to continue what we started at my apartment earlier. The sex is fun, and at one point, still a little drunk, I say in my best sexy voice, "Slap me."

He obliges.

Marc and I keep in touch over text (he says I am "adorable for a toughie") and on Facebook he sends me links to articles like "Love in the Time of Darwinism: A Report from the Chaotic Postfeminist Dating Scene" and "The 'Menaissance' and Its Dickscontents."

He asks if I'd ever want to grab a meal, but I'm more interested in the sex. Depending on what or when I message him, he asks, "Are you drunky?" He's been sober for years, I know, but I guess he's used to dealing with train wrecks like me.

When he does come over again, however, I'm stone-cold sober.

During sex, he repeats what I asked him to do last time—he slaps me.

"What the fuck?" I say.

He gives me a look straight out of *Curb Your Enthusiasm* that says, *No good?*

Then I remember.

"Oh, right, because I asked you to do that before," I say. "Sorry, I guess I fuck differently when I'm not wasted."

We talk about comedy a little bit after, and he says of me, "I think you're funny when you don't know it."

Which makes me feel the opposite of good, but whatever. He's probably right.

After sex, he peaces out, but I get a knock on the door a few minutes later.

"Yeah?" I ask.

"I think I . . ." he says, and comes into the bedroom and picks something up off the ground.

"Wow," I say. "You fucked your AA chip out. That's pretty good."

After he leaves, I follow up on something I'd mentioned I would do, and I email Lazlow from *Grand Theft Auto,* introducing him to Marc about podcast tech stuff.

Marc replies, "Thanks, stud. Nice of u. Nauseous in cab now. Great bein with u."

I don't feel like a stud at all. Well, maybe when I don't know it.

. . . .

ONE THING I am certain of: Nothing is off the table anymore.

Who knows—maybe I'm a lesbian?

After meeting a charismatic psychic named Adi, I spend a long, stoney weekend with her. If anything, she makes me appreciate just how hard it is to make a woman come.

But the next morning when I sober up, I tell Adi the bad news: As much as I enjoyed all the nonbinary fluidity, I just don't think I'm gay.

This inspires Adi to freestyle a song about me: "You wake up in the morning, and you tell me you're not gay / But you're touching and you're teasing like you really want to play / Experience Girl / Experience Girl / In it for the experience / Experience Girl."

She has me dead to rights.

Not too long after, I run into an S&M couple, Edward and Elizabeth, I once interviewed for research on a story about kink. They make me an offer I can't refuse.

"We're going to pick up some coke," Edward says. "Wanna join?"

Cocaine is something I've never done before, and I know exactly where it leads. But I just don't care anymore.

Back at my place, Edward unloads a bag filled with $2,000 worth of S&M gear—giant dildos, collars, and sundry sex toys—

for a porn shoot they are doing the next day. Then he rolls up a twenty-dollar bill, metes out several lines on my Green Day *Dookie* CD, and says, "Welcome to hell."

The first three lines I snort hit me immediately. I want it all. I can't get enough. It's like every doubt I've ever had about myself is gone. I can do no wrong. I am unstoppable. I fucking love cocaine.

"I should totally write about this night for this HBO show I'm going to do," I say, talking a mile a minute, grabbing my computer and pulling up my *Spinster* "concept" document.

Elizabeth reads over my shoulder a little bit and then lashes out at me in disgust.

"What the fuck?" she yells. "What is this *Sex and the City* bull- shit you're writing? You wouldn't say this! You would never say this! This needs to be trashy, sexy, in your face! What is this right here . . . a semicolon? *You would never use a fucking semicolon!*"

My eyes glaze over as I watch this dominatrix really take my punctuation to task.

"Hey . . . so, uh, do you guys want to, like, actually dominate me?" I ask.

I look at my reflection in the mirror, and I see my pupils are the size of Alaska.

"Showtime," Edward says, standing above me.

To prepare to dominate me, Edward looks around the room and ignores the $2,000 of assorted porn props they have brought, and instead grabs my Sporty Spice neon yellow bike jacket, which I bought during a brief healthy-living phase. He ties it around my eyes. Then Elizabeth pulls off my pink Victoria's Secret lace pant- ies and stuffs them in my mouth. It's a nice touch, I must admit.

"Do you think you're a little starlet?" Elizabeth hisses as she spanks me. "You think you're a little star, don't you?"

I find this entire dynamic hilarious. This is pretty much the opposite way to dominate me.

"Yes!" I agree enthusiastically. "Totally!"

But now Edward is trying to get in on the action.

"I'm going to fuck the shit out of you with my huge cock," he snarls, and then leans into my ear to whisper so only I can hear, "I've wanted this for so long."

That sobers me up—a little. I strip off the blindfold to see him standing there, revealing his sad, flaccid coke-dick. For once, I am so grateful to the gods of impotence. Thank you, Jesus.

"Edward, we have to go," Elizabeth says, disgusted. "We have the shoot tomorrow."

It is now 4:30 a.m., and in their rush to leave, some of their porn props are still scattered around my apartment, which is also littered with empty beer cans and cigarettes. When they're gone, I am pacing the room, ready to jump out my window. I log onto Craigslist and post an ad on Casual Encounters. "Need to get fucked now," it reads.

A million replies flood my in-box, and I click on one that catches my eye. Ken, an engineer, includes a link to his professional website. I watch a reel that attests to his professionalism and work ethic. Yeah, this is the guy.

Before Ken arrives, I light a red-and-gold glitter Wiccan love-potion candle I've purchased to help me find my soul mate and fix my love life. Seems to be working so far!

I change into some black sheer Wolford thigh-highs and dance around to Weezer until the doorbell rings. When Ken arrives, I answer the door wearing only the stockings.

"Oh, hey, let me do, like, a fashion show for you," I tell my new suitor, pulling Ken into my living room before digging through my closet to try on various Halloween costumes. I change into my slutty nurse outfit. Then my slutty pilot one. Then my slutty Sacagawea.

Before I can find slutty nuclear physicist or whatever comes next, Ken lifts me up to carry me to my bed. But my feet stretch out and knock over the Wiccan candle, splattering red and gold wax all over my cream carpet.

"Fuck!" I say. "That's my love-potion thingy. I *need* that."

Ken shrugs and sets me down on my bed, but as he does, something catches his eye. Ken looks a little freaked out. I look over and see what he is seeing.

"What the hell?" he says.

One of the porn props Edward and Elizabeth left behind that fell out of their bag is the most enormous dildo you've ever seen in your life.

Ken picks it up off the ground with a sly smile.

"Oh, that's not mine," I say by way of explanation. "It belongs to this S&M couple who were over here earlier. We had a failed three-way, and I did coke for the first time."

"Sure," Ken says, shaking his head in disbelief. "That makes sense."

As debauched and ridiculous as the evening is, I love the debauchery and ridiculousness of it all. I tell myself I am a sort of modern Hunter S. Thompson with a vagina. I tell myself these stories are gold. I tell myself that I'm in control because I'm the one doing this. But there is no control. I'm just lost.

Not long after, I have a few more Casual Encounters with men who are seeking "snow bunnies" (women to do coke with) or "girls to show off." I even answer an ad where the guy offers "100 roses," which means dollars. But I can't bring myself to take the

cash at the end of it. So instead we watch *Apollo 13*, and I lecture
him on "repetition compulsion theory" and how I totally know
what I'm doing with all of these seedy sexual encounters before
I leave.

Another night, I go to a high-rolling *Post* party where I arrive
stoned, and a lawyer plucks me right off the vine, kisses me, and
takes me back to his place. He orders coke, and I do it off a plate
while he watches patiently before carrying me into his bedroom.
When I leave, I don't want the night to end, so I answer an ad on
Craigslist from a guy who posts only a JPEG of his dick.

It's like "Choose Your Own Adventure: Sex Death Wish Edition." He lives at a Central Park West address, and when I arrive I
think we are each somewhat relieved that we are both fairly normal. He's an investment banker (of course he is). Only when I tell
him what I do, he starts to get nervous about how high I am already
and how much of his coke I want to do.

"I don't know," he says. "I don't want a *Post* reporter to die on
me, man."

I wish I could say the same.

. . . .

NOTHING REALLY FILLS me up anymore, so I decide I might as
well just say yes to everything.

As I'm on my way home to my apartment one evening, carrying
some groceries I've just picked up at the store, a good-looking man
approaches me.

"Excuse me," he says.

"What?" I ask, looking into his eyes, which approach a color
close to blackness.

"I wanted to ask you," he says, looking at me and my bag of groceries. "Would you want to get a drink sometime? I find you very attractive. My name is Carlos."

"How does now suit you?" I ask.

With me still carrying my bag of now-spoiling groceries, we walk together to Spring Lounge.

"I should tell you something," Carlos says when we sit down. "About three years ago, I hit on you when you lived in Park Slope."

He then repeats line for line everything he said and how I reacted. I have to admit, I'm a little weirded out.

"Wait, you didn't, like, follow me and find out where I live to hit on me again, did you?"

"No," he says. "Nothing like that."

I'm not entirely convinced, but he can't be any more dangerous than all the assorted strangers I've kept company with of late in my little apartment-cum-sadness brothel. Fuck it. Who cares.

But when the two of us finally go over to his apartment, I see laid out on his desk a bunch of clippings from the *Post* scattered around, *Homeland* theory corkboard style.

"What the hell," I say. "You *are* stalking me, aren't you?"

"You think too much of yourself," he says.

We go into his bedroom, which is painted completely black, and lie down on his air mattress.

"Can you grab me a beer?" I ask. "I think I need to drink in order to hang out with you."

We drink and talk and drink and talk, fool around a little, get naked, come close to having sex, and eventually we are talking again. He asks me why I got divorced.

So I tell him how my ex cheated on me and then maybe I veer

off into sadness, talking about being sad and trying to have the courage to be an authentic human being.

"I want some attention," he says. Then he gets on top of me and thrusts his uncircumcised cock into my dry vagina. He groans and it's over fairly quickly.

"What the fuck," I say. "I wasn't ready for sex."

"That was not sex," he says. "That was rape."

I turn to him, aghast.

"It was a joke," he says. "You do not get my sense of humor."

No, I get it all right.

Then because he had not gotten his fill of debasement, perhaps, he grabs one of our empty beer bottles and penetrates me. I don't say no. I am not forced. But it is bleak, man. I would say the whole experience feels like a "consensually abusive" romp.

"I don't want to date you," I tell him eventually. "This is over."

"Well," says Carlos, always the master troll, "if I shoot myself in the head two months from now, it is not because of you."

I shake my head and leave. He follows me for a little bit, but eventually, I lose him.

. . . .

I WISH I could say that all these twisted and depraved sexual misadventures were wake-up calls for me. But no, all they do is make me wax nostalgic for my days as the secret girlfriend to a rich dude whose biggest relationship skill was in wasting a few years of my thirties. How the hell is Blaine anyway? On a whim, when Fashion Week rolls around, I invite him to a big supermodel party at Rose Bar. I don't want to date him again. But I think that looking in his eyes will remind me of a simpler, depressing-for-totally-different-reasons time not so long ago.

When I spot Blaine across the room, I make my usual nightmare-grade inappropriate small talk ("Hey, guess what, I tried cocaine for the first time!"), and all the while proceed to slam down martini after martini. I find him boring, and I want to make sure he knows that. So as Blaine watches, I begin to flirt with everyone in the immediate vicinity—his friends, the caterers, my cowork-ers, gay men just trying to get out of my way—until eventually the night kind of blurs out. But I do have the photographic evidence to document what happens next. Because I go home with an actual photographer.

We apparently go to several more bars that night in which I pose and smile with empty dead eyes and duck face. The next morning, I come to consciousness again. I didn't fall asleep this time. I was just—not there at all—even though I seemed like I was.

When I realize that this photographer is fucking me without a condom, my stomach turns.

"I think I'm going to be sick," I say, and race to the bathroom and begin vomiting.

As I'm puking my guts out, Garth the photographer compli-ments me all the while.

"I don't think you realize how hot you are," he says, which just makes me puke even more. "I'm never going to wash my fingers again."

When I finally lift my head off the toilet, I tell him why I got so drunk, how stupid I am, how I invited Blaine to the party, and ap-parently all of this makes a very memorable impression. Because, I kid you not, a few days later, Garth texts me a picture—of Blaine. Garth runs into him at some socialite party he's covering, and somehow, Garth puts two and two together that Blaine is the ex I told him about in between vomit takes.

"I told him I was shooting for *Gawker*," Garth explains via text, "and he said he had a friend who had an ongoing battle with them who writes for the *Post*. To extrapolate, he mentioned your name, and I said we met once."

God, how I love the coded message of man speak. "A friend." "We met once." *So good.*

But I have to be honest, I do *kind of* love that Blaine can't help but bring me up at parties. I know him well enough to remember how he was always bragging about famous or interesting people he knew when he got a little bit of a buzz on.

That means I won, right? I'm now the girl he can't help bring up when he's tipsy. *I rule.*

But the next day, Garth sends me one final update. It turns out one of the pictures Garth snapped of Blaine at this benefit for the preservation of money or whatever the hell it was is now going to be published—on fucking *Gawker*. The gossip site that used to write about my column all the time and that Blaine lived in terror of being outed on.

"So I emailed Blaine to tell him he was in one of the shots," Garth texts me, "and he asked me not to mention you. Nice guy, yeah."

You know that feeling when you think you have finally achieved amazing washboard abs but then it turns out someone has actually sucker punched you in the stomach? That's how I feel. So. Much. Ouch.

Of all the symbolic interactions I've had with Blaine, this one beats them all. Fucking Blaine brings me up. Fucking Blaine mentions me. Then fucking Blaine begs the fucking photographer he mentioned me to in the first place to "please please please don't say I dated Mandy Stadtmiller." Good God, man, stop being so afraid of life.

And me? Maybe I should start being a little *more* afraid of it.

Because I'm freaked out I woke up with this photog rando who wasn't using a condom, I make the necessary Plan B purchase, but I also decide I need to make some kind of change. I know what I need to do, obviously. Stop drinking. So that's what I resolve to do. It's not like I have to go to some depressing AA meeting or anything. I'm not some weirdo alcoholic. I'll just . . . stop. On my own. I've done it before.

Not too long after *Gawker* runs their beautiful non-Mandy-associated photo of Blaine, I get an email from him out of the blue. I've just written a groundbreaking feature on the "hot new trend" of threesomes, and what do you know, Blaine read the piece.

"Was reading the *Post* at the gym today, nice article on 3sums," he writes. "How are things going, what are you wearing for Halloween?"

What am I wearing? I want to punch my fist into the computer screen. That's what the fuck I'm wearing. Instead, I write a terse passive-aggressive reply: "I'm wearing a costume that says, 'Garth, please don't mention that I dated Mandy Stadtmiller if you post that picture of me on *Gawker.*' Things have never been better. Take care."

I think it's fairly clear in that email that I'm pissed, right?

Instead of offering any kind of acknowledgment as to how this was yet another insult in a long line of them, Blaine replies: "Garth seems like a nice guy though I guess discretion is not his middle name! Funny picture and saw no need to advertise it, hope all is going swimmingly with you. Can you help us out with an event in December we are doing?"

So fucking tacky.

I've never felt so glad to be single. No matter how much I am spiraling out, I feel a weird sense of freedom in knowing I refuse to ever sink as low as that relationship brought me again.

....

BUT . . . LET'S BE real. I am so, so spiraling out.

The newest wrinkle in my sex life is that I have now recruited my friend Bianca (who I met while on retreat with Amma, the so-called hugging saint of India) to be my partner in crime. It's so perfect somehow that I met her at this super-hippie patchouli-scented spiritual convention, and that instead of praying or whatever, we end up having a bunch of creepy sex romps. We have one, then two, then five three-ways. We're definitely not average on the Kinsey scale to be sure, but neither of us is really all that into pussy. No, I would say these three-ways are our sad aging-party-girl versions of slumber parties where we get to dish on the man afterward—and not feel dumb when he doesn't call. I suppose, in some ways, they are also my meager attempt at having love and consistency in my life.

But that isn't even the spiral-out part. Where it gets really dark is when I begin an affair with a married man—something I said I would never do.

The night we meet, I don't go home with him, nor does it even come up—but he does roast me in a way that is slightly thrilling. He is an award-winning comedy writer whom I've met in the course of covering the scene. I go to see him perform at his suggestion, and afterward we grab a drink at the bar . . . talking. Because you know, that's beyond reproach, right? Nothing wrong with that. Men and women do that all the time.

When the bartender comes to get my drink order, I proudly

stick to the no-alcohol rule I've kept up for a few months now since the *Gawker* photographer no-condom debacle.

"I'll get a water," I say, and then apologetically offer by way of explanation, "I stopped drinking a few months ago. I'm just so over the top as it is, you know."

He looks at my six-foot-two frame.

"You're a pretty big girl."

"Whoa." I laugh. "Don't ever tell a girl she's 'big.' I'm tall. And I fucking hate it when people give me shit about my height."

His eyes twinkle.

"Why?" he says. "Just because your height makes you a mutant, is that what you mean?"

I laugh. I am amazed, horrified, delighted. I like dickhead funny when it is actually funny.

"Yeah, I just try to look like a model," I say. "That's what I can only hope a guy will fetishize, you know. Being pretty and skinny."

He glares at me. A glimmer of a smile.

"But you're not," he says. "Pretty or skinny."

"Man," I say, laughing louder than I have in a while, "I love what a cocksucker you are. That's hilarious. It's fun to be eviscerated in such a clean, asshole-y way."

That night he requests me on Facebook, and we keep in touch.

When I write a satirical piece in the *Post* giving advice to men on how to have an affair—based on the shit show of a tabloid story that is ESPN talking head Steve Phillips's cheating scandal—not too long after, with perfect irony, I get a message from the Married Man.

"Excellent article," he writes. "You certainly know your infidelity."

I lie to myself and think: *Wow, this guy thinks I'm really funny*

and what a great ally he'll be to me in the entertainment industry.
Instead of the truth of the situation: *This is chum. He wants to have
an affair.*

This guy doesn't like my talent. He likes my insecurity—and
my fear that I have none.

Soon after, the text comes. "Want to get together tonight? My
wife is out of town."

"Wait," I text back. "You're married."

"Yes, I am," he replies. "Want to come over?"

So now the moral question is laid out in front of me with perfect transparency.

I can't decide to do something like this on my own. I need some
kind of magical realism outside person to blame for what I do or
don't do. So I duck outside of the *Post* and call an old married
friend of mine who is *the* perfect husband, thinking he can talk
me out of it.

"I don't know," my friend says. "I don't necessarily think it's
such a bad thing."

"Wait," I balk. "Do *you* cheat on your wife?"

I can hear his hesitation on the phone, and because I'm a
human bullshit detector, I know.

"Well, clearly you do," I say. "Let me just give you some advice.
If your wife ever asks, don't pause—not even for a second."

I end the call, stare at my phone, and write the Married Man
back asking what time I should come over.

I've just been given the "everything is shit anyway" mental justification I was looking for in talking to my friend. When in reality,
I'm the one who is actively making things shit myself.

When I was married to James and found out about my ex-
husband's affairs, I recoiled, emailing these women years later at

2 a.m. from my work computer at the *Post* with the one-line message "Just wanted to say you're a cunt."

Oh, how wrong I was. I am the cunt. The Married Man is the cunt. We are all the cunt. Anyone who has ever cheated (and the statistics are utterly depressing) is a huge fucking cunt.

That night, the affair begins. When I arrive at the Married Man's apartment in central Manhattan, his eyes are already ablaze from several bong hits. He leads me into his study, overflowing with Emmys. One of the globes has come off, and he rolls it around in his hands.

"That's the problem with these things—they break," he says.

Then he tosses it to me to catch.

"Nice move," I say.

Then he hands me his bong.

I haven't been drinking or drugging for a few months now, but I know I'm about to do something wrong—really wrong. I need some plausible deniability as to why I did it, right? Alcohol and drugs are so great for that. Without a moment's hesitation, I lift the bong to my lips—and inhale deeply, feeling the wash of simpleton fluidity. Such a relief not to think.

Just like that, my weak-ass attempt at sobriety is blown. I cough, and he hands me a beer to wash it down.

"It's good, isn't it?" he says.

I nod through my coughing fit. Yes. It's good.

He keeps checking. "Are you high yet?" he asks. "Want some more?"

"Yes," I finally say. "I'm high."

He comes over to the couch where I am sitting, looks at me with sickness and excitement in his eyes, and kisses me.

"I was afraid that might happen," he says. He starts taking off my clothes and says, "Let's go to the bedroom."

He is so hungry, so out of control. He presses his face into mine, asking, "Did you think about me all day? Did you feel it the instant we met? I want to fuck you all the time. Say it. Say you'll fuck me all the time."

That's when it hits me: *Oh my God. This is an ego fuck. I am fucking his ego.*

"Yes," I say. "Yes."

Afterward, we smoke cigarettes on his balcony.

"Holy shit," he says. "Now I'm thinking about what I've done. I just did a horrible thing. *You* are a temptress."

Not really. Just a fellow self-sabotaging depressive, but whatever.

The next time I see the Married Man I meet him at a Thai place near the *Post* for dinner, and he dryly brings up the newest cheating scandal dominating the headlines.

"Can you believe this Tiger Woods thing?" he says with an angry straight face. "What kind of a scumbag cheats on his wife?"

I laugh, hate myself, feel aroused, and hate myself some more.

Any moral high ground I ever held over the Other Women who fooled around with my ex-husband is wiped out. Everything I've done—everything I'm doing right in this moment—is unjustifiable, unredeemable. It provides such a surprising sense of relief, too. It feels like freedom. No burdens. No moral questions. Say yes to every bad idea and accept that you are a bad person. You can't get lower than that, right?

But eventually my conscience does catch up. I ask the Married Man if we can just be friends. No, he tells me. He's not interested in that.

This makes me angry in a very specific way. Why do I have to lose out on this guy's friendship when I try to do the right thing? Fuck it. I'll just make things even worse then.

So instead of shutting it down, I bring my three-way companion Bianca into the mix.

"Want to get a hotel with me and my friend?" I text him one evening after one of our most recent trysts at the St. Marks Hotel. His reply is instantaneous. When and where?

I'm riding high now on just shrugging off any kind of consequences or responsibility. Because, I mean, society is so fucked-up and a guy who I thought was the perfect husband is cheating and the gun control problem and 9/11, so why bother, right? Everyone is terrible and we're all going to die. When you make everything into this big awful incredibly gallows humor joke, you can pretty much justify anything.

"Let's go shopping," I suggest to Bianca. We stroll into American Apparel, and the young gay clerk keeps bringing us boring outfits until we finally tell him what's up.

The clerk smiles. "Three-way with a married guy? I know *just* what you're looking for."

I buy a sheer body stocking and Bianca gets a barely-covering-her-ass blue mesh dress. Now fully costumed, we meet the Married Man at the Standard in the East Village.

"I told my wife I was at *Avatar*," he says.

As I kiss and undress Bianca, I ask in a nauseating infantilized voice, "How do you like the movie?"

We all get stoned, and it is fun for about a minute. But when he begins fucking Bianca, it's like I have disappeared completely. Of course that happens. What the hell did I think would happen? She's fresh meat. So after a few minutes, I just bolt completely.

A few weeks later, Bianca comes to see me perform at Jon Friedman's *Rejection Show* at the Bell House in Brooklyn, and she comes up to me at the bar, glowing and flush with the scent of sex.

"Dude," I say. "Did you just come from seeing him?"

Bianca beams and says, "We have a new place. The Liberty Inn!"

I snatch my phone and send the Married Man a text with just the name of the hotel and a question mark. He doesn't write back, which is unusual.

It is Valentine's Day. His wife found the phone. His wife read the text.

I have just completely devastated this man's marriage.

Neither Bianca nor I ever see him again.

Of all the shitty things I've done, I think hurting his family is perhaps the worst of all. But I also very much believe that it is the hiding of our secrets that create our sickness. There's no excuse for what I did. There's no excuse for what he did either.

It wasn't all for naught, though. Because I am positive that after that disaster, the Married Man never cheated on his wife again. Most men never do—when they realize just how close they have come to losing everything that really matters.

....

FORTUNATELY FOR MY career at the *Post*, I have nothing that really matters.

One day I get a more-urgent-than-normal email from my new editor.

"Let's discuss a nutty adventure story that's come up," she writes. While I highly doubt there could be any adventure that's nuttier than the state of my current personal life, my editor quickly proves me wrong.

It turns out everyone in the media is talking about the announcement of "Markus," the very first legal male prostitute in America. Markus just gave an interview to *Details* about his thoughts on his role, an interview in which he, no lie, compared himself to Rosa Parks and Gandhi. They've stopped letting him do press because of this, so instead I book an appointment posing as an excited sex tourist.

Within the next seventy-two hours I have made a flight and car ride, eventually arriving at the tiny dusty yellow brothel known as Shady Lady Ranch in the middle of the Nevada desert.

Markus comes out to greet me, wearing a blue satin shirt, and guides me into a humble suite with a little Buddha statue. Then he asks me for $500 and tells me that we will first need to "inspect each other in the shower to make sure there are no discrepancies."

Holy crap. A shower immediately? I've already decided I have no interest in sleeping with this guy. Hookers just don't really do it for me. I'm all about the ego fuck, too, when it comes right down to it. But who am I kidding? I'm not going to blow this assignment just because I don't want to stand naked in the shower with the guy.

Dignity? Never met her.

The two of us stand together awkwardly in the water, and I do a barely glancing "inspection" of this twenty-five-year-old Alabama native with an eight-and-a-half-inch dick who looks a bit like Steve-O. I know how the sex worker industry works. They keep tighter standards than most guys you meet online. Markus looks me up and down and shares his assessment.

"Wow," he says, "you're like an eight or a nine."

So good. If I did write a Yelp review of the experience, I would be sure to add: *If a lady is paying half a grand for your time, maybe just go for bust and say ten.*

I quickly put my clothes back on, and we move to the bed, but his unrelenting pressure for me to touch him is irritating. There's something bittersweet about the fact that even when you hire a guy to be your companion, it still feels like a shitty second date in New York.

"I love oral," Markus says, showing me various ribbed prophylactics. "I love eating. I'm telling you, you're not getting the full experience. You will come your pants. I'm serious."

As romantic as that sounds, I decline. So he tries a different tactic.

"Or I can put a condom on, and you can give me oral? Or . . . I love to be stroked."

"Yeah, it's just . . . I don't think I'm that good at it," I say, thinking about how good at it I am. "But I think it's hot when guys get themselves off. I want to see how you touch yourself, because every time I've done it I've messed it up."

"Sweetie," he says, beginning to jerk himself off, "you've paid for this. You just stroke in a slow rhythmic motion."

I fully embrace the virginal rube character I'm doing now. "Doesn't that hurt?" I ask.

"No, that doesn't hurt at all," he says, laughing. "This is a learning experience for you. It's soft and hard *at the same time.*"

As he jerks off, Markus waxes on philosophically about politics and psychology and literature and Buddhism. Then he asks me to "stroke him off"—once again.

I'm starting to get a little worried he's suspicious about my complete lack of interest in doing anything sexual. So I give him a half-hearted hand job and call it a day.

When I fly back to New York, I am immediately put on deadline for the story. Around 6 p.m. I sign off on the final proof of my pages. But while reporters are shown the mock-up of their story inside the newspaper, if the story ends up on the front page—or "the wood" as it's called in tabloid parlance (because it used to be set with wooden slabs)—we don't really see it.

While I never have reason to go up to the tenth floor where the A-1 page is set and designed, Mackenzie does. So, as she's upstairs doing some important editor stuff, she just happens upon the next day's cover all mocked up and ready to go. "Would You Pay $500 to Have Sex with This Man? Our Reporter Did!"

Mackenzie does a double take and finds the designer. "You guys, Mandy *didn't sleep with him*. You guys know that, right?"

It gets changed last-minute to "Spend the Night." Better. But it doesn't really matter. Because the next day, the pickup on the piece translates like an international game of telephone. By the time it reaches Turkey the translation is "US Reporter Sleeps with Male Hooker for News" and leads to a lot of fan mail in broken English saying things like, "Best journalism! Very hard working assignment looking good." In Asia, one of those creepy yet hilarious animations is done, featuring me and Markus taking a shower, making passionate love, bickering—and making passionate love again. The press requests are insane, and within a span of a couple of hours I've had to turn down *The View* while making appearances on *Inside Edition, Joy Behar,* and tons of radio from around the world.

At the end of this very long day, I head to Langan's alone to get a drink. I've gotten only a few hours of sleep and am fried. As I sip on a Maker's, I check my email at the bar and get a Google news alert that *Gawker* has written a follow-up piece to their morning link to the story.

"Should the *New York Post* Hire Hookers? Media Types Spend the Day Jeering."

Meanwhile, Markus, whose real name is Patrick L. Norton, actually loves the attention. He writes on his Facebook, "If I can help and be satirized so be it. . . . I've never felt so important in my entire life."

I feel happy for him and betrayed by whoever the hell is sending in tips about me. But whatever, that person at *Gawker* is just doing their job, too. I get it far too well.

Over at the other end of the bar, I spot a Fox reporter I've chatted with before, and we joke around about the prosti-dude until I realize how spent I am. Which means I have two choices: self-care . . . or ensure that the night provides a distraction enough from the self that so badly needs caring for.

"Give me one good reason to stay," I tell the reporter.

He has an answer at the ready. "I have really good drugs." Yeah. That sounds right.

So we head into the Langan's bathroom and begin sharing an eight-ball, and I feel that same spinning, speeding rush of asshole invincibility I love so much. When I tell him I need to head back to the *Post* to pick up all my shit, the two of us have the brilliant idea that I should definitely do a bump off my desk. Because: story.

When we get back to his place in Midtown, I can't stop rambling. Everything about the day is so preposterously heightened already, but that's not enough. Nothing is ever enough for me. I want to go darker, weirder, sadder, kinkier, more. So I ask him if we can role-play.

"How about I pretend I'm . . . fifteen," I suggest. "And let's, like, make it really crazy."

He "yes ands" my shitty sexual improv in the most hilarious way possible.

"Okay, yeah," he says. "Yeah . . . and, uh, if you don't sleep with me . . . I'm going to fucking kill you!"

I fully burst out laughing.

"Okay, maybe not *that* extreme," I suggest.

"You're a whore," he says.

"Sure," I say. "That works."

. . . .

DURING THE COURSE of writing the prosti-dude piece, I become friends with one the *Post's* top lawyers, and soon, sexual partners with him, too. It's becoming clearer and clearer what a dangerous game my life is becoming.

Back at his place, as we are sixty-nining in his bed, I whisper in a sickly little girl voice, "I'm going to file a sexual harassment claim against you!"

"Just . . . please . . ." he says, "stop . . . talking."

Is it fun? I don't know. Is self-harm fun? You be the judge.

When I leave his place, I limp back home and try to figure out what the hell I'm even doing with all these degrading hookups.

I can't help but remember what a friend once told me about how he had been sober for several years. At the time, I surprised myself with my reaction. "Huh," I said, "I should probably do that." He told me if I ever wanted to check out a "meeting" to give him a call.

This time, I think I might finally be ready.

Because things are getting weird. I can see that. I'm acting rashly. I'm making stupid decisions. Not only have I hooked up with a company lawyer, I have also fooled around with News Corp's very hot maintenance guy in his giant office (no idea why that dude had such a giant office) while he told me secrets like knowing who was going to get fired first because he handled key card deactivations.

Something has to happen. Otherwise, how long until I've

worked my way through the entire News Corp building and am fired in some kind of spectacular scene, then carted off to rehab?

Trying not to overthink it too much, I call up this sober friend, and we make plans to go to a lunchtime AA meeting on Houston Street. As soon as I walk into the slightly run-down but very lovingly cleaned old building, I feel like I'm entering church.

These people seem like they've seen some shit. These people feel like my people.

Near the end of the meeting, there are only a few minutes left, and while I didn't intend to speak, I shoot up my hand impulsively. "My name is Mandy," I say, and then, without even realizing I'm going to, I identify myself for the first time in my life, "and I'm an alcoholic."

The moment the words come out of my mouth it feels like such a huge weight has been lifted off me. It's like a different kind of rush. But I don't treat it with real respect. I don't think about what it means. And in the days that follow, I don't actually go to another meeting. After eight days of not drinking, my "sobriety" is starting to feel like something dangerously familiar. It's starting to feel like one of my stories.

But no matter. All I have to do is just not drink. One day at a time. Everyone knows that.

I even shine a little brighter from not drinking. When I go to a Page Six going-away party, it doesn't even surprise me when a gorgeous twenty-seven-year-old Leonardo DiCaprio type named Alex starts talking me up for what seems like hours. Everything feels so great and fun and free. Hell, I'm even *meeting* amazing guys in sobriety.

Alex flatters me by asking me a lot of questions and expressing endless interest, and I launch into my balls-to-the-wall, trying-to-impress, super-extreme-honesty, sexual-anecdotal Tourette's mode, telling him some of my greatest-hits stories to just do it up, lay it all on the line. My closer is, of course, being on the cover of the newspaper with the gigolo.

"Wow, I love it," Alex says. "You're not like a normal girl, are you? You're *unusual*."

I beam proudly. Man, this guy *really* gets me. I *am* so cool. It feels so nice to be seen, to be recognized, to be appreciated.

"You know," Alex says, looking at me with measured intensity, "there are these swinger parties they have. Except you need a woman to go with, and I've never met a girl cool enough."

Ah yes . . . there it is.

I have not been working this guy. This guy has been working me—the whole time. His follow-up statement reveals just how obvious a mark I really am.

"It's so funny," Alex continues, "there's actually a party tonight."

I look at him and I feel naked already. Like my clothes have been ripped off and every shameful flaw is on display. My heart drops a little. I glare down at the nonalcoholic water I'm holding in my hand and have been dutifully drinking like some asshole. I feel a flash of rage. Who am I kidding? Everyone knows who I am, even strangers I've just met.

I'm the girl you take to a sex club.

"All right, you little shit," I say, harder than before. "I'll take that drink now. Because I'm not drinking water if I'm going to a fucking orgy."

Before we reach the club in the Meatpacking District where the dubiously named One Leg Up party is being held, Alex grabs my hand and whispers: "I'm your boyfriend now."

I laugh, but it also secretly delights me. Of course, I know what he's doing. He's just trying to ensure we appear to be a real couple and will be let inside. Versus the reality of what happened, which is that he is a single horny guy who wants in to the party, so he plucked a chick off the street whose self-worth is so in the gutter she's literally up for going to a last-minute sex orgy—like, within two hours of meeting.

Outside the mysterious China One club, Alex gives the password ("I'm naughty") and whips out two hundred-dollar bills for entry. One for him. One for me.

We head down the stairs to the lounge below, elliptical Moroccan music encircling us, and he takes my hand again, guiding us to the bar to get drinks, then to a maroon velvet banquette on the side. The two of us sidle up next to a buxom British chick who is pouring out of a tight red dress and snuggling up next to some dashing Peter O'Toole–looking motherfucker.

The Absolut I'm downing is starting to take effect. I'm feeling loose, brash, and free.

"We should play a get-to-know-you game!" I say to this ridiculously attractive couple. "Like truth or dare or something."

"Ooh yes, okay, me first," the man pipes up. "How about, I dare you . . . Mandy, is it? I dare you to go down on Sylvie here. Sylvie just loves girls."

"No problem," I say, smiling and empty. As I walk over to Sylvie, a small crowd begins to form, which includes the resident coke dealer—whose job is to obviously know where the action is before anyone else.

No one wanted to buy any coke.

"Oh, that's okay," the dealer says to me, "I just want the visual so . . . I'm going to give you a bump to do off that girl's big-ass titties so I can have that burned in my brain, okay?"

I do the line greedily, then dutifully lift the bottom of Sylvie's dress and slowly lick her clit, all the while perking my ass up in order to best pornify the whole encounter for Alex and all our new friends.

"Oooh, my turn!" Sylvie cries out. "Mandy, I want you to go down on Alex!"

The energy changes a little, and Alex looks annoyed.

"Sure," he says, clipped and less confident than I've seen him all night.

I soon see why. Alex is adorable, but this is his best—his biggest—attribute.

There are times like this in life when you are really forced to woman up to be who the man you are with needs you to be. And I am *not* going to let Alex down.

"Oh yeah," I say, summoning every acting lesson I've ever had. "Mmm, give it to me."

I get on my knees, count to a hundred Mississippi, and do the best object work of my life.

Yeah—my first attempt at sobriety is not going well *at all*.

. . . .

EVEN WORSE THAN blowing my eight days of sobriety is the unbearable guilt I feel at having totally blown eight days of sobriety. I hate more than anything the feeling that I've done something wrong. It's a debilitating kind of perfectionism I've had since childhood where I'm so afraid to have done something wrong that I stubbornly stick to whatever wrong choice I've made—all so I can avoid the shame of having to admit I screwed up in the first place. So instead of returning to the rooms of AA, I stick to my guns that

I did the right thing in going back to partying. Besides, you never know, Alex the sex-club boy might . . . actually . . . be interested in me?

I am so dumb. But, truly, from the moment Alex grabbed my hand and said, "I'm your boyfriend now" and talked about going on a "sexual heart of darkness" journey with me, I thought there might be a real connection. That he would call. That he would want to hang out again. That the drinking and the partying and all of it was worth it—the *right* thing to do. It had to add up to something . . . right?

But the sun still rises in the east, the sky is blue, and of course he doesn't call.

That doesn't mean I can't talk about the experience, though, to get the whole thing out of my system. Which leads me to a conversation with a man who is a friend of friends. When I spill to him the details of that crazy night, he tells me that he, too, has been to sex clubs. He seems to accept my weirdness, and I like that. He gives me weed and booze and coke, and I like that even more. It's an escape. That's all I'm seeking. Just one more escape. Just for a little while.

But the higher we get together, the darker our encounter becomes. He slaps me, insults me, and jerks my hair in a way that feels like my neck is snapping. It doesn't feel like playful S&M. It feels sinister.

When I finally sober up to realize I need to get the fuck out of his apartment, I rush to get dressed in the dark. I don't want to have sex with him. I don't want to be this fucked-up. I don't want any of this. As I'm walking out the door I ask him weakly, "Can we just be friends?"

"I don't think so," he replies.

His rejection confirms all my worst fears. He knows what I am good for—and when I don't give him that, I'm good for absolutely nothing. As I walk home in the rain as the morning light starts to break, my mind races as I chain-smoke and stare at the disgusting pavement below. None of this is fun anymore. *None of it.* I feel like I am offering myself up as some kind of human sacrifice for a story that has long since lost the plot.

When I wilt into my crumpled-up pile of sheets at home, I grab my phone and study the cracked screen. Someone inside my iPhone must genuinely care about me, surely. But I don't want to burden my friends. I know my family doesn't want to know how bad things have gotten. I don't want to break everyone's heart.

Scrolling through my contacts, I swallow my pride and dial a sober comic I know who's given me really straightforward advice in the past. Truthfully, though, I feel like a jerk for even reaching out, because I spoke to him a few weeks back when I tried sobriety the first time around—and he congratulated and supported me. Then, of course, I cockily updated him on exactly why sobriety wasn't for me and how I obviously had to drink because of my super-legendary swinger's club night. That time, he was still nice, but his response was more distant and polite.

No worries, Mandy. Sounds fun.

This time around, I drop the act entirely.

"I don't understand why . . . I just feel so incredibly sad," I confess over the phone, my eyes closed, my voice choked and thick with grief. Why is this all hitting me so hard this time?

He isn't cold to me in his tone, but he isn't indulgent either. Instead, he gives me what I need more than anything else: a cut-through-the-bullshit lifeline.

"You know, Mandy," he says, "you can keep calling me up every few weeks, or you can change your life."

Wow.

This lands—so, so hard.

You. Can. Change. Your. Life.

His words strike me like a thunderbolt. I know right then and there that if I don't decide this moment, this day—June 28, 2010—is truly my "low point" that I might not come back at all.

The next morning feels different when I wake up. I have a purpose. A goal. I can change my life. I can decide things. No one else. No matter how tempting drinking and drugs are, no matter how much they feel like an inevitability or a necessity—I can always choose to stay sober. I see that now. I see what I did wrong. And it's okay that I have been wrong so many times. The very next day, after work, I go to an AA meeting in SoHo, where I weep and tell a story that only makes sense to me to a room filled with strangers. I see the beauty, the peace, the freedom in admitting my weaknesses and my flaws. I feel how powerful it is to admit how truly powerless I am. Someone gently gives me my first twenty-four-hour coin, and I put it in my purse like the precious object it is. One sweet girl suggests to me a meeting that's good for newcomers. That meeting leads to another and another, and for a few weeks, I'm really doing okay. I'm doing pretty good.

I have twenty-two days of sobriety. I have a new life. And then—I finally hear from Alex the sex-club boy again.

There is another "party" coming up, he says, and we should go. The male-validation pull is strong with this one. Convince me to go, I tell him. After a few texts, he does.

The night of the party, this time at Macao, this time with the password "ultimate fantasy," we have an incredibly tame evening. I don't even kiss Alex. I just observe and have a genuinely fun time making observations and interviewing people. I ask a tiny Asian woman getting fucked from behind, "So what do you do for a living?" She replies, "I'm a CPA!" The guy fucking her says, "And I'm a corporate investigator!" It is all very normal.

At one point Alex brings up the fact that I went to Northwestern, and I'm genuinely surprised he remembers. He responds, "Oh, I have a little app on my phone that tells me which school the girls I take to sex clubs graduated from."

Over the course of the evening, five things occur that do not seem like accidents.

1.　The bartender brings me a free drink that I did not order. I refuse.
2.　At the entrance to the party, the organizer squirts vodka into people's mouths. I refuse.
3.　Inside the party, they squirt vodka into people's mouths. I refuse.
4.　Inside the party, Alex brings me a drink. I refuse.
5.　After the party, Alex and I go back up to the bar, where I order a Pellegrino. I am brought a champagne.

The gesture feels like some sort of cruel joke. I have literally never had alcohol forced on me so many times when I didn't ask for it.

Could it be a sign? Maybe it is a sign. Maybe I should just keep drinking. Maybe . . .

I look at the alcohol. I look at Alex. I don't say no. Justifications in my mind are hitting me rapid-fire now. Instead of picking it up, though, my hands instinctively fumble around inside my purse, and without realizing what I'm doing, that's when I feel it: the twenty-four-hour chip.

I cling to it like it's a life raft and stare at the champagne, stare at Alex. This guy doesn't give a shit about me. I know that. My fingers rub the coin intently, turning it over in my hands, and I think of all the women in AA I've spoken to over the last few weeks. Women who don't even know me, but I can already tell want to protect me more than I'm able to protect myself.

I don't want to give that up.

chapter eight

The Rebirth

2010–12

The "pink cloud" is real. That's a term in sobriety where you float around in a cloud of happiness, redemption, and seeming magic. I begin killing it at work and in my personal life.

One day I'm getting the first American interview exclusive with the Winklevoss twins, who've sued Mark Zuckerberg for stealing the idea of Facebook. Another day I am splashed in the *Post's* pages next to the *Guinness World Records* titleholder for world's shortest man—measuring in at twenty-two inches—who is visiting from Nepal. He asks me on a "date" as a swarm of photographers click their shutters to document me literally cradling this man-baby in my arms. (By the way: Never discount the world's shortest man for his lack of follow-up game. Five years later he messages me on Facebook: "Hi Mandy. You remember this picture?" And then, "You are bad." And then, "Or are not you?")

Overall, in my life, I feel largely unstoppable.

I get a sponsor, and I even start to make amends, which is kind of the worst—but hey, I'm unstoppable, right? The hardest one to make is with Hannibal Buress. The thing I have to make amends for is basically just me acting like a drunken idiot, but when I whisper the confession to my sponsor, relaying the excruciating details of it, my head hangs as if I'm confessing to a cross-state killing spree. Why do sometimes the smallest mortifications impact us the hardest? Maybe, in some way, because they are so real and cut to the quick of what we hate the most about ourselves.

What happened with Hannibal occurred near the end of my drinking days. After several hours spent smoking weed and chugging beer, I ran into him at a party. He had by this time gotten a job at *Saturday Night Live,* and, thinking I was being totally "hilarious," I approached him and started yelling accusingly, "I know more famous people than you!"

Yeah. I actually said that. With, like, multiple witnesses.

Needless to say, we didn't speak for months.

Now sober, apologizing to him and eventually making things right somehow represents a tiny redemption for me—and shows me that maybe it is possible to dig myself out of even the deepest ditches, instead of just finding new ones to fall into.

Unfortunately, this profoundly honest moment is also the exception. Getting sober isn't like a "buy groceries" to-do list where hey, you picked up the chicken so who cares if you forgot the pot to cook it in—you'll live . . . right? But I treat it that way—with blind flippancy and naïve disrespect. Because, honestly, it feels too painful to peel another layer away from the onion. So instead, I remain superficial about examining all the problems underlying my behavior. Instead of attempting to untangle the many mixed-up addictions at play, I decide to just pretend to be someone else entirely.

Of course, I didn't realize any of this at the time. But looking back, it's so completely clear.

I simply slipped from one costume to another.

I've now dropped the archetype of cocktail-party-flitting fake wife for Blaine. And I've given up the role of coked-up party girl who will do anything for debauched good time.

Now—I decide to be the Temptress. What the Married Man had once called me, I essentially drape on as an identity because hey, I'm sober now—and I'm definitely never going to fuck another married guy again—so it's okay, right?

Right?

Besides, playing a role protects me—from feeling any hurt I might feel if I was just being myself.

And so, without quite realizing what I am morphing into, I strut around the city and my job at the *Post*, playacting the jaded, conniving femme fatale. I use sobriety like a drug. It gives me superpowers of cognition and hyperawareness, and I take these enhancements as video game–style "boosts" to sidle up not just to rich dudes anymore—but now to the rich and famous.

Which is how in 2010 I start dating three men in media and celebrity who are all strangely interconnected—Aaron Sorkin, Keith Olbermann, and Lloyd Grove.

While the old nihilistic me would hash out the entirety of this gossip (and I could fill several books), I now realize that's the same person who didn't think she was worth anything on her own. This is perhaps the biggest realization I've had in writing all of this.

You don't need to "attach" yourself to anyone. You just need to make yourself someone who you can stand to be with—alone.

So instead of going deep-cut, I will only relay the highlights of this love triangle—and leave it as the final word on the matter.

Before I do, though, I suppose I should explain how I even met all three of these guys in the first place, as I'm by no means normally lounging at the Chateau Marmont or wherever the hell A-listers hang.

So I need to go back a few months to before I finally got sober, when I was a party-hopping maniac, often accompanied by my favorite companion: the comedian Wayne Federman. (If you google him and he looks familiar, you may know him as Garry Shandling's brother in *The Larry Sanders Show* or from his arc on *Curb Your Enthusiasm* or as being the guy from all those Judd Apatow movies. Incidentally, he's utterly fucking hilarious.)

Wayne and I had a very brief flirtation, but, in the end, the chemistry was off. We came to call it a whirlwind forty-eight-hour romance.

"What do you think is a bigger disaster," I asked him afterward. "This date or the *Titanic*?"

"Number one, the movie *Titanic*," he said. "Number two, this date. Number three, the actual *Titanic*."

And that's how we became friends.

When I was at my lowest, Wayne always made me laugh. In the months before quitting drinking, I told him how scared I was because I had gotten back test results for an irregular pap smear. Instead of indulging in my self-pity or piling even more anxiety on top of my own, he went totally deadpan—and provided a hugely cathartic laugh.

"Wow . . . that is exciting," Wayne replied. "This could be *it* for you."

Even remembering it now gives me this deep sense of relief that only the darkest of comedy can ever provide.

Wayne and I went to *SNL* after-parties together and watched as
Kristin Wiig did karaoke at 4 a.m. at Sing Sing and had several wild
nights at the Comedy Cellar. During one of these, he watched as I
had the world's most awkward encounter with John Mayer.

Buoyed by alcoholic confidence, I asked Mayer what he was
doing after the show.

"I don't know," he said. "Maybe I'll be waking up next to you."

When I watched Mayer onstage, I quickly sobered up as I realized he was referencing me being in the crowd.

"Page Six is here, by the way," Mayer said. "So I'd like to tell
everybody that I just fucked, um, Kate Hudson, yes, using—using
Megan Fox's hand. I thought that was quite crafty of me."

After quickly downing a few beers to have the nerve to approach
him after his set, I watched as his entire demeanor changed. Mingling with Dave Chappelle and Jeremy Piven, I waited for my
opening—and went for it.

"So, uh, could I get your . . . info?"

He glared at me.

"Why," Mayer asked, "are you still talking to me?"

And that was that.

But with Wayne by my side, the humiliation never felt quite as
intolerable as it might have alone.

As soon as I got sober, Wayne noticed the change in my outlook
overall. One night at Carolines, I told him how I was sick of acting
like this groveling low-status person all the time, and that I was
going to quit doing it.

"Actually," Wayne said, "that sounds like an excellent idea."

Cut to the first few months of sobriety.

During this time, I am assigned multiple stories on the film *The*

Social Network. When I interview the movie's famously mercurial producer, Scott Rudin, I keep the pledge I made to Wayne, and at the end of the call, instead of gushing all over Rudin as I might have in the past, I end the call by saying, in a monotone, "Well, good luck."

I get a concerned call a few days later from Rudin's assistant asking if there is anything else I "needed for the story." Amazing what just a little bit of projection of worth does for your status. After the piece publishes, I call Rudin and ask if I can get on the list, plus one, to New York Film Festival's opening-night party. Impressed by my moves, Wayne says I am like a "master-level chess player." I bring him to the party (and Wayne repays the favor by inviting me to take in the Yankees in Lorne Michaels's box seats when neither he nor Jimmy Fallon can use the tickets).

"Oh my God, there's Sorkin—I'm going to try to talk to him," I tell Wayne as we mingle after I nab a photo with Justin Timberlake, who says, "You're with the *Post*? You guys write shit about me like every day."

I literally dodge and weave Sorkin's assistant, and reach out to shake his hand.

"Oh, I kind of screwed that up," I say, laughing.

"Should we do it again?" Sorkin asks.

"Well, we could do the Bill Clinton double handshake," I say, imitating that. "Or the really creepy handshake."

Then I wiggle my finger into his palm. And hand him my card.

I get an email about an hour later—from Sorkin. I'm still at the party, and I show it to Wayne, my mouth open.

"Mandy, I'm really sorry I couldn't answer your questions tonight," he writes. "I hope you had a good time at the movie and the party and I hope I get to see you soon."

I also meet Lloyd Grove, who had been for a long time the *Daily News*'s answer to Richard Johnson. I ask him if he's interested in seeing the script for *The Social Network*, which one of the Winklevoss twins sent me. "Definitely," he says.

A few days after that, Wayne is again my plus-one at a party for the release of a Bill Hicks documentary. We are sitting in the audience still, watching folks head out of the Paley Center, when he says, "I think that's Keith Olbermann."

"Hey, Keith!" I yell, and Olbermann turns around.

The three of us spend the next hour geeking out over Bill Hicks's legacy and old Bob and Ray audio recordings. After a while, Keith offers to walk me to the subway, where he kisses me goodbye. I get a complimentary email from him with photos we took together and a friendly warning that he followed me on Twitter.

In the meantime, Lloyd asks me out, and he tells me all about interviewing Sorkin, which led to raised voices and tensions. I email Sorkin, feeling like I'm the cleverest person on the planet, saying, "I hear there was yelling? Sounds exciting . . ."

Sorkin replies, "Ah Mandy, Mandy, Mandy—if we were on a date and off the record, I would tell you all about it, but since we're neither, all I can say . . . 'What yelling?'"

"But I'm like the queen of off the record," I write back.

"And I'm the king of getting my ass kicked by Page Six," he replies.

With all this potential for self-created drama, I have found my new addiction.

So instead of figuring out how I can, you know, be a better person, I instead take to reading Robert Greene books like *The 48 Laws of Power* and *The Art of Seduction,* which recommend greasy soul-dead tactics like creating an aura of desirability through love triangles, instilling a "shared feeling of guilt and complicity," and trying to stir up regression by dabbing milk on your breasts—just in case a guy has a mommy complex.

I never get around to the milk part.

Essentially, I may be sober, but I'm still rotten on the inside: completely disingenuous in my interactions with men whom I want to please, trying to play some heartless seductress—because it feels like a role that is safe and powerful and can't ever be broken.

Instead, it's perhaps the most fragmented and phony I've ever been.

While Lloyd tells me why he doesn't like Olbermann, I also start to really fall for him. He's so able to laugh at himself and the moment he does the most searing imitation of Howard Stern mocking him in a very put-on affected voice, I think: *This is the guy.* When I tell Olbermann that I can't see him anymore because I'm going to be dating Lloyd exclusively, Olbermann replies, "Good grief, my mortal enemy."

Lloyd and I eventually do break up, but he treats me better than anyone up to this point in my life. There are so many hilarious moments during the relationship (I mean, the guy was good friends with that most scathing wit of all, Christopher Hitchens), and there are several inadvertently hilarious moments, too. Like when he takes me to the White House Correspondents' Association dinner, and at the MSNBC after-party we run into disgraced governor Eliot Spitzer. After listening to me prattle on for a few minutes, Spitzer turns to Lloyd and says, "She must be a handful."

Or when we go to a Midtown bash where Gerard Butler is the guest of honor for *How to Train Your Dragon*. Having once joked with Butler after he came onstage at the Comedy Cellar to shout down a rude heckler, I really thought I knew the room and that we were pal-ish. Boy, did I ever read it wrong.

Thinking he was Mr. Laugh at Himself Crude-Sense-of-Humor dude, I way too familiarly reference something about a *Post* story portraying him as a womanizer. I think I am teasing. This is the most fatal mistake that people make status-wise with showbiz types. You never, ever try to level up by saying anything remotely negative. Ever. Never. Ever. Bad move.

Butler proceeds to curse me out and demonstrate how shitty such allegations are. "What if I said to you, 'Wasn't that you who I saw getting fucked in the ass in a back alley?'"

I pause, think for a minute, and respond with a big smile, "Yes—that was totally me!"

Butler just shakes his head and walks away.

After Lloyd and I break up, it's not long before I am back to my old love-triangle ways and dating Olbermann again. When I do it this time, though, I dangle this fact to Sorkin, who replies, "I'm glad you had a good time with Keith, but I'm better." Olbermann, who initially tells me he likes Sorkin, reverses his opinion severely after *The Newsroom* premieres and words he has said to Sorkin are used in the show.

There are several surreal moments during this era. I'm aware, for instance, that Sorkin is spotted out with Kristin Davis (who played Charlotte on *Sex and the City*) around the time I am also seeing him on and off every few months. When he invites me to his mansion above the Sunset Strip to watch *The Newsroom* premiere with him, I cockily text several girlfriends, "I've never felt more Samantha!"

Or when he creates a character in *The Newsroom* based on one
of our dates where I bemoaned to him over dinner having to exco-
riate a celebrity as part of my job.

"I have to write this takedown piece on one of those Real
Housewives, Bethenny Frankel," I had told him. "But I really like
Bethenny. I respect her. She sent me a freaking vegan-muffin bas-
ket one time, for crying out loud. I tried to get out of writing it, but
I can't."

It was a very meta conversation to have: trying to explain the
heartlessness of your job in celebrity gossip trafficking to someone
who has been the victim of said gossip.

"What exactly is a takedown piece?" Sorkin asked.

I explained how it is a faux-populist, folksy, "we're not going to
take it anymore," tabloidy, STFU rant for whatever winged creature of the moment has flown too close to the sun.

The celebrity in question usually has done three recent things
that are not so good. And maybe another reporter has an anecdote
or something. And you know how journalism works, don't you?
Three things make a trend. A trend—or a takedown piece. In explaining this, part of me felt a weight off my shoulders revealing
the stomach-twisting paradox of life as a gossip peddler who also
happens to be, very inconveniently, not a short-game sadist. There
was also a part of me that was glad he could get a glimpse of how
the other half lives—when the other half is trapped and needs a
fucking paycheck.

"It's . . . you know . . . it's a takedown piece," I explained.
"That's what we call them at the *Post*. That's what we do. It's a
formula where you talk about all the things the public is pissed
off about. But sometimes it just feels toxic when the controversy is

more manufactured than anything. But I can't get out of writing it. I really tried."

"So . . . it's just bitchiness?" Sorkin asked. "What if you suggested five different alternative stories?"

I laughed.

"It's the *Post*," I repeated. "Have you ever read the *Post*?"

Later that night at the Four Seasons, completely apropos of nothing, I turned the conversation away from me and tried to focus it on him. I have this bad habit of offering unwanted advice, ever so arrogantly, on exactly how I can "help" someone. You know, because I'm so self-actualized and shit. Both my parents are therapists. I've been through a lot of therapy. So you can see where my heart lay. Sorkin interrupted my rambling.

"Don't try to fix me," he said.

I eventually, of course, wrote my stupid story on Bethenny. It comforted me somewhat that she is a very smart, very savvy woman and knows exactly how the game is played. Sorkin emailed me later from LA about the role our date played in an upcoming episode of *The Newsroom*.

"THIS CHARACTER IS NOT YOU," he said right off the top. "In fact, in the writers' room, when talking about this story, we call the character 'Bad Mandy' (as opposed to real Mandy) because I haven't named her yet. I thought it was worth reemphasizing that."

Of course, I was thrilled. Normally I am very stingy with giving away ideas. As a well-seasoned idea vulture myself, I know exactly how this trick works. Next time that old friend who is now a TV writer calls you up just to "shoot the shit and hear some of your crazy stories," tell them absolutely, and you in return would love points. See how that goes down. But this was different. This was Aaron Sorkin.

But when I finally watch the fourth episode of *The Newsroom*, called "I'll Try to Fix You," and Will McAvoy (played by Jeff Daniels) meets gossip columnist Nina Howard (played by Hope Davis), and she says, "You just passed up a sure thing," oh my God, I felt like such a fool. (Later, Sorkin emails, reiterating again the character was not me, but the resonance of feeling like I was throwing myself at him—just like Nina—burns in my brain.)

What hurt the most is realizing that maybe it is supposed to be "the opposite" of me—in reality, there was a close-to-the-bone nailing of all my worst qualities at this time in my life. The sexual forthrightness. The heavy flirtation geared toward a very specific brand of money, fame, power, and intellect.

Meanwhile, in dating Olbermann, there is—fortunately—no Bad Mandy character creation.

But the dates with him are equally, if not even more, unlike anything I've ever experienced. All positive—just, you know, it's Keith fucking Olbermann.

When I bitch about fighting with one of my bosses at the *Post*, he laughs and says it's like looking at a reflection in the mirror in terms of the burning-bridges tendency. When we go back to his apartment, I get a small glimpse of his truly amazing baseball memorabilia collection, with an original piece of a now-torn-down baseball field set up right inside his apartment. He even shows me the coolest thing of all, and lets me hold Babe Ruth's bat for a moment in my arms. His place looks kind of like Will McAvoy's stunning fictional apartment on *The Newsroom*, with flabbergasting views of Central Park, eight bridges, Coney Island, and both Yankee Stadium and Citi Field.

At one point, we head outside on to his balcony, where he tells me he likes my height, which is refreshing.

"You're a good kisser," he tells me.

"Thank you," I say.

After a beat, he asks, "What about me?"

"Oh, definitely," I say.

I don't relate that detail right now to make fun of him—but to show that whatever you think of celebrities whom you regard as being nothing but celluloid mannequins, they are in fact real human beings. We all want to know if the feeling is mutual.

Less surreal—and more expected—is Olbermann's inevitable expression of distaste for me. Not me personally, of course, but just why he unfollowed me on Twitter.

"I'm not prudish," he says, "but the tweets lately have really pushed against my 'line' for good/bad taste."

Yeah—I get that a lot.

In fact, I think my life pushes those same limits.

Indeed, my correspondence during this time is enough to blind any man, woman, or child. Here's an incredibly painful little sampling:

- "I'm a terrific person to date. My qualifications include: appropriate quotient of Madonna and whore; mastery of positions including reverse cowgirl but with the naïveté and wide-eyed wonderment of first-time cherry loss; power dynamic fun; psychological fucking ability; ego blow job at the ready; actual blow job at the ready; anal; and natch, cooking."

- "Is it all right that it makes me wet just to write you? I hope that's okay . . ."
- "Still thinking about how you played my body like an instrument, making me writhe like a demon possessed by heaven, making me gasp out for more, more, more."

I think that's enough to make you sufficiently lose your lunch without me needing to provide any further examples of more, more, more.

But oh man, such good stories, right? Know what's great to cuddle with at night? Stories.

And, in case it's not clear, for the record, whatever flaws any of these guys might have, the only jerk in this entire situation is me.

All three are hugely talented and impressive men—who were essentially in the crosshairs of a (while highly delightful at times) newly sober hyper-opportunist who had substituted her old addictions with a new one: trying to hitch herself to a powerful man in order to avoid the hard work of looking at herself. (And for context, to be clear—I dated Lloyd very seriously for almost a year and saw Sorkin multiple times over the course of several years. Olbermann and I only went on a few dates because my relationship with Lloyd took off, but it was hardly comparable. Still, the fact that I actively tried to pit each guy against the other still makes me cringe.)

Essentially, I might have been sober, but I was doing everything I could to avoid feeling some of the pain that was coming up for me.

After this saga of romancing the A-lister trifecta ends, I throw away all my Machiavelli-inspired Robert Greene books, and resolve to be more authentic overall.

I am pleased to discover in the process that I have developed one firm boundary I never have before: my sobriety.

Near the end of the year, I meet a very charming man in his thirties: Jackson, a wealthy artist who is also sober and pretty much seems too good to be true. He can't provide any media introductions. He can't get me a killer agent. And I lay off all the shapeshifty "please project onto me any fantasy of what kind of woman you want me to be so I never have to actually figure out who I am" rhetoric that I had been shoveling prior.

After I've been dating Jackson for a few months, we spend an evening watching *Saturday Night Live* together at his beautiful Central Park West high-rise. It feels like a perfect night. He feeds me a whipped-cream-covered cherry from an ice cream sundae, then he pulls out what is to be the real dessert: weed. I watch as he packs a pipe, lights it up, and inhales.

"I thought you were sober," I say, my palms sweating and my heart racing.

I love getting high. I love getting high. I love getting high. That's all I can think.

"So, you're sober-sober?" he asks. I didn't know there was any other kind.

I observe as he laughs so much more easily at the show we're watching. I miss feeling like that.

"I wish you could see it like I'm seeing it," he says, taking another drag off the pipe.

I leave his skyline-view loft and head back to the *Post*, shaken up a bit.

This is the most I've ever been tempted by drugs since getting sober.

Maybe I *should* get high with him? Maybe it doesn't count? I think about the last time I decided marijuana was okay, which spiraled into me in a sex club, snorting cocaine off a stranger's breast for the delight of a crowd.

But maybe this time it would be different? I like this guy so much.

I want to belong. I want him to like me.

I can't stop obsessing about it, so I write up a list of all the men I've slept with over my lifetime—and next to each I write "drunk" or "high." Every single one.

It's the biggest revelation I've ever had. My addiction is inextricably linked to my entire sexual history—starting from the moment I lost my virginity. I've been re-creating it ever since.

In a move I'll never be able to quite explain—except that I think I am trying to save myself from falling into drugs and drinking again—I email the entire list of men to Jackson.

As much as sending it is pure kryptonite and renders me forever unwifeable in this guy's eyes, I'm operating in pure survival mode now.

I won't go back to who I once was.

I refuse to. Even if it means never finding love again.

. . . .

I STOP DATING almost entirely and decide to focus solely on my career. It seems to pay off—and the synchronicity between what I'm reporting and what happens in my personal life blows me away.

When I'm assigned a big story on Courtney Love in the *Post*, not too long after, I run into her at a Cinema Society party downtown, and she starts chatting me up like a long-lost friend.

I sit and listen to Courtney talk *at* me for thirty minutes nonstop about a romantic entanglement she's currently in the middle of. She details the guy's reactions and goes off on hundreds of associated tangents.

". . . and then I had a dream about this big penis that was like a shark . . ." Courtney says midway through, and I don't know what comes over me, but for some reason, I feel like I can be brutally honest with this woman, whom I have been fascinated by since I was a teenager.

"You need to shut the fuck up," I say when she finally takes a breath. "You must drive men nuts."

Some kind of a fire lights up in her eyes—and she smiles, like she sees me for the first time. "You need a ride home?" she asks. Before Courtney's town car drops me off, she scrawls several phone numbers and her email address in my reporter's notebook.

Several nights thereafter, Courtney invites me over to her house in the Village, and we talk until seven in the morning. Giant amethyst crystals are everywhere, and as I chain-smoke with her, I convince myself that perhaps these "healing" crystals are taking away the toxic qualities of cigarettes. Everything with her is a whirlwind—an intoxicating mix of highbrow and lowbrow conversational crack—like if Page Six and every other gossip column in the world were put into a blender along with Socrates and Proust.

Her assistants bring us fresh mango juice and cookies. Her daily schedule is taped on the mirror. Couture gowns are draped everywhere. On the floor is a giant white sheet with various bits of information scribbled everywhere along with to-do lists and pictures of crying girls she sketches at will.

Everything with Courtney is a nonstop stream of names and conquests and mind games.

Being friends with her is a trip. At her house, we play with her dollhouses, watch old movies about Marilyn Monroe, and root through her insane $10 million collection of clothes. Other times, she'll send me on wild-goose chases throughout the city, telling me to meet her at the SGI Buddhist institute in Union Square; then the location changes again. It's like a shit test of the ultimate proportions.

"Do you want a coffee?" Courtney asks me late one night.

"No thanks," I say, and as the words come out of my mouth, I watch as she proceeds to make me a cappuccino and slide it over.

I drink the cappuccino. Of course I drink the cappuccino.

"My friend Peri is coming over, she's a psychic, so just like throw her sixty dollars if you want to do a reading."

I try to enlighten Courtney about the state of my financial reality.

"I'm broke, Courtney," I say. "That's why I'm basically stuck at the *Post*, even if I wanted to leave. Because I need the paycheck. I'm barely surviving in New York. I'm even thinking about doing bankruptcy."

"Do Chapter 7 if you do it," she says, without missing a beat. "Chapter 11 is so pedestrian."

I have no idea what this means, but she's got a bunch of gold records on the wall, so I'll take her word for it.

"You know, I used to be really broke when I was young," she says. "But then I started chanting 'Nam-myoho-renge-kyo,' and within two months I had two million dollars. I'm serious. Don't fuck around. It's the only thing that really works. Here, let's chant."

We chant for a few hours before psychic Peri Lyons comes over, and she does that thing that all psychics do where they look into your eyes and tell you how hard you have it. Don't get me wrong, I think some psychics are legit "touched" (like the ones police use, and Peri does pro bono for them I find out later). I count Peri as part of that group. But it always makes me laugh how every single one starts out by validating how very special you are in all of your utterly unique pain and victimization.

"People put a lot of shit on you," Peri says. "You've had a really hard year, huh?"

I don't know what all of it means, but whenever someone seems to acknowledge the loneliness of how I feel, it makes me tear up a little.

"Yeah, that sounds right," I say, trying to keep my composure. "I'm just kind of . . . I don't know what to do next."

"You're a phoenix, babe," Peri says. "You know what happens with phoenixes, right? Death and rebirth, rising from the ashes. You're on your way back up."

It's 3 a.m., but before I go, Courtney drops me three hundred-dollar bills and tells me to get a haircut.

She abides by my number one rule for people: Never be boring.

One evening I accidentally run into Courtney downtown when I'm on a setup date with Rex, an artist who is a friend of a friend. He's scruffy and sexy and exudes sex and Leonardo DiCaprio just bought one of his paintings. I'm impressed, and I love artists.

Before meeting up with Rex, my friend doing the setup did

warn me, "He might be kind of crazy, though. Like he might choke you to death, but the sex will probably be great."

I'm not scared, though. I'm just too cool to be scared.

"That guy was hot," Courtney texts me as we are checking into Chelsea Inn together.

I haven't been with a guy in what feels like ages (but is probably, like, a month), and I'm looking at an evening with Rex as being like a trip to the sex gym. Stupidly, I've also just gotten a spray tan. Rex and I fool around for a little bit, and it's fun and exciting at first, but right before we're about to have sex, the guy turns to me—and he spits on me.

This has never happened to me before. And I'm sober now.

I start crying, and now there are big zebra stripes on my face from the not-quite-set spray tan and the awfulness of realizing the situation I've just put myself in. I get the fuck out of there before I can listen to this dude finish his speeches to me, which start with saying the spit was a compliment and ends with calling me a crazy bitch. Eventually, I take a cab home, crying.

Finally, I text back to Courtney, "Cute yeah . . . But he was awful. That guy SPIT on me. What the fuck. I mean I guess he knew I was meeting up with him just to have casual sex so maybe I kind of set myself up . . ."

Courtney texts back immediately.

"NO! Shut the fuck up! A guy has to ASK before doing something like that. IN NO WAY DID HE HAVE A RIGHT TO DO THAT. What is his name I will fuck him up and ruin his life . . ."

Then she sends me a million pictures of her artwork featuring crying girls bleeding from their hearts. I hear her—and feel the protection. I also hear the really big questions she is asking of me.

Why am I so comfortable with abuse? Why did it even enter my mind that his behavior was okay? It's not okay. Nothing like this from a man has ever remotely been okay.

I need to have boundaries with sex the same way I do with drugs and alcohol. The very next day I attend a Sex and Love Addicts Anonymous meeting for the first time.

"Hi," I say, "my name is Mandy, and I'm a sex and love addict."

I even set for myself within that first meeting exactly what my sexual "bottom line" will be: I will never put myself in a situation that I sense is dangerous or makes me feel unsafe again.

I will never accept abuse again. I will never justify abuse— including that which I give myself.

. . . .

THE NEXT TIME I see Courtney is the first time I get to meet Jane Pratt.

On the promise of writing an item for Page Six, I get an invite to the launch of *xoJane* from the president of the site's parent company.

When I get to the Jane Hotel, bursting with press and catered with adorable miniature cupcakes that no one really eats, I wade through the flash of lights and step-and-repeats and run into Michael Stipe. I realize this is my two-minute window of opportunity to get an item. I remember reading something about him and Kurt Cobain being sexually linked when I did research for a *Post* story about the twentieth anniversary of *Nevermind*. It's an awkward subject to bring up, but whatever. I just straight up ask him to confirm or deny.

"So did you guys ever . . ."

"Let's set the record straight on Page Six," Michael says after I relate to him what I read. "Kurt was a really sweet man, and we never had sex. All right? There's your exclusive."

The gossip trade is such a humiliating business. For everyone involved.

At the party, I introduce myself to Jane, who is glowing and gorgeous, and I ramble on to her about my deep connection to her legacy over the years—from when I was a finalist in high school for Sassiest Girl in America to only nabbing an internship at the *Washington Post* because of a comprehensive college newspaper article I wrote documenting the cultural import of *Sassy*'s sale. But I'm pretty sure I say one sentence too many, because at the end of my impassioned soliloquy, I have that gross feeling of when you've overstayed your welcome after a one-night stand.

At the party, I end up talking the entire time to Courtney Love, who starts stealth smoking within the venue and shows me how to sneak cigarettes when you are indoors. Afterward, her driver takes us back to her West Village house, and we keep talking until four in the morning. She pulls tarot cards for me, and even writes Jane a note about how they should hire me. She's got my back. The text is typical Courtney and an example of one of countless epic screeds she is infamous for sending among anyone who has ever befriended her. You need to have a brain that is also juggling two hundred million ideas, tangents, and brainstorms in order to successfully decipher.

"Its court your text cheered me up, get mandy to do this and we can do it shes efficient and really good writer whereas im longwinded and will getmyself in trouble, and thank you for paying her dont

worry about me at all just bail me out if i get arrested for jaywalking or something, ha, i want to blog about alot, this week, why me and anna dont like each other, and the seating at the testino gala, anna mario kate winselt model me josh hartnett facing stefano tonchi carine steve ghan donnatella , it was FUNNY^ and there were times it qwas just anna and me w a gap between us, her in a statement fur and marni fucking marni, me in a beaded cavalli they gave me and after plkatying amfar w the worklds worst band and seeing this cote d azur crowd of rich people , with beading beading beading, fucking bhedazzkled, blingin g blazing yuck, yiou know those gap /collezion couture mags you buy when you start your line in your head? and you see some libyan or lebanese couturier and thik" well halle berry worked that one elia saab i could work this " and try to get the area code for libya? well all i couidl do was see littlke napalese fingers falling off, i never wanbt top sere beading again, seriously beading beading beading, yuck, and there i was all beaqded and beadazzled in cavalliu and a marchesa bag beading blinging blinding, going to biennelle which om clueless about, seriously just beinbg tourista anyway clearly im a scatterbrain and id like qa voice on your blog abnd itd be good fgopr you too, but mandy has to help her writing is efficent and reader funny lets think of a name for mine that doesnt involve the name courtney love, ims o sick of that dammed name, its boring me. hope your well, biggest kis from turkish delight istanbul court"

A few weeks later, I get an email from Emily McCombs with Jane copied asking me to ghostwrite some columns for Courtney, which essentially involves typing out what she's saying and then bringing it together with a through-line so it's readable for anyone who doesn't speak Courtney.

The opportunity *only* comes because of Courtney sticking her neck out for me.

She's not afraid. She's never afraid.

She is also one of the first people in my life to break through to me about men and how I treat myself.

....

NOW THAT I am sober, nothing quite "fits" the way it used to. I don't want to subject myself to guys I might have given a chance to before. I don't want to go out to parties that leave me feeling empty inside where I'm networking the whole time, with no tangible result in sight. And more and more, my job at the *Post* no longer feels like it fits either.

If I was still working with Mackenzie, Steve, and Katherine, I think I could have eventually found my way as I floundered around like a child, figuring out my new sense of sober boundaries. But the days of working with all of them are long gone. There's new management, and I don't feel the human connection that once made working there so extraordinary.

I know I'm not the only one who feels it either. In his final days at the paper before retiring, V. A. Musetto (most famous for writing the headline "Headless Body in Topless Bar") would roam the floor wearing the yellow Santa cap he kept on year-round, muttering things like, "This place is turning into a women's magazine." I empathized with where he was coming from. There's a certain neutered interchangeable voice of the stereotypical lady-mag that is never something I've identified with, writing-wise—and why I always loved the magazine *Jane* so much in the 2000s and *Sassy* before that.

Turns out sobriety is a huge pain in the ass if you're not completely happy in your job. I can't stop questioning everything. Like, why did I have to do that piece on Bethenny when I objected? Why am I doing anything in my life that I'm uncomfortable with at all?

Your far-too-clear sober brain starts to feel more ownership over the scope of your whole life. Like, if I can choose not to drink and stick with that, what else might I do?

While I actively seek out creative new job opportunities—including with *xoJane*—no one is hiring. *Check back again with us later, okay, thanks.*

I decide that if I can't find a new job, maybe I can focus on getting help for my soul in the evenings instead.

After asking around, I'm referred to an unassuming therapist named Sherrye, who has several decades of sobriety, and she listens to me intently during our first session. When I talk about how lucky I am to have my job and all the opportunities in my life, and how guilty I feel for even trying to find a new gig, my voice cracks. The more I talk to my therapist the more I realize that the problem is not the *Post*.

The problem is me. The problem has always been me. The *Post* is the *Post*. If they want to be more corporate, good for them. I don't have any say in that.

"You react to things childishly," my new therapist agrees with me when I tell her about conflicts I'm having at work. "Because you are still in a 'child ego state.' If you do not have a proper 'adult ego state' modeled to you, then you don't ever progress into learning the healthy skills of understanding how to deal with adversity. You're still acting out and throwing tantrums like a child."

I quote to her one of Blaine's lines that I am a drama queen and that nothing really bad ever happened to me. Is that true? Is the hurt I feel inside unjustified?

"You've been through a lot of pain," Sherrye stops me. "But I want you to look at something. Do you see that you can only even talk about yourself in comparison to other people? There is something called the 'looking-glass self,' where you judge your self-worth based on what you think other people think of you. You base your identity off the love you perceive others can give you, and then you readjust your opinion of yourself accordingly."

When Sherrye says these words, my opinion of myself shifts once again. I've never realized how utterly penetrable such a thing was.

"Here's the key," she says. "You don't actually know what I think of you. You are, in essence, guessing what I think of you. And then based off of that guess, that's how you are determining your self-worth. Do you see how dangerous that can be?"

That's what I have been doing my whole life, I realize. Always looking outside of myself for validation that I am okay, that I am worth something. Never believing that the key to self-esteem lay inside myself all along. You can't drink it into yourself. You definitely can't fuck it into yourself. You can't work it into yourself either.

The more I trust her, the more I start spilling to Sherrye all of my unspeakable stories. She pours me glasses of water and hands me tissues to calm me down. She nods attentively, but I can see clearly from her questions what is happening as she tries to follow along.

"Now . . . who is this again? Okay, this is another person? And what is Twitter exactly?"

Sherrye can't keep up. Hell, I can't keep up either. I'm using all these meaningless transitory details to avoid articulating feelings that are so difficult for me. Eventually, after a few sessions of trying to constantly steer conversations away from my early life to prattle on about the minutia of some *Post* assignment, Sherrye confronts me.

She wants to know why I won't talk about my childhood. Why have I been ignoring for so very long that little person inside of me who has been hurting and acting out?

"My inner child?" I repeat, and then I laugh bitterly. "What a bunch of bullshit."

I haven't heard from that little girl in years. She knows her place. I've made sure of that.

Sherrye never takes any of my dismissive or angry bait. She never "reacts."

"I understand what you mean," she says compassionately. "But it's a lot more than that."

I cry through my anger. I let myself actually feel the sensations that I did as a little girl and how frozen I become when even thinking about criticizing my parents or acknowledging any pain. It is my job to protect them. Why can't people see that?

But week after week, Sherrye persists. As she gently guides me through the story of my life—to the most difficult parts—I realize that the little person is still there.

She hasn't left me. She's just completely terrified.

....

ONCE I OPEN myself up to all the feelings I never let myself acknowledge as a child, it feels like a dam breaking. The tears never seem to stop. The softness feels too soft. I think I am in danger of disappearing completely. The world becomes harsh, painful, ugly . . . *dangerous.*

"I can't take it, I can't take it, I just can't take it," I yell at Sherrye, sounding exactly like my father when he's in a rage.

"You can," Sherrye tells me. "Pain is not going to kill you. You're not betraying your family by talking about them. It's okay to acknowledge what you feel inside."

But when I do, it feels like all I am doing is reopening old wounds.

I call my dad one night and tell him I'm trying to do my Fourth Step as part of my AA program, where you look at resentments you've carried throughout your lifetime. I write out a list for my father, and it's late at night when I call. Instantly, my father snaps at me when I tell him what I'd like to do.

"Do I want to hear what a shitty father I was? No, Mandy!"

I hang up the phone, shell-shocked and inconsolable. How stupid and naïve I was to think such a thing was even possible. The next time I see Sherrye, when I try to tell her about what happened, I can barely speak at all I am crying so hard. This is all one giant bad idea, I tell her. I'm only making things worse.

"Okay, you need to go to an Al-Anon meeting," Sherrye says. "You. Have. To. Go."

But my dad isn't a drunk. And Al-Anon is a twelve-step group for friends or families of alcoholics to deal with their volatile behavior. Hell, my dad wasn't even allowed to drink for a long time because the doctors thought it would affect the metal plate in his head. But both his birth parents and his adopted parents were alcoholics. And his head injury has caused him to have the mood swings of one.

"Fine," I relent. "I'll go to yet another twelve-step meeting. Pretty soon my life will be nothing but fucking twelve-step meetings."

When I arrive at my very first Al-Anon meeting on the Upper East Side inside a sterile office space, I notice that the pained, nervous smiles of everyone around me are communicating a code of sorts. We all seem to share a secret language of perfectionism and extreme self-criticism. We want so badly to be loved. We want so badly not to be rejected. We are on high alert constantly, crippled by hyperawareness, trying to sense what might be the alcoholic's (or dysfunctional person's) next move in order to accommodate that or dodge the chaos.

It's a strange, unsettling feeling.

My face must betray my discomfort. Because a little old lady sitting next to me leans over and pats my leg.

"Everyone's really nice here, don't worry," she assures me. "My name's Anna. We can talk afterward if you'd like."

When the meeting ends, Anna turns to me and asks if I want to get a coffee. She's my mom's age, and her kindness is so disarming, so comforting, so unexpected.

As we sit in one of those neon-lit Café Metros, each knowing only the other's first name, I tell her a little about the disaster that calling my father was the other night. I try to explain why getting yelled at felt like reliving childhood trauma all over again.

"I understand," Anna says. "You know, there's this principle in Al-Anon that may be helpful to you. Have you ever heard of something called 'detachment with love'?"

I shake my head no.

"Think of it like this," Anna says. "You can still love your father as much as you always have. That never goes away. But you don't have to keep engaging in the same way again and again with people who have hurt you, hoping for a different result. You can protect yourself first. But you don't have to stop loving them either."

We exchange numbers before she leaves, but I never see or talk to her again. This happens all the time in recovery meetings. People give you little gems of wisdom that dramatically impact your entire journey, and that is your onetime exchange with each other, human to human.

I take Anna's (and Al-Anon's) life-changing lesson and start applying it to the *Post*, too.

The conflicts stop. It feels like I'm no longer thrashing and bashing around, creating problems and expecting a different result.

I love the *Post*. But I can detach from it, too.

············

OF COURSE, I don't stop looking for another job completely.

One late night at Carolines, I start talking to Scott Einziger, a TV guy who used to be a producer on *Howard Stern* and was a showrunner on *The Amazing Race*, and he tells me about how he's started investing in and forming new companies. Boldly, I tell him that he should invest in me. What would the investment be? he wants to know. I think about it and suggest something I've been reading about a lot online: the self-publishing industry. We could create an e-book company together, I suggest, and he listens to my on-the-spot business plan I'm literally imagining right then and there.

Scott has to fly back to LA soon, but we spend the next few weeks emailing and talking on the phone all day long, exchanging ideas of how such a situation might work.

Within two weeks, Scott feels enough confidence to respond to my suggestion that he should invest in me. He is game. He says I should quit my job so I can move to LA, and he'll pay for expenses. But there is a complication at play. We like each other quite a bit. At one point, he tells me that he thinks he may just have found a soul mate in me. I like him so much, too, and I could see myself falling for him. So I don't let the potential for personal and professional entanglement scare me off.

I'm just so excited for a new chapter. I don't even fully believe what is unfolding until one day my phone rings at work with an alert from PayPal. "You have $8,000." I can't believe it at first. No one is around, so I actually fall on the floor of the newsroom in disbelief. I am going to have a whole new life. I can't stop smiling.

I quit my job a few weeks later. My last day is February 12, 2012. Realizing that this is an opportunity to also unburden myself from all the debt that I have accrued during my insane partying days, I take Courtney Love's advice and declare Chapter 7 bankruptcy to rid myself of the more than $55,000 in debt I've accrued in the last few years.

I'm going to have a fresh start, and none of this could have happened if I was out drinking and getting high and not believing in myself enough to take control.

But as much as I can't wait for this new venture, I'm also a little bit scared. I'm going to be living rent-free in a studio apartment that Scott is paying for, doing a business I've kind of pulled out of my ass, and also, he tells me after his last trip to New York, he thinks he might be falling in love with me. I feel emotionally bonded as well, but I'm also nervous.

"Won't that complicate our business relationship?" I ask.

"You're right," Scott agrees. "We'll slay dragons in business, and we can figure out what happens after that."

I really don't want to screw this up. I just want some kind of magic bullet that will make me have the perfect mental health for when I finally move to California to start my new life as an entrepreneur. But panic attacks occur fairly regularly once I no longer have the routine and scheduling of the *Post*. I no longer have the daily assignments to distract me from the full weight of all the awareness that sobriety has brought into my life.

When I visit Heather Spillane, an extraordinary acupuncturist who saw me at my absolute worst, I tell her all about various regrets from how I acted before I got clean. As I lie on her table one day, I ask her, "How do you stop thinking about things that you could have done differently? That you've messed up?"

"You know what 'shame' stands for?" Heather responds. "'Should Have Already Mastered Everything.'"

I am stunned. Heather's words flood over me like a cool tonic of healing and forgiveness. They're so simple and so true. No one has mastered everything. We just have to keep learning, getting better, trying to be our best selves.

Heather tells me she learned it from the "Caron Institute." I write down the name, google it, and read all about this drug and alcohol facility in Pennsylvania that specializes in intensive group therapy in something they call their "Breakthrough program." I realize this is exactly the missing link in my recovery that I need. Something that will help me be able to live with the at-times-crippling realizations that sobriety brings as you look back upon your past and creates a bridge for you to move on to the next phase of your life in a healthy, stable way.

I ask Scott if it's okay if I use part of his money to do Caron's Breakthrough program—at a cost of $2,600—and he fully supports it. Soon after, I spend one week in a tiny town in Pennsylvania, learning from morning to night about what unhealthy relationship dynamics I might be re-creating in my life and how to advance my recovery to a better place.

Part of the experience includes writing letters to my parents, expressing what I wish I could have gotten from them when I was younger—versus the reality of what I did receive.

"Dad," I write in my letter, "I didn't just want to hear that I was valuable. I wanted you to show me I was valuable through your actions."

In a small nondescript room with sunlight streaming through the windows, I stand up, wearing no makeup, no designer clothes, and I read this entire letter aloud to my group. Except when I get to that line, the therapist stops me cold.

"Wait," he says. "I want to try something."

In order for me to really reflect on the meaning behind my words—and how they relate to my own self-treatment and care—he assigns another group member to play "me" so that I can then read that statement back to "myself." We did this sort of thing at Caron a lot. It sounds so silly, but for some reason these "psychodrama" act-outs can make you see a desire you are articulating in an entirely new light. Which is exactly what happens.

"I wanted you to show me I was valuable through your actions," I tell the woman who represents me, sitting in a chair a few feet away. As the words come out, as I tell "myself" that I wanted to be shown that I was valuable through my actions, the impact is overwhelming.

Mandy, I wanted you to show me I was valuable through your actions.

Do you see? Do you see what I saw?

It's like a layer of film was lifted from my eyes. An often-repeated principle of sobriety is the notion of "taking care of your side of the street." Meaning, I can't change my father. I can't change anyone. I certainly can't go back in time. But I can change myself.

So why have *I* been treating myself so terribly?

A few months later, at the beginning of June, I make my big move out to LA to stay in the apartment set up by Scott, someone with whom I have only spent three hours in person.

He's a remarkable individual, one of the smartest, greatest men I've ever met in my life, but our relationship is complicated. I'm so consumed with my sobriety and self-care during this time, going to meetings all the time and without any kind of structure or schedule, the progress I make on creating this company I pitched him is fairly pathetic.

But I tell myself that it's okay because I know that he is also shepherding my recovery, and he fully supports that. He loves me, after all. He told me that. But Scott is separated and going through a divorce at the time, and ours is not a true business relationship. I am his fake wife, and when on the night of my second-year anniversary of sobriety I crash the car he rented for me, he lashes out in a way that makes clear how dangerous the blurring of personal and professional can be.

Suddenly, the close emotional bond we have developed is nowhere in sight. Now he is a raging boss who is disgusted with me as an employee who has failed to deliver. It leaves me feeling shell-shocked. I have never seen this side of him before. It feels like a combination of the rage of my father and the vitriol of my ex-husband combined. It is extremely jarring.

"Where is the work you promised me?" Scott yells. "What is wrong with you? Why are you so full of shit?"

When I try to speak, he interrupts me and mocks me mercilessly.

"I'll pay you back the money," I tell him, my voice going monotone. "But I'm not going to accept this. I don't let men talk to me this way in my life anymore."

I tell him I am moving home to live with my parents in San Diego.

"Keep the money," he says. "I don't expect anything. But I'm disappointed in you for giving up."

Scott says I need to get over his rage outburst and just pretend it didn't happen. But I can't do that anymore. My gut tells me that I need to get out. His anger at me is completely justified at my utter failure as an entrepreneur, but the rage he directed at me triggers a sense of fight-or-flight protection I can't ignore. It feels like a switch has gone off. One minute our relationship is no expectations, take your time, focus on your self-care. The next minute I am deserving of the most brutal and demeaning of his anger. I realize I need to triage the situation before it gets any worse.

I'm happy to say that in the months that follow, a healing occurs. We become good friends again and recognize that the entire thing was a mistake, sparked by both of us being in such transitory, uncertain periods in our lives. I am still fairly new to sobriety, he is in the middle of a divorce, and I suppose both of us were so desperate to cling to something that felt positive and warm and good, we jumped into a whirlwind situation that unsurprisingly self-destructed within a very short span of time.

One of the things that I love the most about Scott and this experience is that never once did we share any physical intimacy. It taught me so much about how deeply you can connect with a man when you don't muck the whole thing up with sex from the get-go. And it also taught me that establishing boundaries isn't the end of the world.

But it is tumultuous. On a hot July night, I pack up my entire life once again after only two months in LA. I arrive on my parents' doorstep at 1 a.m. with a U-Haul stuffed with my now incredibly stripped-to-the-bone belongings.

I am thirty-six years old. I have $279 in my bank account. I have no job prospects. I have no romantic prospects. I have nothing. And it feels like such a relief.

I am a phoenix, just like Courtney Love's psychic predicted, starting over from ashes once again.

....

RETURNING HOME AS an adult woman is like nothing else I've ever experienced. It is awful and beautiful and extraordinary and like being given a time machine to understand some of the keys to surviving my childhood.

As a sober woman, I am now able to give myself something I

couldn't when I was just a child growing up in my family's unpredictable household: compassion.

Seeing my dad yell and scream one day, set off by his cup
being moved slightly, I react so differently as an adult. I still
jump. I still feel scared. My insides still freeze. I still feel afraid.
But I no longer absorb it like a sponge. I no longer feel like it is
all my fault. Returning home helps me give so much love to the
little girl inside me who didn't have anyone watching out for
her so many years ago. I think about what Sherrye the therapist
told me, about connecting with that little person inside of me.
I'm starting to get it now. It's starting to make sense finally. You
can re-parent yourself. You can give yourself what you've always
needed. You don't have to define yourself by the scars of your
past.

In order to keep attending AA and Al-Anon meetings, I with-
draw fifty dollars from my ever-dwindling bank account to purchase
a used, barely working bike off Craigslist so I can cycle around the
city and make meetings. At every single one I attend, I tell my story,
and it feels so different from the ones in New York, where, despite
the emphasis on anonymity, many people still discuss their very
high-powered Manhattan-specific jobs in theater, in media, in PR.
This kind of thing never gets brought up in San Diego. The pace
feels so easygoing and languid. Like, you can actually feel how
close the ocean is, and we are all so peaceful just because of it.
There is nothing transactional about any conversation. I don't want
anything from them. They don't want anything from me. We are
just trying to be better people.

I also find out, now that I have been gone from the *Post* for a
few months, who my real friends are. Anyone who has ever worked

in a job where you can do something for people—like provide press or perks or whatever—knows the experience of what happens when you leave that gig. Folks who email you all the time acting like you're besties often disappear entirely when you are no longer a "favor friend." And other people, ones who you never imagined would be there for you, suddenly come out of the woodwork, revealing what they care about: you.

One person who I never expected to speak to so much during this time is my friend Taylor Negron. He's passed away now, but he's a comedian you may know from *The Aristocrats* or *Fast Times at Ridgemont High* or any of his other seventy roles in movies and TV. I first met him when I did a character actor profile on him for the *Post*, but we kept in touch afterward, and during my time in San Diego, we talk on the phone frequently.

Every time we do, Taylor effortlessly improves my mood and corrects my perspective.

"This time is a gift for you, Mandy," he says. "Don't you see, you've been so addicted to drama and chaos all your life without realizing it, and now that's all gone. It's you and your family and California. Take a walk outside in the San Diego sun, and see if you can get addicted to a flower. I'm serious. I want you to actually try it. Take a walk, and just find a flower and appreciate it. Think of all the excitement you can get from it and feel that peace."

I do that, and a sense of calm and appreciation bubbles up that I haven't experienced in a while. It feels a little like . . . wonder. Like the kind I had so much of as a child. At night, I sleep in my mom's study on the ratty old pullout couch and cuddle next to my dad's guide dog, who, like all guide dogs, is a special kind of angel.

One day, when I check my email, I get a press release that reminds me of another time.

Amma, the Indian hugging saint whom I first profiled in the *Post* so long ago, is coming to New York for her annual visit to see her followers.

I may not have the flash of the *Post* anymore, but I still have the connections. For the hell of it, I decide to email Arianna Huffington, Courtney Love, and Jane Pratt to give them all the personal cell phone number for the swami who handles media and can hook them up with a personal guru visit, skipping lines that stretch for hours—just in case they're interested.

It's a strange instinct to have, but I find that those are sometimes my best ones to follow through with and act upon. At least in sobriety they are. About a week later, the butterfly effect begins.

I've rekindled Jane's memory of me from a year before when I applied for a full-time gig, and a few weeks later I get the call. *Finally*, they do have an opening. They want me to come on board to replace Cat Marnell, who quit months before. I do a test piece for them on deadline about how to achieve the appearance of "just been fucked"–style makeup and hair. Two days later, I am hired.

I'm going back to New York again, this time a completely different person.

I'm thrilled and in awe of this unexpected and exciting turn, but I'm also nervous to leave what I've built in San Diego. There is so much peace and softness and authenticity in my life now. I don't know what will happen when I return to the city where everything went both so right and so wrong.

. . . .

2012–15

GETTING TO WORK with Jane Pratt and edit first-person stories from women around the world is a dream come true. Finding myself alienated from my friends and family is not.

It's hard to understand how I go from a place of love and healing and understanding with my family to what happens next, but the repercussions of directly tapping into the vein of my personal life to write about traumas or regrets is unsettling for people who are much more private individuals, which everyone in my family definitely is. One of my earliest pieces for the site is about losing my virginity to rape, and there is a tremendous amount of awkwardness in discussing the piece with my parents. It feels a bit grotesque, exhibitionistic, and unprocessed. Of course, I'm still proud of the piece that I wrote, but it's a double-edged sword. There is also a part of me that is sacrificing my own emotional boundaries for the sake of my new job—and Internet clicks.

Every bit of my personal pain becomes commodified and packaged, and sometimes the experiences and revelations don't go over well with my family. My mom is horrified when I write about her obsessive-compulsive disorder. (We've gotten past that now, obviously.) My sister thinks I'm revealing too many things about my life and tells me she feels uncomfortable with the whole thing.

All the "feel the peace in a flower" sentimentality and ease I felt before is trampled. Now there are fights with my family and friends, who wonder: *Why am I airing all my dirty laundry for the world when I haven't even finished examining it myself?*

When my mom mentions offhandedly to me that maybe *she'll* write something I won't like in the comments, I block her on Facebook. She doesn't understand how the Internet works, that there are plenty of strangers out there who make an active hobby of hating me online already. The last thing I need is that kind of threatening vitriol from her. My sister and I eventually stop talking because she is squeamish about some of the stories I am writing, so I angrily unfriend her on Facebook, too.

My dad and I barely speak at all.

But none of that matters, really. Because who needs to talk when you have thousands of anonymous avatars to interact with for hours on end with a constant feedback loop that never stops? New comment notifications pop up rapid-fire everywhere I go, and it feels like a mob of faceless people—some friends, some fans, some haters—who are constantly following me around commenting on the most deeply personal aspects of my life, soul, and mind.

It's hard for me to even write about this period—and I've obviously condensed it dramatically—by virtue of having had to already dissect every little thing that happened in my life at that time either within *xoJane* or on the weekly podcast that I eventually start called *News Whore*. I realize that almost every single relationship in my life has now returned to the completely transactional variety.

It is the anti–San Diego.

There is a true irony that people who are blogging or podcasting all about the minutiae of their lives are sometimes the loneliest people of all. I rarely date or get out of the house. I sometimes go to therapy and meetings, but my workaholism is a mask for not actually having any kind of life. If something doesn't lead to a post I can write ("It Happened to Me: I Had Fun Catching Up with an Old Friend Who Actually Kind of Gives a Shit About Me" is not quite clickbait gold), then why bother?

I just don't have the time. I'm online and on the phone all day from wake-up to pass-out, finding stories, slinging stories, editing stories, writing stories, promoting stories, trying to keep those clicks up, up, up.

When a news story breaks, I reach out to those involved the instant that I can—individuals who are (like me, in some of the highly personal pieces I write for the site) still in the middle of processing whatever it is they are going through. When I speak to Sydney Leathers about writing a piece for the site reflecting on her role in the explosive Anthony Weiner scandal, we speak for a few hours and she really opens up.

"I just fired my manager," she tells me. "She wanted me to do porn. I was like, no."

Then the other line rings mid-conversation. It is Sydney's manager calling.

"I have to take this," she says.

I never get a return call from Sydney, although we reconnect years later. Her manager only lets me communicate through her, tells me Sydney *is* in fact going to do porn and now will only do a piece for us if we can pay $500, which is ten times our (admittedly, not very great) rate.

That piece teaches me something about the rapid-fire pace of the world. In a matter of a single hour, someone can literally become a porn star and her entire life trajectory will change. Eventually, Jane approves the fee—and the piece publishes.

Of course, it is a big traffic hit, as are many first-person pieces I secure and edit for the site: important narratives from rape survivor Daisy Coleman, who went on to do a Neflix documentary; Tuesday Cain, a fourteen-year-old who went viral for her "Jesus Isn't a Dick; So Keep Him Out of My Vagina" sign at a pro-choice rally; revenge porn crusader Charlotte Laws; Steubenville gang-rape blogger Alexandria Goddard; and Shauna Prewitt, who wrote a searing open letter to politician Todd Akin about being a rape survivor and then bearing the child (destroying his narrative that a woman can't actually get pregnant if she is the victim of "legitimate rape"). Over time, these viral stories become expected of me as the rule rather than the exception. Instead of any kind of financial compensation or reward, the metric of expectations for my job performance simply changes: Give me *that*—all the time.

When I secure two exclusives from Duke University student Miriam Weeks, aka porn star Belle Knox, Miriam and I work together all through the night (writing, rewriting, and getting the proper permissions). And I'm very proud of the result: a sex worker's ongoing manifesto on feminism and double standards for men and women in society. Largely as a result of these hugely viral pieces from Belle Knox, in a single month in 2014, traffic jumps up from a few million uniques to seven million. When I joined the site in 2012, traffic was at eight hundred thousand uniques. While undoubtedly every person who works at *xoJane* is responsible for this traffic growth, there's also a gnawing reality. Especially with the Belle Knox stories, there's an undeniable charting of just how significant these stories are in raising the traffic—and how they have originated from a lot of extra hours I've logged. It's hard not to feel increasingly resentful that I have not received a raise in that entire time.

When I finally meet with someone from our parent company about compensation, her suggestion is to reduce my base salary by $20,000 (with theoretical sky-is-the-limit bonuses contingent on big traffic hits). It feels like such an insult. I'm barely keeping it together on the salary I do make, so this is about the worst possible thing I can be told.

Instead, I take to laughing bitterly at the idea of transparency espoused at the site as I complain to friends. Long hours are spent Gchatting with one of the site's many talented editors, Lesley Kinzel, until I find myself sobbing and bereft.

"Just talk it all out with me," Lesley tells me. "It's healthy. I understand."

I tell her how enraged I feel to be working at a company that sometimes runs at the speed of molasses—and I can only write things like "Hugs! Love you! Hey lovies!" because that is our brand or something (even when I feel utterly demoralized).

When I try to have a straightforward conversation about this, I discover a doublespeak that feels maddening. At the *Post*, you are told directly if something is a problem—even if what you are told is hard to hear. At *xoJane*, it's more like "I love you, babe" but said with a slightly different tone of voice you are expected to decon-struct, decode, and respond to accordingly.

I've seen the site parodied a lot, but I think *BoJack Horseman*'s "Girl Croosh" nails it most of all. There is a constant rallying cry of girl power, which overlies a culture of secrecy and backbiting. Don't get me wrong. I'm as guilty as the next person, but it was demoralizing at times.

Jane's original tagline for the site is famously "A place where women go when they are being selfish, and where their selfishness is applauded." But in reality, the site is only referring to a very specific kind of woman. She is liberal. She is not snarky or sarcastic about celebrities (I know this sounds strange, but it was a literal rule if you were writing for the site). She doesn't diet. And she never challenges rhetoric that has been mass-accepted by the collective feminist majority.

At one point, when I commission a piece from author Jo Piazza, who describes trying to lose weight before her book party launch, I am actually reprimanded and told that we can "do better." Jo is a hugely successful author whom I was lucky to convince to even write a piece for us at all. I am baffled. I of course support body acceptance and fat acceptance, but why can't you both be a feminist and desire to lose a few pounds in a healthy way? It makes no sense to me.

But I learn that talking about any kind of hypocrisy is not really welcomed. The best bet is just to keep your head down, never raise any issues at all, smile, and do what you are told regardless. Part of this is accepting what your role at the website is.

Jane doesn't like to talk about editors who work there; rather, she refers to us as her "characters," whom she has cast. I actually don't realize what my "character" is until one day a reality production company comes in to observe all of us interacting with one another in a rollicking, freewheeling staff meeting. They are considering doing a reality show based on the website. By way of small talk in our meeting, Jane reveals exactly who she believes my character to be. "And Mandy," she says, "is the girl you love to hate."

"Oh," I say, forcing laughter. "Okay, I didn't know that."

I feel so naïve. I never realized that all the self-hatred I wrestled with internally would one day become my "brand" at a fucking feminist website. I was really trying to work on the self-love thing, actually.

Still, at the end of the day, all of these complaints are trivial. Any frustrations I feel are always diminished—and rendered entirely insignificant—when compared with the gratitude I feel for what Jane created in providing one of the most important meeting places for women I've ever seen (including giving me the good fortune to work with the tremendous editors I learned from during my time there: Emily, Lesley, and Corynne Cirilli—formerly Steindler, whom I worked with at the *Post*—and so many more). Jane is an indisputable genius. She completely changed the news industry. Her staple "It Happened to Me" has been ripped off and adopted by pretty much every mainstream news organization nowadays. She pioneered first-person journalism. Not to mention she also gave me one of the biggest breaks of my life, which doesn't make her a genius, but does make her a godsend to me personally.

....

THERE IS A little bit of irony to the fact that I write so much about so many of my most personal issues on a website read by millions, which sometimes leaves me with no time to deal with those issues in real life. Sure, I go to SLAA meetings. I go to AA meetings. I go to Al-Anon meetings. But it takes years sometimes to break out of patterns of self-hatred and self-abuse.

That initial pink cloud from my early days of sobriety is long gone. Now I am just stuck with myself, and the magic is starting to feel dull.

I am not drinking or drugging or betraying my sexual bottom line, but to be quite honest, all that heady elation from my early days of sobriety is so long gone that "recovery" sometimes feels like a chore. Still, I keep doing it. I know that as long as I am sober, that is in itself a victory. But it never looks like the third-act everything-is-suddenly-perfect reinvention that is portrayed in the movies. Sometimes the process is the most unglamorous, irritating process imaginable. Sometimes getting healthy is a drag. But it's still the right thing for me to do, and I have to remind myself of that daily.

My absolute favorite part about *xoJane* is the platform it provides for women to shatter stigmas and fight back against the subconscious shaming of women's lived experiences. That's what I hope some of my favorite pieces for the site achieve.

I write one called "I Don't Think I Can Have Casual Sex Anymore Because the Power Balance Shifts So Dramatically," where I chronicle what is to be my last one-night stand ever. I reveal that at the last minute I took a young man I met on Tinder with me to a media party I was invited to, which was held at a strip club and riddled with porn stars. This was after I'd gotten blown off by a proper OKCupid date. After the young man and I fooled around for a while, I asked him if he'd want to do it again in the future, thinking maybe he could be my new "healthy" friend with benefits. I didn't want a relationship. Not at all.

"Well, you have my Tinder chat," he responded, getting up to leave.

"Yeah," I said. "I get it."

He left, and I went to my phone and pressed my finger on the app until it quivered. *"Are you sure you want to delete Tinder and all its contents?"* Yes.

I realize that casual sex feels like I am trying to invert, like a spiky umbrella, that loss of power I felt when I was young by angrily protesting through my actions: "You want to see whore? I'll show you fucking whore. You will never have any ownership of my soul. Guess what, what you got was a character. There is no intimacy there, and yet, I saw you inside and out."

But I'm only contributing to a pattern of debasement.

Maybe, I start to realize, my hero's journey is in transforming and healing myself sexually. My sword can be wielded to cut my attachments to the men whom I've let into my precious energy space without regard for how it affects me and the aftermath of what I've let inside. My resurrection is in revealing my heart, and only revealing it when someone has proven themselves worthy of being in my ordinary world.

....

AS MUCH AS I may occasionally pop up on TV (oh hey, there I am on *Dr. Drew*, check it out, I'm on *Inside Amy Schumer*) or take photos with celebrities here and there for my job (I'm booked on a panel with Issa Rae, oh hey, it's a party with the cast of *Orange Is the New Black*), the reality of my life is as unglamorous as it gets.

The only real companions I have are my dogs, Sam and Trip. Sam is a pit bull I took home in 2012 from the shelter after a Facebook friend posted his picture, telling me he'd be put down the next morning—and I was his only hope. I am gun-shy about pit bulls in general from coverage of so many incidents on every newspaper job I've had, from Florida to New York, but I figure I can at the very least help buy the dog a little more time. Trip is a Cavalier

King Charles spaniel I got from a breeder after my vet suggested a companion might help Sam.

But from the first night I took Sam home, his unpredictable aggression scared me. Out on a walk that first night, he bit a stranger. It wasn't long before he bit me, too.

And so begins the journey of a very complicated and abusive love story.

If you were to look at the relationship in the perspective of a domestic violence situation, you would never say of a man hurting a woman, "It's your fault." But with my pit bull, that is exactly what happens.

"You need to make sure you don't do anything that might upset him . . . like seeming tense or worried," a stranger tells me as I sob in the middle of the Washington Square dog park after Sam bites my calf, leaving a dark purple welt. "You need to do better and be more careful how you look at him, because it might alarm him."

Sam is often such a sweet dog, and I know he doesn't mean to hurt anyone. When he is loving, he is so loving.

I spend thousands of dollars on multiple trainers and a doggy day care (until he gets kicked out), and eventually bring home the happy-go-lucky Trip, whom Sam takes to immediately. The two of them play all day long. It helps a little bit, but the incidents never go away completely—and now trainers are starting to tell me that I'm putting myself and others in danger.

When I use a muzzle on Sam, he thrashes it into my legs, creating deep and lasting bruises. I can rarely have company over. But despite all of this, I've never loved a dog so much.

"He's a ticking time bomb," one trainer says.

"Why do you think he was surrendered in the first place?" another says.

"You're going to get sued," everyone tells me.

One friend emails me the story of Darla Napora, mauled to death by her pit bull when she was six months pregnant despite doing everything seemingly right and participating actively in pit bull advocacy groups. Another pit bull owner tells me that it hurts the reputation of the entire breed when you don't immediately surrender or euthanize the dog after the first bite.

"The first bite happened before he even arrived at my home," I say. "Don't you think with training he'll get better?"

"He might," she says. "But you're putting your life and others at risk."

But these two dogs are the only loving constants I have.

Everything reaches a boiling point when Sam bites a neighbor one day. I call multiple animal sanctuaries, and every person I talk to tells me the same thing.

"No one will be able to accept him," they tell me. "I know it's painful, but putting him down is the right thing to do."

I still can't hear the message, though. When I call my parents crying, it is my father who finally gets through to me.

"Sam wouldn't want to be responsible for hurting someone," he says. "You are protecting him, too."

I call the vet and am told euthanasia costs $431. Crying and numb, I don't think I can even afford doing what everyone is telling me to do. I go through my wallet and then my change drawer. I have $431 exactly. I call my dad one more time. I feel like I cannot keep putting off what so many people have told me is inevitable, even though it is the hardest decision I've ever had to make. As I hold Sam close as the euthanasia is administered, he lets out one final breath, and I am devastated—unable to stop weeping.

"Think of the good times," the vet tells me as I sit, inconsolable, paralyzed with sobs. "Think of the good times."

I did not expect this level of obliteration.

When I return home, I feel out of my mind with grief. My other dog, Trip, senses my despair, and he regresses to the old behavior he exhibited before he was trained. He, too, seems miserable and alone, pining for his best friend. I cannot bear to see him so unhappy every day. After speaking to several friends who work with animals for a living, they suggest that rehoming Trip might be the best option. I speak to several potential families, and I find a beautiful one, with a little boy who has always dreamed of a spaniel. When I bring Trip over to see how he likes it, the difference is striking. Trip has a bigger space to run around in, a cat to play with, and a little boy who is his new best friend.

After I transfer Trip's papers to the family, I am left sobbing once again.

This may be the responsible thing to do, but I've never felt so alone. Now I have nothing—except a job where I feel increasingly alone, too. I've come a long way, but something clearly needs to change.

chapter nine

....

The Guy

2015

Aftter several years of *xoJane*, I am more burned out than I've ever been.

Yes, I'm very proud of a lot of what I do. But the workload of the website is 24/7, and when I write about my own life, everything feels phony and constructed now.

I try a few relationships on for size. I even go back to my old starfuckery ways with Donal Logue. Donal and I talk for hours while he drives cross-country on his trucking routes; he sends me videos of his remote cabin away from Hollywood; and when he's in New York for TV, I help him run lines for his recurring role on *Law & Order: SVU* before he's cast as a lead on *Gotham*. But he's not relationship potential. Obviously. There's a reason why they call it starfucking. No matter how much of a gentleman the person is, you are inherently making yourself small in the process.

Eventually, I just give up on dating.

I don't want to be hurt, disillusioned, or alienated anymore.

I spend most of my date nights counting down until I can come up with a fake reason to leave. One guy spends the whole evening complaining about how difficult it is dealing with these desperate New York women who are so eager to "trap" eligible guys like him.

"Especially the ones on OKC," he confides to me over drinks. *OKC? Wow. He must save so much time not having to say "upid."*

"Yeah," I say, trying to get in the commiserating spirit. "Totally."

I've long given up on the idea of getting married. I'm too old—I'll turn forty near the end of the year—and the prospects out there are too vanilla to even see possibility.

I'm sick of crushed expectations, and I just can't with the boring guys. I'd rather be one of those cool spinster New York ladies than feel like I am forced to spend night after night with someone who lacks a sense of humor or, even worse, thinks he has one—and doesn't.

I realize that in order to have the one thing that makes me happy—authenticity and connection—that means I can no longer hide parts of myself from anyone.

I have a realization during this time that changes my outlook on love entirely.

I almost write it all up as an *xoJane* piece, but it feels too precious somehow. I want to nurture it just as I might that little person inside of me.

One day when I am walking to an AA meeting after a long day at *xoJane*, as I cross the street, I begin absentmindedly praying to one of the saints I've always felt most connected to in life: St. Anthony, who is known as the patron saint of lost things. As I pray, I ask the question silently to myself, again and again: *Will I ever find my soul mate?*

Because maybe, I think, my soul mate is just lost. Maybe that's all it is. Maybe he just got bad directions.

By the time I reach Forty-Second Street and walk up the stairs to a run-down theater building in Midtown to make the 8 p.m. meeting, the answer to my question comes to me in a flash. I actually stop walking and laugh out loud.

Me. It is me.

I am the soul mate I have been looking for all this time.

I am the only person who can decide if I am the good guy or the bad guy in my story. I am the only person who can decide that I am worthy of love—all the time, even when I am falling down on my face yet again or when I am trying my absolute best.

As I think about this concept, I start exploring and investigating, and the possibilities feel like beams of light and love are shooting into the most bruised and battered parts of my soul. What if I were to truly focus on giving myself all the love and compassion and forgiveness I've longed for from someone else all my life? What if I no longer beat myself up? What if I learned to treasure the idea of taking care of myself and my heart and my boundaries, even when it felt unnatural and uncomfortable? What if I accepted and forgave the ugliest parts of my history—every guy, every drug, every deception—and stopped terrorizing my heart with impotent regret?

What if I was forgiven and free? What if I always had been?

Maybe all the costumes and disguises and posturing along the way didn't matter. Because the only self that ever existed could be explained in one single identity.

I am a survivor—and I can and will always be there for myself, no matter what.

After having spent so long chasing some external source of relief in the form of sex and food and drugs and work and even shame itself, realizing that I alone can give myself reprieve feels like the most beautiful gift of all.

I will never let that go. It will never be lost again. I feel unified at last.

. . . .

I TELL MY friends. I tell my therapist. I tell my parents and my sister, with whom I've finally reconnected once again as I begin to develop more boundaries in my writing and sharing.

But I am also more open than I have ever been. I am open to the prospect of meeting someone who will support and love me the rest of the journey. That's what a good partner does.

So when an online dating site called Plenty of Fish offers me $20,000 to blog about finding the perfect Valentine's Day date while promoting their business venture online, I see a financial— and possibly even a relationship—light at the end of the tunnel.

Initially, I'm told I cannot take the gig by someone at *xoJane*'s parent company. When Jane finally intervenes on my behalf, she turns the project around. She understands how much I need it—in more ways than one. Jane, once again, is my guardian angel.

This online dating experiment—which we end up calling "The Mandy Project"—includes the game plan for me to "test out" thirty different relationship clichés in thirty days before V-Day. These relationship adages include "Put yourself out there" (which I test out by walking around Times Square with a sandwich board that says, I'M CURRENTLY SINGLE) or "Play hard to get" (wherein I create a scavenger hunt for my beleaguered suitor).

The schedule proves to be grueling: multiple dates a night, filmed stunts, social promotion, blog entries, and lots of corporate check-ins—along with nonstop writing and editing at *xoJane*, not to mention freelancing I've taken on at *TimeOut*, *Penthouse*, and *Maxim*, and the recording of my weekly podcast.

Within the first two weeks, I get so sick, I can barely get out of bed.

The majority of dates are pretty fun—like the guy who takes me on a helicopter ride or the man who plays along as we have to abide by assigned first-date topics—but others are less so. One man I meet on the rooftop of the Delancey, and a few drinks in, I ask him if he's ever been to prison. I'm totally joking.

I don't expect his answer to be anything but "Of course not." And then we will laugh.

"Once," he says, with a completely straight face. "For assault with a deadly weapon."

Trying to keep from puking on the guy as the fever I am fighting burns hot, I focus on trying to placate him instead.

"Oh well . . . I'm sure that was all a big misunderstanding," I say cheerfully. "Hey, can you sign this release form in case I end up writing about you?"

It's not quite the Carrie Bradshaw dream I'm being paid to make it out to be.

When I get home, in between vomiting spells, I reach out to my friend Dr. Belisa Vranich, a talented psychotherapist who is in fact the amazing friend who hooked me up with this incredibly welcome gig in the first place.

"Some of the guys are kind of sketchy," I complain. "At this point, I'm just trying to keep my shit together to even finish the project."

"Well," she says, "it's not like you have to only date guys from the website. Why don't you meet up with a couple of men you know in real life and write about dates with them?"

"That's a really good idea," I say. "I never even considered it."

So, for one of my final dates, scrambling to meet my quota of stunts, I think of possible candidates. My first thought is to reach out to a comedian named Pat Dixon, whom I met a few months earlier. We were both hanging out at a comedy club called the Stand when he approached me and said that he was a fan of mine.

"You are?" I asked.

"I am," he said with a smile.

I don't know much about him, but I thought he was cute and funny. Still, that usually spells out the kind of too-cool-for-school comic who will roast me on the date—and later on social media or in his stand-up act.

I tap out all the numbers to call Pat, but chicken out at the last minute and hit the X on my keypad instead. I try to think of other candidates.

I call up four platonic guy friends who I know will be safe. But the answers are all no for various reasons: "I'm married now." "Moved to San Fran." "Have a girlfriend; she wouldn't like it." "Out of town."

Fine, I can take a sign. Besides, this isn't the kind of magical realism justification "sign" where I try to convince myself—after being offered alcohol five times in a row, say—that I should drink. This would be a healthy risk for me, asking out a guy I like, where the only real danger is that my pride and ego might end up wounded if he mocks me afterward.

Fuck it. I'm calling him. What do I have to lose?

I already have my soul mate, after all.

Pat answers his phone after a few rings in his deep newscaster voice. "Hello?"

I talk a mile a minute when he answers.

"Hey, oh, hi Pat, yeah, it's Mandy Stadtmiller, wasn't sure if you have my number but yeah, I'm doing this weird paid dating promotion thing so I was wondering if I could ask you out and then write about it for the thing and I realize it's kind of weird but don't worry it's like a stunt date so—"

"I'd love to," he interrupts me.

The assurance in his voice stirs something in me I can't quite pinpoint. It feels something like hope.

Before the date itself, I have to prepare. True to the Mandy Project thesis, on this outing I will be testing out the dating cliché of "Don't play games."

Ahead of time, I've written out a list of relationship expectations that I'm going to give him before we even have small talk on our "date"—to see how he will react.

As I joked ahead of time to one of the corporate consultants managing the Mandy Project, "This will go down in history as the two-minute date."

I arrive a few minutes late to meet Pat at the restaurant I've selected, the Grey Dog, a down-home joint in my neighborhood.

When I enter the restaurant, I see Pat around the corner, sitting down at a table waiting for me.

Dressed in a trim gray suit, he embodies the antithesis of the sloppy, not-trying aesthetic so popular among performers, and when his eyes are on me, my body is on fire.

I feel attracted to the point of embarrassment. I have to look away and down and to the side. I never expect to like guys anymore.

Not *really* like them, that is. Not look-into-their-eyes-and-feel-like-my-goddamned-heart-is-going-to-explode like them. I have never experienced this kind of chemical pull before. It feels like I am seeing someone who I have been looking for my entire life without even realizing it.

"You know this is, like, a stunt date." I quickly try to diminish my eagerness when I sit down next to him.

"Okay," he says with a smile. "I like your scarf, by the way."

I touch my neck. I'm wearing a red-and-white silk scarf Belle Knox gave me as a Christmas present that I threw on at the last minute because in my dating-project-onset sickness, I fell asleep with a humidifier on my chest, and the steaming-hot water spilled on me.

"Oh, this," I say, clutching at it. "Thanks. I'm covering up a burn."

"Are you okay?" he asks.

"Oh yeah, totally, totally," I say, cutting him off from getting too deep into the conversation. "Listen, before we start talking like, you know, normal people, I have to ask you to read this."

I slide over to him my fresh-from-my-printer piece of paper with a big bold title at the top that reads "Mandy's Relationship Expectations." My cheeks are flushed hot. Maybe this *will* go down in history as the two-minute date. And that means there's ninety seconds left.

Pat picks up the paper and starts reading.

Welcome to this date with me, the note says. *I want to be straightforward and let you know what all of my expectations are if we end up having a relationship together. Please take a moment to review:*

1. *When I feel bad, I want you to make me feel better.*
2. *When I am sad, I want you to comfort me and/or care.*
3. *You must say "I love you" first. Please note: This does not apply if you do not in actuality end up loving me.*
4. *I would like you to spontaneously and organically give me at least one compliment a day.*
5. *It is a deal breaker if you cheat on me or blatantly flirt with other women in front of me in a way that it is humiliating.*

Pat is quiet as he reads the note, seemingly studying the words. I am dying as I realize this is definitely too much.

"I don't know," Pat says, and then a smile breaks through. "This all seems fairly reasonable."

"Oh, thank God . . ." I say, exhaling. "It's so weird doing this whole thing. It's like I've gone from never dating to doing it so much I can barely function."

"So, I'm curious," Pat says. "Have you ever been in a real relationship?"

"Married once," I say. "A few relationships after that. What about you?"

"Married twice," he says. "And one woman tried to murder me."

I laugh out loud.

"No, seriously," he says.

"Wow," I say. "Seriously? You might have more red flags than I do."

Offhandedly, I mention to him that dating has changed since I got sober a few years ago.

"You too?" he asks. "This April it'll be fifteen years without a drink."

Synchronicity. I did not expect this. I veer into my dump of inappropriate background information.

"I was crazy when I drank," I say. "So, how many guys do you think I've had sex with?"

Pat jokes, "I don't know, like a hundred?"

"Oh my God, no!" I say, and then, without thinking too much about it, I blurt out, "I mean, I've probably sucked a hundred dicks."

The sentence just hangs there. There is no taking it back. I sit there, flushed, recoiling in quiet horror at myself. Okay, maybe this won't be the two-minute date. Maybe it'll be the two-minute-and-two-hour date.

"You have great stories," Pat says, not taking the bait. "You know, I've always been a fan of your writing."

He doesn't respond with lewdness, but instead offers . . . respect.

That's about the last thing I expected. There is no trace of judgment or leering dismissal. He treats me like a peer.

We are quiet for a while, and then he says, "You're a lot sweeter than I expected."

"I am?"

"You are."

As I'm talking, without realizing it, I am nervously ripping the napkin in front of me to shreds, and little bits of detritus are covering the table, my food, everything.

Without a word, Pat removes the napkin from my hands and sets it aside. He places his hands on mine, holding them with gentleness and warmth.

I stop talking. What is this sensation flooding my body? I feel giddy. High.

"Jesus," I say. "I feel like I'm in the seventh grade."

This guy makes me want to drop all of the bravado I'm wearing like a costume on Halloween. Even if it makes me look like a fool, I know I need to communicate what I'm experiencing inside right now. Because I haven't felt something like this in a long time.

"Listen," I tell him hurriedly, "I know I come across kind of . . . strange. But I feel like I should tell you . . . I would date you."

The urgent rush of sincerity is embarrassing. Like I just wet my pants right there at the table.

"Thank you," he says, his face softening. "I'm glad you told me that."

We walk back to my apartment because I tell him I need to get a photo to write about the date—and I've forgotten to bring the photo release form with me.

"Sorry," I say. "I realize this whole thing is so weird."

We enter my tiny studio, and he looks around to take in the view.

I've "decorated" the place with a pile of clothes in one corner and an unwieldy stack of letters, packages, and assignments in another.

Most of the place is inherited from the girl who lived here before me, and it shows. A green suede headboard hints at a cute frilly girliness that I have never embodied as a single woman. You can even see the slats in the wall where she once displayed her vast hanging high-heel collection. The pièce de résistance, however, was her framed wedding announcement next to the sparkly stiletto-heel trinket she had hanging on the door.

This studio was her true-to-life *Sex and the City* paradise, and I've tarnished her tradition by filling it with wrinkly clothes, a paltry kitten-heel collection, ungodly stacks of reporter's notebooks, and the near certainty I will never achieve her endgame.

"What do you think?" I ask Pat.

He looks around at the disarray and says, "All your place needs is a woman's touch."

I laugh, and Pat walks over to the side of my bed, next to the scratched-up black desk I also inherited. Atop my desk is a side-by-side display: an unwashed Bullet vibrator, a half-empty plastic carton of orange juice, and ten gold and silver plastic boxes of "S&M kits" a publicist has sent me. Pat sidles over to the assortment, and, as if making his choice in a Showcase Showdown, lifts up the orange juice and takes a swig.

His total authority over my apartment turns me on. I hand him the release form to sign, and then we go out into my stairwell to snap a photo for the blog entry I have to write. I extend my iPhone to capture the moment, and Pat puts his arm around me—then turns to give me the best kiss I've ever received.

It feels like a slo-mo sequence of chemical reactions, from excitement to lust to a little bit of fear.

"Do you want to come inside for a little bit?" I ask.

When we sit on my bed making awkward small talk, Pat encircles his fingers around the Belle Knox scarf and plays with it for half a second. When she gifted it to me, Belle wrote on her card, "Hopefully, you can use this for something dirty and fun."

Belle Knox gets her wish.

Pat pulls the scarf toward him and kisses me again in a way that is slow, deliberate, and done with a confidence I haven't experienced in a lifetime of kisses.

We fool around for a few more hours—but don't have sex—and as he gets up to leave, I expect this will be the last time I ever see the guy.

"I like you," he says before heading out the door. "I want to see you again soon."

"You do?" I ask.

"I really do."

. . . .

WE DON'T HAVE sex until a few dates later, because I'm trying to incorporate the lessons from mistakes I've made in the past. When we do, there is a physical connection that feels like something swallowing me whole.

Maybe because we're both sober. Maybe because we're both aware of every breath and kiss and move we're taking. There is nothing more intoxicating than total awareness of every little thing going down.

Pat is the only man I've ever been with who can quickly go from kinky to tender to completely psychological—without ever missing a beat. It's like Sexual Mad Libs, and possibly constitutes the only way that monogamous sex does not get boring.

If there are any people in relationships looking to spice up their sex lives who are reading this, please, if your partner is into it, go nuts when you do the dirty talk. It is the most freeing experience in the world. It's like Disneyland every night in the bedroom. I don't know why it's so freeing—but there's this level of trust involved that is absolutely narcotic. It's like a fucking Scientology audit.

That fun carnality is made all the more precious because he is also one of the kindest, most thoughtful men I've dated.

One day I mention to him how alienating it can feel when you are becoming close with someone new. I tell him how I wish he could just immediately know everything that one of my best childhood friends might know—like, say, the name of my first cat I had when I was a kid. The next day, Pat texts me.

"What was your first cat's name?"

"Rags," I text back, with a huge grin on my face.

We are so close, so fast. Which means we are also contending with our newfound status of "being in a relationship." Neither of us really expected it, and sometimes our resentments bubble up out of nowhere and take on a much heavier weight.

One hot day in Bryant Park after one month of dating, he talks about the black-or-white pressures he feels bearing down on him.

"Sometimes it feels like it's all or nothing if we fight about something," he says. "It's this idea that we're together forever or nothing."

"What are you saying?" I begin, already feeling the anxiety and the anger rising inside me, beginning to strangle any sense of reason or calm. "Because I don't need this, you know. I've done just fine on my own."

"Stop with that bullshit bravado, Mandy," Pat says. "We're past that."

"It's not bullshit," I say, even more defensively. "I'd rather die alone than spend a minute with someone who doesn't want to be with me. You owe me fucking nothing."

While I am in theory sober, my actions are incredibly unsober.

I'm not going to meetings. I'm not seeing a therapist, because I'm trying to save money. And my professional life is falling apart. At *xoJane*, layoffs have just been announced—and I'm a casualty. I feel unmoored, and the stakes for every little decision seem insanely high.

In fact, all of our fighting stems from a conversation started about how I am up for a full-time features editor position at *Mashable*, which would mean editing a features section that does not generate much passion within me, but which would be the safe choice. When I prepared for the final round of interviews, I showed Pat what life might be like, with my sample story idea lists: *Ten different recipes for broccoli that will blow your mind. Why this season's caftan will change your life. Seven belly-busters that will change the way you think about cellulite.*

Instead of taking that job, I decide to look for every possible angle to figure out how I can dodge the corporate route and have more freedom.

"Maybe we could move in together," I suggested earlier before our fight began. "Then I wouldn't have to worry about money so much, you know . . ."

I wasn't really serious when I said it. Okay, I guess I was kind of serious. I was spitballing. Hey, at least I didn't register him a domain name. I shouldn't have said anything. I know that. In fact, I feel shame about having said anything, but now it's out there, and I can't take it back. I'm angry at myself, and I can feel myself directing the anger at him as he begins to speak.

"I care for you so much," Pat says now. "But we haven't built the foundation for the metaphorical house we would live in—for a relationship. I want the stakes to be lower, rather than living in a house with no ceiling or walls, just posts and beams with holes in the ground."

Pat tells me he met his second wife a month after his divorce— and moved in with her, and stayed in that relationship for years because he did not take it slow enough. He doesn't want the same thing to happen with me. This is too important, he says.

"You're a camper," he says. "You want to set up camp. I want to keep what we have intact and see where this goes."

Now, I am in full-on autopilot mode, defensive and enraged at just the smallest whiff of rejection.

"Everything you're talking about," I say, "makes me feel like I'm complicit in your fucking entrapment or something."

My words are violence. Fuck this. Fuck that. Fuck you. Fuck everyone.

After having begun the best relationship with someone I've ever had, I now feel wildly offended at the notion he might want to go slow to preserve what we're in the process of creating.

So I end it. The hesitation and concern and very logical resistance in his voice feel too painful. They sting me, and my pride kicks in.

"I don't want to be a burden," I tell him, even though he never once said that I was a burden. "Thank you for the best four weeks of my life."

"This is your decision," he says. "I don't understand it, but I can respect it if that's what you want."

I don't even listen to him. I shut him out and walk away. I am okay being single forever. Because I am in control. I am the one crashing the plane—no one else.

....

I EMAIL SEVERAL girlfriends and my sister a rendition of breaking up with Pat. Then I call my parents. They all start giving me feedback I am not prepared to hear.

"I think you're ruining a good thing." "He actually seems really emotionally intelligent and like he knows how to deal with some of your shit." "Why are you doing this, dude?"

Then my sister calls me and speaks to me in the straight, no-nonsense way for which she is famous.

"Hey, Mandy," she says bluntly. "This reminds me of when

Mom said to Dad, 'I think I might want to get divorced,' and then Dad was pissed, so he got divorced. Remember that?"

Of course I remember. Against all odds, my parents went on to remarry five years later and have been together since. But my mom acted impulsively. She acted out of rage. Then my father did the same. Shit blew up. Is that the kind of behavior I want to model in my own life?

My sister's insight lands in a way nothing else does.

Examining where I've veered off course is so uncomfortable for me. It is for everyone, I suppose. It requires a level of personal accountability in admitting that you are wrong—and practicing what my therapist calls the art of "defenselessness."

"Okay, I'm going to call him," I tell my sister. "I hope it isn't too late."

"Good luck," she says. "Don't fuck it up."

It's near the end of the night, and I broke things off about six hours before. Pat picks up my FaceTime call after a few rings, and the look on his face is one of amusement.

"Hello," he says. "You're the last person I expected to hear from."

"I screwed everything up," I say. "I'm so sorry. I just shut things down because I was scared that you would reject me so I wanted to do it first."

"Why?" he asks, seeming tentative.

"I don't know," I say. "It's like there's one part of me that wants to be open and vulnerable to love, and then there's another part that's all about self-preservation and survival—and I just want to run from anything that might end up hurting me. Or hurt the other person first."

Pat is quiet, and then suggests a solution.

"What if we came up with two different names for those two different parts of yourself?" he asks. "We could call one 'Deborah.' And the other 'Shithead.'"

I laugh out loud, and it reminds me of the level of joy this guy provides me. He is dark and irreverent, yet I can feel his honesty and openheartedness in the way we communicate. He can make a joke and then follow it up with an insight that speaks to a psychological vocabulary that surpasses my own.

"So," he says, "what can we do so this doesn't happen again?"

"I'm going to . . ." I stall, not wanting to commit to what I know I need to do. "Okay, I'm going to go to my therapist and AA meetings."

Pat's face melts into a smile.

"Good," he says. "That makes me really happy."

He sees me. He forces me to talk about my feelings.

It is a strange thing. So much of this relationship is strange—in the best sense of the word. It is some manifestation of years of work I have done on myself to heal that little girl inside who was her worst enemy in re-creating the chaos with which I was so acquainted. Those twisted familiar patterns that felt like "home" are now being redefined. Maybe home can be a safe place with someone whom I can trust and love and count on.

"Why am I so fucked-up?" I ask him, annoyed at my broken lizard brain, including all of the dark and disturbing sexual scenarios it frequently conjures.

"You know what the most insane, crazy scenario might be for you, Mandy? A man who is madly in love with you and adores you and thinks you're the love of his life."

"Jesus Christ," I say. "I think you're right."

Seeing myself get past my natural inclination to self-sabotage as a form of protection is no small triumph. It feels like a miracle.

....

AFTER SIX WEEKS together—and two weeks after my aborted breakup attempt—we start calling each other boyfriend and girlfriend.

And now I am watching my boyfriend perform onstage. It's a slightly harrowing experience.

"My first two wives were both virgins," Pat is telling the audience as I sit hidden in the back row after asking to tag along. "I guess it seemed honorable, a girl saving her sex for marriage."

Inside Dangerfield's, the comedy club where he is performing, the dim lighting and red-glass-lit tables create the effect of a *Mad Men* dive bar. There are about twenty-five people in the audience, tittering and shifting nervously as he holds court. He pauses to look into the eyes of the audience.

"After two divorces, I'm kind of saving my next marriage for a girl who really likes to fuck."

He smirks at me when he says that, and I squirm in my seat like he's just seen through me with X-ray vision. When I took some friends from the *Post* to see Pat, he did one of his jokes about how he'll never get married again, and city editor Michelle Gotthelf whispered to me, "Too bad."

So I don't take this joke about his "next marriage" seriously at all. Besides, I've ruled that out for myself. I am a realist at heart, and now I'm just enjoying the ride.

"The girl I'm dating right now," Pat tells the audience, "told me she sucked a hundred dicks."

What the . . .

I spit out my Diet Coke. It takes a lot to scandalize me, but here we are.

"Does that seem high to you?" he asks. "How many dicks is a woman supposed to suck? I don't know. She's almost forty, she started 'dating' at fifteen. After twenty-five years of dating, that's about four dicks a year. That's not bad. It's one dick, quarterly. A lot of small-business owners would be grateful for that option."

I'm laughing and burying my face in the table. The waiter brings me another soda and smiles.

"My first wife, she was my high school sweetheart," Pat tells the crowd. "You marry your high school sweetheart, it's like you've said, 'You know what—I've looked all over the school.'"

Pat is unlike any man I've ever dated before. He doesn't give a shit. Doesn't want to impress (or even offend) the right people. Doesn't want to glad-hand those in the right circles. Doesn't want to kiss the ass of the world as a whole. It's scary to date someone who has less to lose than you do, but that's what's unfolding here, and I realize that every minute I spend with the guy.

Then he moves on to the story he mentioned on our first date.

"I had a woman try to murder me at an IHOP," he tells the crowd. "It's true. It's a one hundred percent true story, which I'm opening up to share with you tonight. When I tell women that a woman tried to murder me at an IHOP, they all have the same question. Do you know what it is?"

Four or five women sitting at different tables yell out in near unison, "What did you do?"

"'What did I do?' you want to know," he repeats to the audience. "First of all, thanks for blaming the victim. But if you must know what I did, I fell in love, that's what I did. I was thinking with my dick."

Appreciative laughter, especially from the men. Some women titter, uncertain as to what's to come next.

The story of the attempted murder he's telling is a matter of public record, no matter how unbelievable I found it at first. My mistrusting nature led me to do a search for the 2004 police report, and there I saw it, the woman who had greeted him with a murder-suicide note in her pocket and police-issue Glock 9mm before he wrestled it out of her hands. At that point, she unleashed her fury on him, jumping onto his back, scratching his face, and trying to force her fingertips into his eye sockets.

The woman, who was convicted of second-degree attempted murder, had been his mistress in his failing second marriage. When he cut the relationship off and put all her duffel bags in a hotel room to avoid a face-to-face showdown, she grew obsessive and increasingly unglued. She called his family members, whom she'd never met. She incessantly called his parents, threatening his mother.

Having cheated death that time, Pat resolved to never cheat again.

"Would you like to know why men think with their dicks?" Pat asks the women who shouted out the question to him earlier, asking what he'd done. "Because I'll tell you."

A pause.

"Yes!" one woman cries out.

"It's because," he says, "our dicks have pretty good ideas."

He's killing, and he's won the women over, too—the same way he's winning me over as his girlfriend.

After the show, I see him mingling at the bar with the other comics, drinking a Coke and speaking out of the side of his mouth. He's perpetually unperturbed, his military-close haircut alienating and cold, giving him a look akin to Travis Bickle-cum-*Peaky Blind-ers*, which works, since he has the swagger of a maniac, the guy who could either save the day or light the whole place up, unre-deemable.

"Good set," I say, sounding almost hesitant, which I never am anymore.

"Come downstairs with me," Pat says, and he leads me through a narrow stairwell and into a hidden greenroom with a picture of Rodney Dangerfield hanging above us where he closes the door. Rodney has a look that says, *I get no respect*, and I giggle looking at it. Pat has taken me to a secret place. He swings one arm over my black lambskin jacket and black disco pants and pulls me close.

"You know who you remind me of? Blondie. Not Deborah Harry, the comic strip," he tells me, running his hands up and down my body, which is boosted up and cinched into the tightest outfit I own. "When I was little, I thought Blondie was the sexiest woman in the world, with her figure and the tight dress, the hair. And now here you are with me. Big tits. Perfect face. Blond hair. Long legs . . ."

"Fuck," I say, breathing into his ear. "You don't seem scared of anything."

"What's there to be afraid of?"

I think for a minute.

"I don't know. My past, maybe."

"Your past is what makes you *you*, Mandy. I wouldn't have it any other way."

When he comes back to my place in Chelsea, I go into auto-pilot, switching into a character I can do on cue: The Slut. I try not to do it anymore, but sometimes old habits kick in without my even realizing my defense mechanisms are at play.

"Do you want me to touch myself?" I ask Pat, in a caricature of seduction.

"I want you to cut it out," he says, looking me right in my eyes. "What's this thing you do, where it's like you're doing a show?"

"It's just easier," I say hesitantly. "Sometimes just pretending to be someone else feels safer."

"The only thing that turns me on is seeing who you actually are," Pat says, moving his hand up my body. "Tell me, do you need me?"

"Yes," I say, answering what I know to be true. "I do."

"Why, baby?"

"Because I love you," I say without thinking.

Good God in heaven above.

Did I just say that aloud?

So much for my "Mandy's Relationship Expectations" where the guy must say "I love you" first. Besides, it's only been about six weeks. I try to reel it back in. "I didn't mean it, like, you know . . . it was just . . ."

"It's okay," he stops me. "I love you, too."

Panic creeps in goose-bump inches up my body. This guy *is* different.

"I know you, Mandy," he says. "You were bad, weren't you?"

I nod, eyes squeezed shut tight.

"Nothing is wrong," Pat says, "unless it's untrue.

"Did you fuck a lot of guys?" Pat asks. "You *love* sex, don't you?"

"I have," I say. "I do," I say.

"Tell me everything," Pat whispers to me.

My eyes flutter open.

"Okay."

With every story I tell Pat, he relays to me one of his own.

"Mandy," he says. "I have a feeling about you and me. That we are worthy of each other."

On his way out the door, he hesitates. I'm smiling at him, drunk on closeness. He looks at me, eyes shining, taking me in.

"Will you marry me someday?" he asks.

My heart is pounding. I wonder if I am dreaming right now.

"Yes," I say.

"Good," he says with a nonchalant smile, and walks out the door.

....

THE HARDEST PART about sobriety is realizing that when you open that black box inside of you, the secrets and addictions don't stop their revelations after the first one.

I am a drug and alcohol addict. I am a sex addict. I am a food addict. And the most difficult one: I am a rage addict, too.

"Do you really not care if you lose me?" I scream at Pat one day. This is based on, honestly, no reason at all besides a small disagreement that has now spiraled ridiculously out of control. "You disgust me! You're disgusting!"

"Why are you saying all of this, Mandy?" he asks. "Because I'm not getting upset? I figure you're just saying all of this to get a reaction."

"Well . . . I am," I say, surprised at him calling bullshit on my bullshit.

"Well, okay then," he says.

I sit there, stunned. I've never met someone who knows how to deal with me like Pat does and cut through my defenses. And then he surprises me again, as he always does. Instead of wanting to continue to fight, he has just one request.

"When was the last time you saw your therapist?" he asks.

"I don't have time," I say, looking away. "I saw her after we fought that one time. I did, I swear."

"If you don't have time for that, then we likely won't have a relationship either," he says. "This is that important."

Therapy is, as anyone who takes it seriously knows, not like, say, getting your high school diploma. It's not a "Congratulations, you've graduated" kind of situation. You have to keep going. A lifetime of conditioning doesn't just magically disappear.

When I see my therapist again and tell her some of the cruel things I've been hurtling at Pat, she suggests it's time for me to consider group therapy.

"Will that make me less defensive?" I ask.

"That's the idea," she says.

After a few group sessions, we are asked to do psychodrama and role-playing just like when I went to the Caron Institute in Pennsylvania. In one of the most intense sessions, I am told to role-play my ex-husband while I speak to a chair who is "me." I really get into it. I am cruel. I am scathing. I am relentless. I summon up the worst things my ex ever said to me, and I scream at the chair.

"You're pathetic," I say, pretending to be my ex-husband and spitting the words at "myself" like venom. "You're pathetic!"

I am crying near the end. Because I can hear myself . . . in the way I talk to Pat.

"You disgust me! You're disgusting!"

How many times have I said cruel things—including to my ex-husband—that I may not even remember because I was in a rage blackout? I need to turn everything around. I cannot continue this cycle of victimization.

"I owe you an apology," I tell Pat afterward. "I can see now that a lot of the things I said to you were hurtful and cruel. I don't want to do that. I want to support you."

"Thank you for really trying with me," Pat says. "It means a lot to me."

This, apparently, is how people have a conversation. One person says one thing that isn't a platitude; the other person engages.

"Have I ever told you about my whole black-box theory of relationships?" I ask him.

"Is it anything like the old George Carlin joke?" he asks. "'Why don't they just make the plane out of the black box?'"

I laugh. I am familiar with it, of course. I explain to him the concept: how we have all these internal recordings and programming from throughout our lives that influence future relationships.

"It's so hard to examine all of it," I tell him. "Did you know that I wrote a letter to my future self back in 2012 when I did that really intensive group therapy thing? I can't even bring myself to read it, that's how scared I get about looking at what's inside of me."

I point him to where I keep it hidden away, tucked inside a silver envelope, in a childish blue *Frozen* treasure box above my bed. I mean, it's not like there's anything bad that I could have even written in there—after all, I was sober and approaching some semblance of mental healthiness in 2012. But I still don't want to disappoint Future Me.

"You have nothing to be scared of," Pat says. "Did you know that when I first saw you in New York, you were walking through some comedy club, and I asked someone, 'Who *is* that?' Because I had to know. It was 2007. You were amazing to me even then. You made such an impression on me. You were like this tall beautiful wash of blond hair. I thought you were totally out of my league. You were so striking and confident. At the time, I figured there was no chance."

I'm floored in more ways than one.

"Wow," I say. "I would have been dating Blaine back then. How funny that I didn't feel that way about myself at all. I just thought of myself as this unwifeable disaster who couldn't do anything right."

"Wait," Pat says, looking at me. "Unwifeable? No. That's not you at all. *Unapproachable*. That's what you are."

. . . .

PAT IS FROM Tennessee. I am from California. Our backgrounds are as different as can be, but we are both children of dysfunction, which has made us hyper-attuned to everything around us. As we grow closer, Pat reveals to me the pain he feels watching his eighty-five-year-old mother's deteriorating condition as she lives out her final days in the grips of Alzheimer's. He doesn't agree with the decision to send her to a nursing home, but ultimately it is his father's call, not his own.

We make the long trip together down South first by plane and then by car. As we walk up to the modest care facility, the two of us are carrying bags filled with some of his mom's favorites—fried chicken, Pop-Tarts, and corn along with a hanging plant of lavender flowers—but I can see the spreading sadness on his face. His smile has altogether faded. Pat stops and touches my arm.

"I don't know if I can do this," he says. "It's so hard."

"I'm here with you," I say quietly. "I'm not going anywhere."

As we enter the bright little room, I see his mother, who is frail and delicate, lying like a china doll in her bed. Pat reaches down to hold her in a warm embrace, then sits beside her, stroking her arm. His father is sitting in the corner, updating us on how she's doing lately. She appears so weak. I speak softly and gently, standing above her as Pat holds her. Trying to think of something she might like, I pull up a bunch of pictures of her son to show her on my phone.

"Oooh," she says, touching a picture of Pat holding a mic on TV, smiling broadly. "Will you send me that one?"

She touches her delicate porcelain finger to the screen.

"You promise?" she asks.

"I will," I say. When I look at Pat and her together, I get an idea. As part of getting sober, I studied Reiki, a form of energy healing that is all about channeling prayer and love to someone through touch and intention. I want more than anything else at that moment to love on Pat's mom. I'm nervous about looking like a fool, but I go ahead and ask anyway.

"Hey," I say quietly to her, "would it be okay if I rub your feet?"

She looks at me with a fragile smile.

"Okay," she says in her sweet Southern voice.

I move to sit at the edge of her bed, lift the purple wool blanket off her legs, and begin rubbing her feet gently as I listen to Pat and his mom talk.

Old friends and memories are mentioned, but his mom is confused a lot. People who suffer from Alzheimer's frequently ask about "going home." They regress into younger states. They want to see their parents, who are, of course, long dead.

"Can we see my mother in the other room?" she asks.

"Let's do that later," Pat says. "Why don't we catch up right now?"

"When can I leave?" she asks. "I keep trying to figure out how to go home."

"I'm here, Mom," Pat says.

A yellow star hangs above her bed. I glance at a nurse's chart and see that it stands for "falling star," a sign to the nurse on staff that she might not be able to walk on her own.

"I love you, Mom," Pat says. "I miss you."

When we leave at the end of the night, Pat and I are quiet for a while before we reach the rental car. He turns to me, and his face shows a kind of love deeper than any I've seen before.

"You rubbed my mom's feet," he says. "That's, like, some biblical shit, Mandy. What made you into that kind of person?"

"Childhood stuff," I say quietly. "I think my primary love language is touch."

Pat pulls me into his arms and squeezes me tight.

"I would never put you in a home," he says quietly.

Only a few months later, Pat flies down to be with his mom in her final days. He brings her that photograph she asked for in a small silver frame and places it next to her.

Surrounded by family, Pat sits next to his mom, holding her hand one last time. His father and his brothers and sister and a roomful of relatives are there with him, too. He calls me after she passes, his voice breathless.

"She's gone," he says. "It was peaceful. I love you."

His mom's passing makes me want to introduce him to my family all the more.

"I'm honestly looking forward to it," Pat says. "And I hate meeting parents."

We plan a trip to San Diego a few months away, and in the meantime, I give Pat my dad's phone number so the two of them can talk. But I don't know that I expect him to actually call. I don't want to be disappointed, so I kind of forget that I even gave it to him.

Before they do connect, my dad and I have a conversation on the phone one day where I am gushing all about my relationship—but before too long it ends in screaming and tears.

"I really love Pat," I tell my father at first. "I'm so excited for you to meet him."

My dad is silent.

"Dad?" I ask. "Aren't you excited for me? At all?"

"I just don't want you to get hurt," he says.

"Dad, don't you see that if that's your only reaction . . . just . . . can't you see how hurtful that is to me? How negative it is?"

"Okay, well, I tell you what, Mandy," he says, his voice rising in anger, "you tell me what to say and when to say it and how to say it and I'll forget being honest and spontaneous."

I am shaking. I am so far regressed back to my childhood place of fear and anger and sadness I can't see straight.

"It seems like, you know," I begin, my voice shaking, "I'm trying to tell you about something I'm really proud of, and your reaction is, 'I'm just afraid that it's going to go away.' Do you see how that's immediately just like a lump of coal in my stocking?"

"I'm sick of being the family asshole!" my dad yells. "Fuck it!"

He hangs up the phone, and I throw my iPhone across the room. I didn't detach with love. I engaged with a whole lot of expectations. Honestly, my father's negativity addiction is so all-consuming sometimes I don't think he sees how it affects others. But I just know that if I weren't dating Pat, my dad would be asking me if I was dating anyone—and now, when I do find someone, it feels like he won't give me the approval, celebration, and support I so deeply crave.

Later that night, Pat walks into my apartment using the key he now has, but I can tell he's in the middle of a phone call. He is laughing and smiling, but I am not in the mood. I just sit on my bed, flicking TV channels, my face in a deep scowl—when Pat hands me the phone.

It is my father.

"I just had the best conversation with Pat," my dad gushes. "He's hilarious. He's kind. He's great. I can see why you guys love each other so much."

I burst into tears.

"I'm sorry for before," I tell my dad.

"So am I."

When we finally travel to San Diego to meet my family, Pat charms them all—and is charmed by them in kind. It is the complete opposite of Blaine's standoffishness and frequent looking away from my parents when we visited. It is so clear how much Pat respects them. He notices the sly hilarity of my mom, which no man has ever fully appreciated before, and he says of her bouncy walk, "She's the most youthful woman in her seventies I've ever seen."

All of the strangeness I long sought to hide from others, he just completely gets it. They are hilarious, weird, brilliant, deranged—and where I come from, always.

On our last night in town, my parents and my sister's family all gather together for a big pizza dinner at Filippi's, my favorite restaurant growing up, where I used to play with the dough as a little girl. There are a lot of moments that would normally be very stressful for me—my dad needs to sit in a certain place so he can see very partially out of his one eye, he knocks something over, the waitress doesn't get his sense of humor, they're out of everything. But I don't feel on edge like I did with Blaine. I know Pat accepts me and isn't judging me on any normal scale of *What will the Joneses think?*

The dinner is instead hilarious and fun, with my sister's children taking over my Snapchat, and my dad and Pat swapping jokes nearly the entire dinner. At the end, my father proposes a toast.

"To Pat," my dad says, raising a glass.

"To Pat," my mom says, and then she can't resist adding, "who is one funny motherfucker."

I let out a huge belly laugh and Pat does, too. I feel so much love for her.

"Children are here, Mom!" my sister scolds, and her kids laugh.

Pat is sitting next to me, and as everyone talks, he squeezes my leg.

"Your family is so great," he whispers to me. I feel relaxed, at ease, like all my selves are joining together.

....

ONE NIGHT IN late August, when I am anxiously trying to fall asleep but unable to do so, I get a text from Pat at 2:34 in the morning.

"I just thought of the perfect day we could get married," his text reads.

My heart stops. I reread the text. Marriage? Is he screwing with me? We have been together now for seven months. Is this possible? Is this really happening?

"Yeah?" I reply, realizing that unlike other men who might bring marriage up to mess with your mind, he is 100 percent sincere.

"February 29," he texts again. "We'd have an anniversary every four years."

"That's brilliant," I write back.

"Then it's decided," he replies. "We're engaged."

I'm shell-shocked.

"!!!!!!!" I text back.

I spring up in my bed like I've been hit with a bolt of lightning. I blast Jay-Z's "On to the Next One" and dance around in circles. When I was a kid, my mom would tell me to work out my energy by running around the pool. I wish I could do that right now, but instead I screen-grab his texts and make them my home screen.

Is this really happening?

When we meet up the next day in Bryant Park, Pat greets me with an embrace and holds me tight.

"We're going to do this properly with a ring—the exact ring that you want—and I want you to be able to plan it out just how you want it," he says. "Because this is like the ultimate getting-flowers-at-the-office competition, right?"

I kiss him gratefully. Pat understands how fun it can be to spike the ball.

"I want a ruby ring," I say.

He touches my face gently.

"You do?" he asks.

The ruby ring has a particular sentimentality for us. When we first shared all our stories, Pat told me once about his grandma's ring, which featured all of her grandkids' birthstones.

As a little boy, four or five years old, he would touch the ruby stone and say, "That's me!"

I want him to be able to do the same with mine.

"And we can do the public proposal on the steps of Times Square . . . and we can Periscope the whole thing so our friends and family can watch," I say, on a roll now, so excited at the opportunity to go sky's-the-limit.

"That sounds great," he says.

On the day of the event, we wake up at 5 a.m., and I pick up a copy of the *Daily News*, which shows a picture of us in the top left corner.

"Tune in, see her yes face!" the headline reads, telling people to watch us Periscope the proposal later that day. It is like something out of a million vision boards I would never dare create.

"Mandy," Pat says as a crowd watches on the red TKTS steps of Times Square and another one watches online, "I've been smitten with you since before we met for our first date. I couldn't understand how you could still be single. We met on a stunt date over coffee. You told me stories. A lot of them involving sex. You mentioned how many dicks you sucked. It was magical. After our first date, I was still smitten, but I could kind of understand the still-single part."

I am crying-laughing.

"Mandy, in all seriousness you're the smartest person I've ever met. You're the sweetest person I've ever met. You're the funniest woman I've ever met. You're the person on earth I always want to see the most. I'm still smitten. And I know the reason you were still single is because I hadn't gotten to meet you yet. Because you have the patience and the generosity and the kindness to love someone who is as deeply flawed as I am. So, Mandy . . . will you be my best friend and wife forever?"

I say, "Yes," as I stand there in tears. He puts the ring on my finger and we kiss like it's the first time we ever have, like it's our last night on earth.

I get engaged on October 23, 2015—the very last day of my thirties. I wake up on my fortieth birthday, engaged to the love of my life and unable to believe that I have not only met the man of my dreams, but that I get to spend the rest of my life with him—starting very soon.

As we start to figure out the details, Pat has an idea for how we might do our wedding that he thinks might make the night even more special than just resulting in a marriage anniversary every four years.

"What would you say about getting married," Pat asks, "while performing onstage?"

Nothing has ever sounded so brilliant, honestly. I love nothing more than joining Pat when he performs, and this seems like the ultimate way to tie the knot.

"Are you kidding me?" I respond. "Yes!"

Pat tells me how the wedding will work. Because his stage show has been accepted into the New York Comedy Festival, he's head-lining Gotham Comedy Club on November 11, so we can turn it into the festival's very first wedding-slash-comedy show. Awesome.

But the date is coming up really, really soon, and it's not long before we are both running overheated as we scramble to meet the fast-approaching event. It feels like a 24-style countdown to bring all the pieces together: the minister (check), the performers (check), the vows (check), the rings (check).

I find myself slowly having a meltdown.

"You need to take care of yourself, Mandy," Pat says as I'm try-ing to figure out the perfect dress, the perfect hair, and the perfect everything. "We don't have to get married at the show if it's too stressful. But you have to go to a meeting, see your therapist, something. Because we can't do this at the expense of your personal well-being."

And so, as he runs around the city making last-minute preparations, I sit in a small dingy room with other people who are facing the same demons that I am.

Only today is my wedding day, and I have never felt so grateful.

"Hi, my name is Mandy, and I'm an alcoholic."

Later that night, onstage, surrounded by three hundred friends and fans in a packed comedy club, we recite vows we have written that day.

Pat takes my hands and speaks to my heart.

"You know, Mandy, when we met, everything changed for me," Pat says. "I really didn't know somebody like you existed, and if I had known, I wouldn't have given up on all that shit before."

A wave of laughter ripples through the audience, and tears well up in my eyes.

"You're unlike anybody I've ever met," he says. "It's been the best year of my life. I promise to honor that by never forgetting how bad life was when I didn't know you."

Then he looks in my eyes, pauses, and says, "And I'm never going to put you in a home."

The audience bursts into laughter—at both the irreverence and the surprise of the line—but I know how profound what he says really is. I squeeze his hand.

It is a moment only we understand.

Later that night, when it is just the two of us alone in a romantic hotel suite with roses strewn everywhere, Pat surprises me by pulling out a copy of the letter that I wrote to my "future self," the one I showed him months earlier.

Nervously, I open the seal.

I read it aloud for us both.

"Dear Mandy, what a beautiful experience these past few years have been," I say, fully crying now. "You know who you are. You have a heart filled with love—for yourself and others. And you only partner with a man who has earned the right to be with you."

At that last part, Pat reaches out and caresses the ruby on my ring.

"That's you," I say.

"That's me."

. . . .

IF YOU LOOK deep inside every woman, you will find a black box that records the wreckage of her past relationships.

It's an intimidating excavation, to be sure. Digging through all the dust and debris until you finally find it buried beneath the surface with the ominous seal on the outside reading DO NOT OPEN.

I know better now than to blithely obey.

I am not and will not be afraid to look and to listen and to learn. I want to go there. I need to find the bigger picture, and in the process, myself. While I relive the most terrifying moments recorded, the most disturbing memories, the darkest nights, I can't help but shudder.

But I'm no longer afraid of the fear. I'm no longer paralyzed by humiliation or the notion of what others might think of me. Fear will not kill you. Humiliation holds no real power. But being too afraid to look and listen just might.

At first, the voices sound haunting. Taunting even. But I don't stop. I can't stop. I refuse to. I will go deeper until I find out what I am really made of and where I have been all this time.

> Goddammit I just can't take it!
> This never happened, and if you tell anyone different, I'll deny it.
> I'm disappointed in you, Mandy.
> You're not smart, you're not funny, you're not a good writer, and you're not pretty.
> Do you want me to fuck the shit out of you?
> If I were you, I would have put a gun in my mouth a long time ago.
> Please don't say I dated Mandy Stadtmiller.
> I'd suggest you stay away from marriage going forward?
> You took a little nap. I had to wake you up.
> That was not sex. That was rape.
> I don't want a Post reporter to die on me.
> Are you high yet? You want some more?
> You know, there are these swinger parties they have.

Our black boxes really are such extraordinary devices, built for a level of toughness that is nearly unimaginable. But what we don't know when we are younger is that sometimes what feels on impact like a fiery crash is just the terrifying last moments of an emergency landing that ultimately saves your life. For me, it was rejecting a deeply negative self-concept that became a twisted, masochistic sort of self-fulfilling prophecy.

Yes, I may have felt safe and certain with the concept of "unwifeability." But I never really had any kind of fixed identity. Because no one does. Unless you treat yourself that way, you are always pure potential—always limitless possibility. It was me who felt unworthy. It was me who felt unlovable. It was me who felt unredeemable. So I chose relationships that affirmed my self-hatred. Because if everything is pain, then nothing is.

See that burning wreckage? I did that. That was me.

But empowerment is not self-sabotage—even when you are the one wreaking the havoc. Empowerment, I think, is deciding what you want your final destination to be, developing a plan to protect your heart, and never letting anyone tell you differently.

A funny thing happens the longer you listen to that black box. Over time you can hear how the narrative changes. The more you can take control and confront what needs fixing, the more tolerable the recordings become. What was once a journey of self-hatred and regret becomes the sounds of survival. You start to hear, through the static and the noise, the unexpected connections and daring choices that helped save your life.

> *Mandy, you can keep calling me up every few weeks, or you can change your life.*
> *You've been through a lot of pain.*
> *You know what "shame" stands for? "Should Have Already Mastered Everything."*
> *Take a walk, and just find a flower and appreciate it.*
> *I wanted you to show me I was valuable through your actions.*
> *You're unlike anybody I've ever met.*
> *Will you marry me someday?*
> *It's been the best year of my life.*

We can always correct course.

What seems like certain death can at any moment become certain rebirth. What seems like unforgivable sin can become an unbelievable act of mercy.

If we welcome in the pain of the past, our black box can unlock our shame, freeing us forever. If we face the very worst of it—all the humiliation, all the self-pity, all the anger, all the regret—we will soon realize the answer has been there all along.

Our black box can never be destroyed.

The Upkeep

It's been almost two years since I finished writing *Unwifeable*. And lest my carefully curated Instagram relay a different story, let me just neatly shred whatever tidy bow I may have placed upon the complicated process of emotional excavation right now. Because nothing is suddenly perfect. Life is not now magically easy. Marriage is not without challenges. But finishing a book has meant starting another chapter. How does it end? Good question.

In the time since *Unwifeable* was first published, I've heard from hundreds of men and women around the world who have shared with me their own stories of self-discovery and empowerment. Especially on a hard or stressful day, every single one feels like a gift, a reminder of the power of human resilience and how when we honestly share our challenges with one another, we are never alone. We are *only* alone when we tell ourselves the lie that we are.

Other times they provide a hilarious reminder that men will still hit on you when you have just finished writing a book about how you are now happily married.

But overall, in reading your messages, one thing has stood out. Over and over again, I was struck by the reflex so many of us have to instantly and negatively frame our own self-identities.

"I am unwifeable, too."

"I am unhusbandable."

"I am unlovable."

"I am, well, uneverythingable."

To which I would say: I bet that is exactly what makes you so amazing. Not just amazing. Unbelievable.

....

IN HEARING ALL of your stories, I have realized the impact that comes from being able to flip the script on how we view ourselves—and we all have that power. Hell, consider my story. I could never have found the right life partner if I didn't embrace the "un" I feared for so long.

To that end, I've begun a blog—unyourself.com—to keep exploring this concept.

I've uncovered so many tools that have helped me find solace (or that have made me laugh my ass off, usually at the extremely earnest version of myself I am portraying). While I would sort of like to write about a thousand more pages about it right now, instead, I'm going to share with you my absolute favorite secrets. I'll continue to add to this list at unyourself.com.

And more than anything, I want to thank you as sincerely as I can for reading. Your existence and your courage give me so much inspiration to keep trying. Also, I have seen many of your Instagrams and can assure you this. Unwifeable? No way.

1. Look at jealousy, bitterness, fear, and anger as the teachers they can be. Learn from them.

IF A COMPETITION existed for the most jealous, bitter, angry woman on the planet, there was a time in my life when I could have *crushed* that competition. Forget Miss America. I would be a shoo-in for Miss Jealous, Bitter, Fearful, and Angry. I used to see a peer skyrocketing to success, landing on the cover of *World's Most Perfect Relationship Magazine,* and all I could think was, *Why isn't that me? Why do I suck so much in comparison?*

Now, if I can act against my impulses, then I promise that you can, too. The main epiphany for me came in realizing that success is not a finite, limited resource, and that I was coming from a mentality of lack versus one of abundance. Understanding this is a huge part of the battle.

The more you can recognize that your ego and your pride and your fear are *not* your friends, you can have so much fun engaging in opposite action and seeing what happens next. Instead of, say, sniping to your friends that someone doesn't deserve something or how life isn't fair, experiment with actually giving joy, gratitude, and support to others when it's literally your last impulse to do so. A wild thing happens when you do. You can change your entire energy state. Instead of operating throughout the universe like a black cloud, you become magnetic. People want to be around you.

There are days when Pat is a great resource for reminding me of this. Of course, he says it in slightly different words. Like, "Stand up, take off your bathrobe, and go outside with me. Seriously. I can smell you from here."

But I will tell you what: It works like a charm.

2. *Take what you like and leave the rest.*

"TAKE WHAT YOU like and leave the rest" is a big saying in "the rooms," as so many people call the twelve-step meetings that are offered for free for everyone from codependents to underearners to

AFTERWORD

overeaters to alcoholics to anyone whose life has been affected by
dysfunction.

This fights against everything we've been taught. We are fed
fairy tale after fairy tale *about* fairy tales—about how everything
should be perfect. The conventions of storytelling seep into our
subconscious, and we believe there needs to be a hero, a villain,
a right, a wrong, a black, and a white. And you know what? Most
people and things have so many shades of gray that, if you can have
the empathy to not reject a person or an idea outright, they can
teach you extraordinary things.

This is a tough one for me, so I try to look at it like a video game.
There are times when Pat and I are having such a knock-down,
drag-out fight that I have to stop, take a breath, and remember: Do
I want to be right, or do I want to be happy?

Duh, obviously I want to win. But as it turns out, happiness and
compromise and open-mindedness make life so much better.

And no, this is not all some extensive code that I am down with
anal.

3. *Do guided meditation.*

MY BRAIN IS sometimes like a banshee, screaming with pain,
anger, sadness, jealousy, regret, and self-flagellation. There is one
meditation that has helped me more than any other in clearing
my head when it is in a state of almost total toxicity. It's called
the *metta bhavana*, which means "loving-kindness." Various free
versions exist online, but my favorite is a track off an album called
Guided Meditations for Calmness, Awareness, and Love by an artist
named Bhodipaksa. Other meditations I love are anything by Kelly
Howell or Brian Weiss, and for getting out rage when you really
need an outlet, *Releasing Anger* by Louise Hay.

4. Start morning pages, also known as free writing.

THE ONLY REASON that I ever started to make hugely positive changes in my life, and later on started to have fortuitous ideas that allowed me to capture and harness a moment before it flitted away, was because of the process of doing free writing in the morning in 2004. The idea comes from Julia Cameron's book *The Artist's Way*. This practice alone has saved my sanity on more than one occasion. And I never could have written *Unwifeable* without the hundreds of notebooks stacked up with my messy stream-of-consciousness scribblings about what was happening at that moment in my life. When you are feeling the most incapacitated, writing nonstop about whatever thoughts are swirling around in your brain can be transformative. It has the profound impact of getting it outside of you and onto the page so you can move forward and move on. It forces you to stop lying to yourself when you see something written out plainly in your own words: *I am angry. I am sad. I want to make a change. I am going to make that change. I can't deny it anymore.*

5. Have fun, and find your purpose.

IF YOU'VE NEVER taken an improv class, sign up for one right the hell now. Seriously. I've never met a single person who has not benefited and had their whole life improve as a result. Or go do whatever that thing is that you think would be fun but have been putting off. Make sure you are actually and actively seeking joy. Think about what used to make you happy when you were a little kid, and do that now, as an adult.

When I was at my lowest in writing this book, I checked into a hotel, bought a stack of magazines, glitter, scissors, and glue to make a collage, just like I would have done when I was nine years old. As silly as it sounds, giving my inner kid that sense of play helped nourish what was missing in my heart right then. Write a note and stick it on your wall if you have to: *Have fun.* Joy is right around the corner.

6. *Take one "right action." Then take the next one.*

SOMETIMES THE ONLY thing you can do is get out of bed and force yourself to make a pot of coffee because you know that this little positive movement might lead you to the next. And that's all you *have* to do. Then cheer yourself for doing it. Let your inner dialogue be kind. The next right action will come soon enough.

So often there is this tendency to catastrophize a problem until we feel totally paralyzed by the prospect of everything we need to do to "fix" ourselves.

Our ego tells us the lie that we must not try because trying might mean failure, and at least in the certainty that we are a victim, we maintain control over the narrative. It's terrifying to take action. Because it might mean success, and success is never guaranteed. But if you can become more and more comfortable with that uncertainty, this is how life starts to change. The future is unknown. But it can be anything that you want it to be if you stop needing to control every step along the way.

I used to feel paralyzed every time I messed up. Now, I sometimes ask Pat to engage in gratitude breaks with me. Even though it sounds like the stupidest thing ever, we usually are able to laugh at the fact that I have pulled him away from, say, doing something else he wants to be doing right then, in order to exchange back-and-forth recitations of what we are happy about.

"I am grateful that you finally changed out of that bathrobe."

"I am grateful that I remembered I had a backup bathrobe."

"I am grateful that I am now going to hide all of your other bathrobes."

When you're really stuck, remember: You can never change things that have happened in your past or what someone else's reaction is. But the one thing you can control is how you react to life and how you hold yourself accountable. Do you grow? Or do you stay stuck?

You already know the answer.

Acknowledgments

There are thousands of individuals who even in the briefest of interactions have helped me more than they'll ever know, and to each one, I extend my gratitude. In particular, I am so appreciative of the love, understanding, patience, wisdom, kindness, and empathy of my family: My father, Jerry; my mother, Patricia; my sister, Amie; and the love of my life, my husband, Pat. On a professional level, I am so thankful to Byrd Leavell, Joe Veltre, Hannah Vaughn, and the best editor in the world, Natasha Simons; my publicist Jean Anne Rose and the director of publicity, Jennifer Robinson; editorial assistant Hannah Brown; and the whole team at Simon & Schuster, led by the brilliant Jennifer Bergstrom. There have been so many friends and colleagues who have been particularly amazing, and I'll name several of them here in alphabetical order. If I left you out, please let me know, and I will write a sequel just to make up for the indiscretion. Here goes.

Thank you to: Lexi Alexander, Lindsay Allen, Christina Amoroso, Megan Amram, Fred Armisen, Johanna Aster, Bahar Atvur, John Avlon, Brian Bachner, Joan Baker, Katie Baker, Todd Barry, Maggie Bandur, Amanda Barrie, Suz Bartley, Joy Behar, Greg Behrendt, Jeremy Bell, Sara Benincasa, Ron Bennington, Scott Bixby, Michael Blaustein, Rachel Bloom, Jamie Blynn, Kristin Booker, Alex Borstein, Dave Boyle, Jonathan Brandstein, Abigail

Breslin, Sharon Bridbord, Casey Brodley, DeDe Brown, Stella Bugbee, Dennis Burger, Candace Bushnell, Susannah Cahalan, Charlie Carballo, Erin Lee Carr, E. Jean Carroll, Richard Cernese, Amy Chan, Gina Chon, Amy Chua, Corynne Cirilli, Donna Cochener, Dr. David Colbert and everyone at New York Dermatology Group, Rives Collins, Michael Colton, Margi Conklin, Courtland Cox, Kambri Crews, Danielle Crittenden, Mark Cronin, Anthony Cumia, Kelly Cutrone, Eric Danville, Anna David, Kristin Davis, Mackenzie Dawson, Rachel DeAlto, Jessica Delfino, Juan Delgado, Stephanie DeLuca, Victoria DePaula, Shirine and Tony DiSanto, Kathleen Donohue, Andrea Dunlop, Debbie Pell Dunning, Noam Dworman, Mark Ebner, Scott Einziger, Chris Erikson, Daniel Falato, Stephen Falk, Wayne Federman, Al Fielder, Shannon Fisher, Siobhan Foley, Julie Frady, Maya Francis, Alison Freer, Serena French, Jon Friedman, Paula Froelich, Adrienne Frost, John Fugelsang, Sarah Fuller, Ardie Fuqua, Jim Gaffigan, Joel Garreau, Marianne Garvey, Ido Gaver, Robert George, Hanna Gibeau, Laura Gilbert, Pia Glenn, Ellen Goldsmith-Vein, Evan Gore, Elina Gorelik, Michelle Gotthelf, Joe Grieboski, Lloyd Grove, Joanna Gurin, Isaac Guzmán, Lauren Hackney, Sylvia Haider, Olivia Hall, Charlaine Harris, Eric Hegedus, Sarah Hepola, Jenn Hoffman, Ron Hogan, Jessica Hudson, Joselyn Hughes, Mary Huhn, Gale Anne Hurd, Jenny Hutt, Tamara Ikenberg, Larry Izzo, A. J. Jacobs, Richard Johnson, Molly Jong-Fast, Chelsea Kalberloh Jackson, Don Kaplan, Jill Kargman, Jackie Kashian, Robert Kelly, Caroline Kepnes, Gayle King, Jaime King, Leslie Kinzel, Gayle Klein, Jessi Klein, Larry Knapp, Sarah Knight, Annie Kreighbaum, Natalie Krinsky, John Kupetz, Shinji Kuwayama, Jillian Kuzma, Bonita Labossiere, Destiny Lalane, Anne and Sam Lamott, Artie Lange, Sam Lansky,

Beth Lapides, Enty Lawyer, Beverly Lefkowitz, Michelle Leigh, Warren Leight, Ali Lerman, Lori Levine, Samantha Levy, Tony Leys, Amy Lighter, Courtney Lilly, Mark Lisanti, Courtney Love, Joe and Andrea Lozito, Michael Lustig, Francesca Lyn, Steve Lynch, Peri Lyons, Michelle Madias, Ira Madison III, Cat Marnell, Erin Mater Hogan, Jillian Dolby Mavodones, Molly McAleer, Soren McCarthy, Sheila McClear, Patrick McCloskey, Emily McCombs, Liam McEneaney, Joi-Marie McKenzie, Tara McKinney, Kimberly Rae Miller, Raakhee Mirchandani Singh, Sara Moffitt, Lee Moon-Griffo, Lane Moore, Sonja Morgan, Jonathan Morvay, Polly Mosendz, Allan Mott, Rajasri Narasimhan, Rome Neal, Sharilyn Neidhardt, Lester Nelson-Gacal, Randi Newton, Elena Nicolaou, Brian Niemietz, Jayme Nimick, Hamilton Nolan, Jim Norton, Maggie O'Brien, William O'Connor, Arianna O'Dell, Keith Olbermann, Sandra Oles, Hannah Orenstein, Charity Palmera, Crystal Patriacrche, Peaches, Colette Pervette, Eileen Phoenix, Jo Piazza, Brittny Pierre, Steven Pinker, Lindsay Plotkin, Benari Poulten, Jane Pratt, Liz Pressman, Stacey Prussman, Julia Pugachevsky, Katherine Pushkar, Colin Quinn, Issa Rae, Lauren Ramsby, Katrina Reese, Paola Reyes, Luiz C. Ribeiro, Jim Roberts, Marci Robin, Dana Robinson, Jon Ronson, Alison Rosen, Mike Sacks, Horatio Sanz, Pamela Redmond Satran, Gina Savage, Sue Scheff, Michael Schneider, Ray Schneiders, Amy Schumer, Amanda Schwab, Bex Schwartz, Luke Seemann, Pete Segall, Carrie Seim, Jim Serpico, Noah Shachtman, Susan Shapiro, Rob Sheffield, Kelly Shibari, Tolani Shoneye, Rachel Shukert, Shakti Shukla, Harry Siegel, Sharon Simon, Illyse Singer, Anna Siri, Suzie Sisoler, Ashley Skidmore, Emily Smith, Graham Smith, Jackey Smith, Keri Smith, Kyle Smith, Ryan Smith, Christina Hoff Sommers, Aaron Sorkin, Megan Soto, Lainie Speiser, Heather

ACKNOWLEDGMENTS

Spillane, Rob Sprance, Dese'Rae Lynn Stage, Jerry Stahl, Karrine Steffans, Marlow Stern, Doctor Steve, Nicole Stillings, Molly Stout, Neil Strauss, Cheryl Strayed, Lisa Swanson, Aundria Theocles, Cambrey Thomas, Michael Thomsen, Reed Tucker, Deanna Urciuoli, Dr. Belisa Vranich, Jessie Militare Walsh, Hilary Weaver, Jordan Weeks, Miriam Weeks, Allison Hope Weiner, Gene Weingarten, Farrah Weinstein, Abigail Welhouse, Emily Whitaker, Alice Wright, Franklin Wright, Elizabeth Wurtzel, Laura Yasinitsky, Nikki Yeager, and Ellen Soo Hoo Zurfluh.